RETHINKING PLAY AS PEDAGOGY

The conceptualisation and practice of play is considered core to early childhood pedagogy. In this essential text, contributors from a range of countries and cultures explore how play might be defined, encouraged and interpreted in early childhood settings and practice.

Rethinking Play as Pedagogy provides a fresh perspective of play as a purposeful pedagogy offering multi-layered opportunities for learning and development. Written to provoke group discussion and extend thinking, opportunities for international comparison, points for reflection and editorial provocations, this volume will help students engage critically with a variety of understandings of play, and diverse approaches to harnessing children's natural propensity to play. Considering the role of the learning environment, the practitioner, the wider community, and policy, chapters are divided into four key sections which reflect major influences on practice and pedagogy:

- Being alongside children
- Those who educate
- Embedding families and communities
- Working with systems

Offering in-depth discussion of diverse perceptions, potentials and practicalities of early childhood play, this text will enhance understanding, support self-directed learning, and provoke and transform thinking at both graduate and postgraduate levels, particularly in the field of early childhood education and care, for students, educators, integrated service providers and policymakers.

Sophie Alcock is a senior lecturer in Education at Victoria University of Wellington, New Zealand.

Nicola Stobbs is a senior lecturer at the Department for Children & Families, University of Worcester, UK.

THINKING ABOUT PEDAGOGY IN EARLY CHILDHOOD EDUCATION

Books in this series will serve as critical companions for senior undergraduate and postgraduate students conducting study and research in the field of Early Childhood Education and Care. As well as contributing to the thinking of teachers in a range of countries, these books will also be of interest to policy-makers and thinkers in a range of disciplines including health, welfare, sociology and community-building. Introducing new ideas and differing viewpoints from around the globe, texts take the reader beyond known cultural, ethical and geographical boundaries, to explore children's perspectives as a key component in early childhood pedagogy.

Each book in the series is divided into four interconnected sections: being alongside children, those who educate, families and communities, and policies and systems, to encompass the wide-ranging influences on contemporary pedagogical practice. Editors offer provocations to both link the chapters provided and offer directions for further thought. Grounded in sound empirical evidence, taking a global perspective, and born of critical and collaborative reflection, texts encourage readers to consider ideas which might be applied in their own learning, study and practice.

Series editors: Alma Fleet and Michael Reed

Titles in this series include:

CHALLENGING THE INTERSECTION OF POLICY WITH PEDAGOGY
Edited by Leanne Gibbs and Michael Gasper

RETHINKING PLAY AS PEDAGOGY
Edited by Sophie Alcock and Nicola Stobbs

For more information about this series, please visit: www.routledge.com/education/series/TAPECE

RETHINKING PLAY AS PEDAGOGY

Edited by Sophie Alcock and Nicola Stobbs

LONDON AND NEW YORK

First published 2019
by Routledge
2 Park Square, Milton Park, Abingdon, Oxon OX14 4RN

and by Routledge
52 Vanderbilt Avenue, New York, NY 10017

Routledge is an imprint of the Taylor & Francis Group, an informa business

© 2019 selection and editorial matter, Sophie Alcock and Nicola Stobbs; individual chapters, the contributors

The right of Sophie Alcock and Nicola Stobbs to be identified as the authors of the editorial material, and of the authors for their individual chapters, has been asserted in accordance with sections 77 and 78 of the Copyright, Designs and Patents Act 1988.

All rights reserved. No part of this book may be reprinted or reproduced or utilised in any form or by any electronic, mechanical, or other means, now known or hereafter invented, including photocopying and recording, or in any information storage or retrieval system, without permission in writing from the publishers.

Trademark notice: Product or corporate names may be trademarks or registered trademarks, and are used only for identification and explanation without intent to infringe.

British Library Cataloguing-in-Publication Data
A catalogue record for this book is available from the British Library

Library of Congress Cataloging-in-Publication Data
Names: Alcock, Sophie, 1953- editor. | Stobbs, Nicola, editor.
Title: Rethinking play as pedagogy / edited by Sophie Alcock and Nicola Stobbs.
Description: Abingdon, Oxon ; New York, NY : Routledge, 2019. |
Includes bibliographical references.
Identifiers: LCCN 2018051643 (print) | LCCN 2019002571 (ebook) |
ISBN 9780429454042 (eb) | ISBN 9781138319219 (hbk : alk. paper) |
ISBN 9781138319226 (pbk : alk. paper) | ISBN 9780429454042 (ebk)
Subjects: LCSH: Play. | Child development. | Early childhood education.
Classification: LCC LB1137 (ebook) | LCC LB1137 .R475 2019 (print) |
DDC 372.21–dc23
LC record available at https://lccn.loc.gov/2018051643

ISBN: 978-1-138-31921-9 (hbk)
ISBN: 978-1-138-31922-6 (pbk)
ISBN: 978-0-429-45404-2 (ebk)

Typeset in Sabon
by Swales & Willis, Exeter, Devon, UK

TO OUR MOTHERS, FATHERS AND EDUCATORS EVERYWHERE WHO GIVE CHILDREN SPACE TO PLAY.

CONTENTS

List of illustrations x
Series editors, volume editors and contributors xi
Preface: entering contested waters xviii
ALMA FLEET AND MICHAEL REED
Volume editors' acknowledgements xxi
Series editors' acknowledgements xxii

SECTION 1
Being alongside children 1

1 Playing with digital drawing 3
 JANET ROBERTSON

2 Preschool teachers being alongside young children: the development of adults' relational competence in playworlds 17
 BETH FERHOLT, MONICA NILSSON AND ROBERT LECUSAY

3 Playing in and through the musical worlds of children 33
 MARGARET S. BARRETT

Editorial provocations: engaging readers and extending thinking 47
SOPHIE ALCOCK

CONTENTS

SECTION 2
Those who educate   51

4   Observing and interpreting young children playing:
    reflecting on feelings   53
    SOPHIE ALCOCK

5   Growing playful pedagogies: a case study of educational
    change   69
    ALMA FLEET AND MEL KEMENYVARY

6   The role of context within early childhood education in
    Ireland   86
    MARGARET O'DONOGHUE

Editorial provocations: engaging readers and extending
thinking   101
SOPHIE ALCOCK

SECTION 3
Embedding families and communities   105

7   Recognising and responding to family funds of knowledge   107
    HELEN HEDGES, MARIA COOPER AND TAMAR WEISZ-KOVES

8   Opening the school gates: facilitating after-school
    play in school grounds   121
    MARIANNE MANNELLO, MARK CONNOLLY, SANDRA DUMITRESCU, CHERYL
    ELLIS, CHANTELLE HAUGHTON, SIAN SARWAR AND JACKY TYRIE

9   Pedagogical documentation as 'agora': why it may be
    viewed as a form of citizenship for children, parents and
    communities   139
    ELISABETTA BIFFI

Editorial provocations: engaging readers and extending
thinking   153
SOPHIE ALCOCK

SECTION 4
Working with systems — 155

10 Spinning the kaleidoscope: a conversation around play, learning, policies and systems — 157
    ALMA FLEET AND MICHAEL REED

11 Influences of macrosystems on children's spaces: regaining the paradigm — 173
    MANDY ANDREWS

12 Micro-policies of adult–child joint play in the context of the Finnish ECEC system — 189
    MAIJU PAANANEN AND ANNA PAULIINA RAINIO

Editorial provocations: engaging readers and extending thinking — 205
NICOLA STOBBS

Coda: thinking forward — 207
MICHAEL REED AND ALMA FLEET

Index — 209

ILLUSTRATIONS

Figures

8.1	Preparing the school grounds	131
8.2	Children taking control of the play	133

Boxes

8.1	A rich play environment	127
8.2	Playwork principles	129

SERIES EDITORS, VOLUME EDITORS AND CONTRIBUTORS

Series editors

Michael Reed and Alma Fleet were the driving force behind the production of this six-book series involving over 100 contributors. They shaped the direction of each volume and carefully considered which authors and editors would be best suited to bring their expertise to the project. Both are experienced university tutors and have previously collaborated on a number of projects, including a book on pedagogical documentation, a symposium at the European Early Childhood Education Research Association conference (Bologna) and an international conference on educational quality in North Africa (Morocco).

Alma Fleet is an honorary associate professor in the Department of Educational Studies at Macquarie University, Sydney, with a doctorate in early childhood teacher education. She brings to this series a commitment to educational change as well as her experience teaching both children and adults in several countries, including Scotland and Australia. Previously Head of the Institute of Early Childhood, she now publishes and consults widely, especially on practitioner inquiry, educational change and the transition to school. Her publications include Fleet, De Gioia, Patterson, with contributions from colleagues, *Engaging with Educational Change: Voices of Practitioner Inquiry* (2016) and Fleet, Patterson, Robertson, *Pedagogical Documentation in Early Years Practice: Seeing Multiple Perspectives* (2017).

Michael Reed is an honorary senior fellow of the Institute of Education at the University of Worcester and a visiting professor at the University of Ibn Zohr Business School, Agadir, Morocco. He is a qualified teacher and holds advanced qualifications in Educational Inquiry, Educational

Psychology and Special Education. The series editorship builds upon his experience of writing books, book chapters, research papers and co-edited textbooks. These include *Reflective Practice in the Early Years* (2010), *Quality Improvement and Change in the Early Years* (2012) and *Work-Based Research in the Early Years* (2012). More recently, his work includes *A Critical Companion to Early Education* (2015) and *Effective Leadership for High Quality Early Years Practice* (2016).

Volume editors

Sophie Alcock is a senior lecturer in the School of Education at Victoria University of Wellington, in Aotearoa-New Zealand. She is also an early childhood teacher, which enables her to bring a pragmatic approach to her researching/teacher-learner role. Her research has encompassed children's emotional wellbeing from relational and socio-psycho-cultural perspectives that prioritise the systemic attachment contexts within which children live, play and learn. Sophie particularly enjoys the complexities that emerge when reflexively observing and interpreting children playing. Recent book publications include *Young Children Playing: Relational Approaches to Emotional Learning in Early Childhood Settings* (2016).

Nicola Stobbs began her career in education as a primary school teacher, and then as a preschool educator and manager where she supported staff professional development. She became a senior lecturer at the University of Worcester, at the Institute of Education and the Department for Children and Families. She now holds the post of Course Leader for the BA (Hons) in Early Childhood (Professional Practice). She has written on pedagogical documentation and co-edited a number of books, the latest being Musgrave, J., Saven-Baden, M., and Stobbs, N. (Eds), *Studying Early Childhood Education and Care: A Critical Guide for Higher Education Students* (2017).

Contributors

Sophie Alcock is a senior lecturer in the School of Education at Victoria University of Wellington, in Aotearoa-New Zealand. She is also an early childhood teacher, which brings a pragmatic approach to her researching teacher-learner role. Her research has focused on children's emotional wellbeing from relational and socio-psycho-cultural perspectives that prioritise the systemic attachment contexts within which children live, play and learn. Sophie particularly enjoys the complexities that emerge when reflexively observing and interpreting children playing.

Mandy Andrews studied at Essex University, in England, mingling philosophy, politics and the arts, before becoming a playworker running adventure play, children's play and arts activities. She has been a consultant to arts organisations, an environmental project manager and a children's centre leader. This eclectic mix of experiences and understanding of the diversity of play in different contexts provides a child-and-environment focus and interest in inclusion, empowerment and alternative pedagogies. She has been a lecturer in higher education since 2007, first with the University of Worcester Centre for Early Childhood and subsequently with Plymouth University's Institute for Education, where she is currently studying for her PhD on the theme of 'Children's "landscapes of play": Unsupervised play experiences close to home'.

Margaret S. Barrett is Professor and Head of the School of Music at the University of Queensland, Australia. She researches the pedagogy of creativity, early musical development, engagement in music and arts activity, and music program evaluation. Her research has been funded by grants from the Australian Research Council, the Australia Council for the Arts, the British Council and other commissioning bodies. She publishes extensively, including articles, book chapters and conference papers. Publications include *Collaborative Creativity in Musical Thought and Practice* (2014) and *Narrative Soundings: An Anthology of Narrative Inquiry in Music Education* (with Sandra Stauffer, 2012). Her contributions to research have been recognised through an Excellence in Research Higher Degree Supervision Award (2016, UQ), an Excellence in Research Engagement Award (2016, UQ) and a Fulbright Senior Research Fellowship (2017).

Elisabetta Biffi is a researcher in Pedagogy at the Department of Human Sciences for Education 'Riccardo Massa' at the University of Milan-Bicocca, Italy. She is a member of European and national research projects on pedagogical documentation, child protection, children rights and educators and teachers' professional development. Her research work has included autobiographical and narrative practices as a tool for pedagogical documentation, promoting children's voice and teacher and parent training. She is Co-convenor for the European Early Childhood Research Association Education, Special Interest Group: Transforming Assessment, Evaluation and Documentation in Early Childhood Pedagogy.

SERIES EDITORS, VOLUME EDITORS AND CONTRIBUTORS

Mark Connolly is an educationalist with experience working in a variety of institutional and cultural contexts. At present, he lectures in the School of Social Sciences at Cardiff University in Wales. His doctoral work and research interests include professional identity, children's rights, risk and outdoor education, and the formation of education and cultural policy.

Maria Cooper is a senior lecturer in the Faculty of Education and Social Work at the University of Auckland, New Zealand. Maria's research and teaching interests focus on early childhood education, specifically collective leadership in early childhood settings, early years curriculum, teacher–family partnerships and infant-toddler pedagogy.

Sandra Dumitrescu is a lecturer in Early Childhood Studies with Early Years Practitioner Status, Cardiff School of Education and Social Policy, Cardiff Metropolitan University. Sandra is a registered health play specialist, having worked primarily within health care settings for the last 22 years. Her work has taken her overseas to support children in institutions in Romania, working collaboratively with the support staff, as well as setting up a hospice for children with HIV/AIDS. Sandra has previously held the post of Therapeutic Services Manager at Ty Hafan, the children's hospice in Wales.

Cheryl Ellis is a principal lecturer and Head of the Department for Humanities, Cardiff School of Education and Social Policy, Cardiff Metropolitan University. She is a member of the university's outdoor learning team and regularly works with children and students within Forest School. She holds a doctorate; her research interests include outdoor learning and play, inclusion and additional learning needs. Having previously worked as a primary school teacher, Cheryl has experienced the 'practical realities' of classroom life.

Beth Ferholt is an associate professor in the Department of Early Childhood and Art Education of Brooklyn College and a member of the doctoral faculty of the Graduate School and University Center's PhD Program in Urban Education at the City University of New York. Her research focus includes challenging the divide between method and object in conventional social science; playworlds; *perezhivanie*; and preschool practices in which children are understood as culture and knowledge creators.

Alma Fleet is an honorary associate professor in the Department of Educational Studies at Macquarie University, Sydney. She enjoys thinking alongside learners of all ages. Alma publishes and consults widely, especially with people and projects involved with practitioner enquiry, educational change and the transition to school. She is intrigued by the intersections between the pervasiveness of play and a high-accountability educational landscape.

Chantelle Haughton is a senior lecturer in Education and Early Childhood Studies, Cardiff School of Education and Social Policy, Cardiff Metropolitan University, and a senior Higher Education Academy fellow. Chantelle is a Forest School leader and trainer responsible for developing an outdoor learning centre which has regenerated use of a small, ancient strip of Welsh woodland and concrete patches on the university campus. Chantelle received several teaching awards in recognition of the live, playful, innovative community engagement projects that she designs with students, local children and practitioners.

Helen Hedges is a professor in the Faculty of Education and Social Work at the University of Auckland, New Zealand. She is Head of School for the School of Curriculum and Pedagogy in the Faculty of Education and Social Work. Her research program examines children's and teachers' interests, knowledge and learning, and the ways these combine to create curriculum in early childhood education.

Melanie Kemenyvary is an Australian early years and primary teacher. She has worked across a range of rural and remote locations, including Indigenous Australian communities. Parenthood became the catalyst for her interest in early education. Her career has involved educating children from three-year-olds through the first years of school and a children's centre context, as an educator and mentor. Her interests include pedagogy from preschool to school and the development of dispositions for successful learning.

Robert Lecusay is an assistant professor of Early Childhood Education in the Preschool Didactics Research Group at Jönköping University's School of Education and Communication, Sweden. His research examines the relationship between formal and informal learning in after-school and preschool environments, focusing in particular on processes of schoolification and pedagogisation in early childhood education for sustainable development.

Marianne Mannello is an assistant director (Policy, Support and Advocacy) at Play Wales, a national charity for children's play. Her professional experience of playwork spans over 30 years and includes play strategy and development. She worked with the Welsh Government to support the development of a toolkit to support local authorities to undertake statutory Play Sufficiency Assessments. She is a member of the Wales UNCRC Monitoring Group, an honorary research associate in the College of Engineering at Swansea University, and an associate tutor with the Early Childhood Studies team at Cardiff Metropolitan University.

Monica Nilsson is a former preschool teacher and an associate professor of Early Childhood Education/Preschool Didactics at the School of Education and Communication, Jönköping University, Sweden. Her areas of research are, broadly, learning and development in the context of preschool, and more specifically tools and environments that afford children's play and exploration as well as teachers' professional growth. Her work builds upon the tradition of cultural-historical activity theories.

Margaret O'Donoghue is Course Coordinator and Lecturer on the Early Childhood Care and Education Batchelor of Arts (Hons) Degree program at the Technological University Dublin, Ireland. She has over 17 years' experience in early childhood practice. During that time, she completed a BA (Hons) in Child Family and Youth Studies and a Masters in Child Family and Community Studies. Her doctoral research interest is exploring the implementation of Aistear: Ireland's Early Childhood Curriculum Framework, and the Irish Primary Language Curriculum.

Maiju Paananen is a post-doctoral researcher at the University of Tampere, Finland. Her research interest is in the field of early childhood education and care policies and governance. She is also actively involved in national development work in the field of early education. She is currently part of the Finnish National Educational Evaluation Center's working group that evaluates the implementation of the national core curriculum for early childhood education and reviews plans that steer early childhood education.

Anna Pauliina Rainio is an adjunct professor and a senior university lecturer of Educational Psychology at the University of Helsinki, Finland. Her current research focuses on the questions of student agency, engagement and ambivalence in early education and in play pedagogy, and on theorising the dynamics of institutional educational change. With colleagues, she has published on children's sense of agency in preschools.

Michael Reed was for many years a senior lecturer at the Institute of Education at the University of Worcester and is now an honorary senior fellow of the university. He has an interest in the way young children grow and learn and in particular the way that systems and policy initiatives allow educators to provide effective opportunities promoting children's play and learning.

Janet Robertson holds a teaching qualification and Masters degree in Early Childhood Education. Having worked as a teacher and sector advisor, she became a specialist toddler teacher and then developed the position of Outdoor Educator at the Mia Mia Child and Family Study Centre at the Institute of Early Childhood, Macquarie University, Sydney. She presents at symposiums on early education, with attention to the potentials of the outdoors. Janet is recognised for her work with pedagogical documentation to engage and celebrate children's learning and ways to represent their thoughts and ideas. She publishes with Alma Fleet and Catherine Patterson.

Sian Sarwar is a lecturer in Early Childhood Studies, Cardiff School of Education and Social Policy, Cardiff Metropolitan University. Her research interests include student voice, ICT in education, music education and early language acquisition.

Tamar Weisz-Koves is an experienced lecturer in early childhood education and mentor for newly qualified teachers. She has taught in a range of early childhood and tertiary settings, both within New Zealand and overseas. She works part-time as a lecturer at the University of Auckland.

PREFACE

Entering contested waters

Alma Fleet and Michael Reed

As 'play' is conceptualised as core to early childhood practice, it must be interrogated constantly in the changing early childhood international landscape. There continues to be tension between seeing 'play' as something that passes the time in early years settings, or as facilitating experiential opportunities for growth and wellbeing. The conversation in this case, however, is not so much a justification for 'play' in early childhood settings, as that argument should be well behind us; it is an exploration of what actually is being considered under this umbrella.

Positioned neither as a practical guide for beginners or a post-structuralist critique for theorists, this companion volume offers fresh voices to extend the thinking of growing professionals and to push the boundaries of traditional explorations. This volume, for example, highlights the difference between 'play' as dichotomised from 'work', and the consideration of 'playful pedagogies' which are integral to learning, particularly for those across the early childhood bracket (birth through the early years of school). It draws attention to intersections of children's choices, perceptions, curriculum, digital literacies, adult priorities and policies.

Writing from a range of roles, responsibilities and geographic locations, chapter authors share their thinking, research, concerns and values, offering them as provocations for readers to engage in robust intellectual conversations around the construct of Play as Pedagogy. The work ranges from theoretical considerations to local experiential knowledge – including the following personal view which sits 'underneath' one of the chapters offered here (private communication, Kemenevary, 2018). This reflection from a colleague hints at several threads in this book: the voices of children, conversations with families, thinking by educators, and the often-inscrutable influences of systems.

Only recently, I was saddened by a conversation I had with a parent of a child in her early years of school. Marcia's father had commented that she had mentioned she felt sad because she really wanted to play in the sandpit, because it used to be so much fun, but that she wasn't allowed. When he questioned her as to why she wasn't allowed, her response was that she's at school now and school kids don't get to play in the sandpit anymore. They have too much school work to do. This conversation really played on my mind. At what point in time did the joy of playing in the sandpit (at the same site) become out of bounds to children? I might add that this is not a school rule, but a 5-year-old's perception of what it means to be a school student. In only one school term, this child has been 'conditioned' to the ways of traditional schooling – conditioned out of the joy, awe and wonder that was common place in her preschool setting.

These voices, and the others that follow, may resonate with you, or be unsettling. They provide opportunities for you to question current practices as well as considering your emerging understandings of the issues being offered. This volume, then, is a critical companion for those engaged in early childhood settings, both as learners and those extending their knowledge of professional practice. It introduces differing viewpoints, asks questions and encourages further study. Its production has involved many people, including the children, parents and professionals who allowed us to enter their worlds and capture day-to-day practice. It also involved drawing upon the expertise of experienced chapter authors, publishing editors and administrators working together to make that practice visible and richly engaging. It was a process which took time to come to fruition, involving series editors locating people with expertise who could write about issues relevant for the advanced study of early education. It also involved volume editors shaping and exposing issues within and between chapters in order to provoke critical thinking. The chapters should be seen as a professional invitation to examine existing practice, explore new philosophies and re-imagine practice.

The series is therefore the product of a shared personal and professional community of practice. The growth and wellbeing of all participants in this educative process are key, particularly as the processes engage, support and extend children. The volume itself, as with the other five volumes in this series, is divided into four interlocking sections:

- Being alongside children
- Those who educate
- Embedding families and communities
- Working with systems

The sections represent key influences on pedagogical practice in action and should be regarded as interconnected themes underpinning pedagogical practice. They contain views intended to take the reader beyond known cultural, ethical and geographical boundaries and explore contemporary practice in action. This is particularly important in an early educational world which appears to be struggling to find balance in working to meet national regulatory requirements while developing local educational environments nurtured in relationships. These issues can be informed by and challenged through developing local interpretations of these larger ideas (Fleet, 2017) and considering what 'play' means in an intellectually complex and changing world.

Reference

Fleet, A. (2017). The landscape of pedagogical documentation. In A. Fleet, C. Patterson & J. Robertson (Eds.). *Pedagogical documentation in early years practice: Seeing through multiple perspectives*. London: SAGE (pp. 11–25).

VOLUME EDITORS' ACKNOWLEDGEMENTS

The volume editors would like to acknowledge with grateful thanks the thoughtful contributions of the chapter authors and the unfailing support provided by the series editors in *Rethinking Play as Pedagogy*.

SERIES EDITORS' ACKNOWLEDGEMENTS

Children put their trust in those who hold their hands. From that perspective, we note that the editorial team at Routledge believed in this book series from the start. They and the production team transferred that belief into many small actions which taken together helped us make big decisions. Thanks to Alison Foyle and Elsbeth Wright and everyone who held our hands. The volume editors helped shape and watched over the contributors' playground and made it a wonderful place. The contributors themselves generated energy, shared their knowledge and shaped the play space. As series editors, we very much enjoyed the opportunity to play with this collection of diverse, warm, supportive, intelligent and creative individuals.

Our thanks to all.

Section 1

BEING ALONGSIDE CHILDREN

1
PLAYING WITH DIGITAL DRAWING

Janet Robertson

This chapter considers that 'other' sheet of paper, an interactive screen, as a drawing surface, and the possibilities of meaning-making with and for young children. Digital drawing is another vehicle for children to become familiar with and utilise those techniques to tell us what meaning(s) they are making of the world. This 'interactive agency' (Lenz Taguchi, 2009), with teachers being alongside children, broadens children's abilities to connect with others. Unfortunately, this common-sense approach has become entangled with concerns about too much 'screen time' depriving children of other forms of explorative play and experiences with nature.

Exploring digital drawing is exciting. As David Hockney says, 'Picasso would have gone mad with this, so would Van Gogh. I don't know an artist who wouldn't, actually' (cited by Gayford, 2011, p.191). The reticence of early childhood teachers and the panic about 'screen time' have perhaps clouded what digital drawing is. The screen is simply another surface to make marks on, an alternative piece of paper.

The thinking and stories retold in this chapter occurred with children under five years of age at Mia Mia Child and Family Study Centre, Department of Educational Studies, Macquarie University, Sydney, Australia, a long day programme from 7.30am to 6.00pm, five days a week, 49 weeks of the year, where the author has been the outdoor teacher for 17 years.

Stepping back from the ruckus of 'screen time' and realising the importance of children using digital drawing becomes simple when viewed from this question: *Would you limit children's use of traditional drawing materials in an early childhood school?* If the tools offered are simple (gimmick-free, no novelty pens or rainbow nibs), the early childhood profession would be aghast at the suggestion that students could only draw for ten minutes a day. The profession knows that mark-making is the essence of externalising thinking (Bruner, 1996, p.23) and is shrouded in early literacy memes. Digital drawing affords children a landscape upon which and with which to think. As Kress notes, 'makers of representations are shapers of knowledge' (2010, p.27). The essential point is that children must be able to use the app, not the app use them.

An exploration of the techniques and affordances of this media will be examined in this chapter, noting the differences between paper and screen. The surface upon which we make marks is as important as the implement we make the marks with (Vecchi & Ruozzi, 2015). Manipulation of digital colour is immediate and captivating; the possibilities for colour overlay, clarity of colour, immediate erasure and recording of marks in the making support the value of a 'child as creator'. The digital platform used influences the child's agency; some software is cluttered, with multiple options, so the child engages with the functions, creating 'a child as consumer' rather than 'child being in charge'.

> Play-based learning is a context for learning through which children organise and make sense of their social worlds, as they engage actively with people, objects and representations.
> (Department of Education, Employment and Workplace Relations (DEEWR), 2009, p.3)

In my childhood, the invention of the 'texta' or marker pen astonished me. The solid vibrant coloured line was so surprising to someone used to the pale markings of colour pencils and wax crayons. Perhaps digital lines might astonish contemporary drawers? They certainly astonished David Hockney, who says:

> Using this medium means you miss some things – you miss texture – but you gain a lot ... the freedom to alter things. With this you can move things about, change, make them bigger and smaller. The black is like nothing else you can print. It's fantastically dense.
> (cited by Gayford, 2011, p.97)

Let me be clear: digital drawing should not supplant pen and paper. It is simply another way to make marks and thinking visible. The ability to draw one colour over the other without colour compromise, the ease of erasure, the simplicity of changing line width, the opportunity to draw on solid colour backgrounds and that the hue stays true are all affordances offered by the media.

Drawing movies

Finding simple cheap digital drawing software is possible. In 2013, I began using the software Explain Everything (https://explaineverything.com/), and in Ursula Kolbe's book *Children's Imagination: Creativity Under Our Noses* (2014) I described our first encounters. It is software more usually used with older school students; however, I worked with a group of four-year-olds.

To avoid children being dazzled by the array of effects, I showed them a basic screen only. I wondered at the time if this was ethical, but reasoned that I would not have allowed children all the art shop supplies, a photography studio, cameras, lenses and filters plus GarageBand in one go. It seemed to me the opportunity to draw with white on a black background was innovative enough. The restricted colour palette meant children paid attention to details in representations rather than playing with colours. I'd often given children black markers and white paper to explain some idea they were thinking about, so this seemed the logical extension. Once past initial exploration and now using the black and white drawing affordances (a matter of days), I explained the other functions. This included the ability to create a simple rotation, an expansion and contraction of each drawn character ... creating a moving illustration. It was not real animation, only giving movement to marks, as was soon understood by savvy four-year-olds, as was the understanding that the software was cumbersome, fraught with operator sequence failures, and needed an adult alongside coaching and commiserating when drawings were 'lost'. (It took weeks to remember the order of icons to tap). I showed children the final effect, which was the opportunity to record a voiceover and capture the movement of their marks, then replay the result ... and short 'movies' were possible.

Aidan and his brother discovered the app's ability to expand. I had been intrigued by a game of astronauts they had created in a complex block structure on the veranda with the large wooden outdoor blocks, playing there for 90 minutes with that deep inward look of children engaged in rich imaginary play. I took a photo of the building and the next day I offered Aidan the photo, inserted in the app, asking him, 'Can you draw the game for me?' He drew, building the known components of the game, or at least the ones that had been obvious to an observer, of a pilot and passenger. To my surprise he included another plot, underneath the photograph, drawing and narrating an underwater world, with ocean, octopus and scuba diver. Aidan was able to do this as he could expand the size of the page, adding room for the rest of the narrative and its imagined landscape, moving beyond my offering of the photo as 'task-scape' (Ingold, 1993, pp.152–174). This drawing gave me insight into the depth of the imaginary play the day before (Kolbe, 2014, p.83).

The first movie was Kevin's. As a marine enthusiast, he'd covered the 'page' with fish, then inserted an underwater photograph as a background. We projected it onto the wall and his drawn and verbal narrative of fish scuttling away from a fearsome shark was embellished by contributions from the audience.

In recent years, the background photograph has become less important, with the animation and immediacy of the narrative influencing the work more. Oscar created a movie of his father burning sausages on the barbeque, the smoke occluding everything at its conclusion. Cate's movie of the internal life of bubbles, peopled with fairies whose hazardous existence required rescue whenever a bubble burst – eventually coexisting inside one giant bubble – clearly illustrated her competence and imagination. A series of simple shark movies, with appropriate dangers to other sea dwellers or users, captivated a group of shark enthusiasts. The pressing desire to depict the thrilling adventures pushed these children's representational skills beyond their usual comfort zones, hybridising and appropriating each other's accomplishments to create detailed sharks and prey, outdoing each other's narration.

The additional ability to record the narration highlighted for us the skills required to compose a story, to sequence and vocalise it with expression, using theatrical effects such as pauses and sounds and working to end with an appropriate dénouement. I knew that a story often accompanied paper drawings, but listening to these renditions made me realise the further potential of narration and animation to increase the complexity of children's thinking (Bruner, 1996). The limited movement easily given to characters (back and forth, up and down, rotation, expansion and contraction) I could see, on reflection, had also existed in previous paper drawings. When children lifted a page off the table, flapping it or running about with it, this too was movement, an embodied animation of the marks. Now digital movement was added to the movement repertoire.

A user-friendly app

In 2016, I introduced a simple drawing app for children aged birth to five, Seesaw (https://web.seesaw.me/). This app was much easier to use and did not require the adult support Explain Everything had needed, so children's agency was foremost.

A note here: this app allows for the digital transmission of images to other users. We did not and would not enable this function as we are aware children's digital footprints and histories are valuable and vulnerable. We also realised this new frontier for communication and thinking was relatively manner-less, that societal codes for politeness, privacy and respect which adults might understand had not been articulated to young children, so we taught the children 'digital manners'. The children were used to opening parents' phones and rummaging through the apps, looking for the familiar and interesting. The school iPads were different; if the children were given an app to use, the teacher's expectation was that children would not leave that site. The children soon understood that pressing the 'home button' was not acceptable on our iPads. We also found that children had assumed it was okay to take a photo of another person without permission, so we taught them to ask, as we always did, before taking photos of people. Another rule, respecting refusals, as the teachers did, and not sneaking photo shots, was well policed by children.

The early photos were of things, covered with lines mimicking the object. It took only days before children began to cease this *photo as colouring book* genre and moved on to adding imaginary elements. The first element was the addition of blue and white lines representing rain on a photo of the lawn, which had been taken and drawn on a dry cloudless morning. This imaginary invention was greeted with hoots of laughter prompting a rash of other imagined events, such as 'rabbits hopping about in the puddles' being also drawn over the lawn image.

Photo-drawings with three- to five-year-old children

Typically, however, children chose to take snapshots of each other and transform (with permission) those images. Their work reflected immersion in 'life', revealing intrigue with superheroes, popular culture, hetero-normative gendered families, and fantastical creatures. We teachers disrupted and engaged in critical reflections about these important tropes. In discussing creation of images, Eisner (2001, p.130) refers to 'the limits of the material with which they work and their technical repertoires'. The surface the children used was both the screen and the photo; creating a platform for their lines to make yet another surface of meaning. We are yet to understand the role these photo-drawings have in the graphic traces children use to make meaning of the world and relationships. We remember that, 'Of course, how an image is handled is not only a function of purpose; it is also related to children's technical repertoire for making such representations possible' (Eisner, 2001, p.113).

First marks

Grace at 13 months had already frequently explored mark-making materials: chewing on the ends of pens, dropping them to the floor, stuffing them in another container, crumpling and patting paper, rolling crayons on the table, tumbling them about, relishing the sound ... but making few marks. Her inability to hold the crayon/pen and press down limited her capacity to make a visible mark. Certainly, she created phantom marks when she held the crayon and made a movement across the paper, or unexpectedly while tracing her finger through rain puddles on the veranda, but no intentionally visible marks were made. On the iPad, sitting in an adult's lap, we captured Grace's exploration of digital line-making. We watch as her finger explores the screen surface, as if getting to know it. We see her surprise, her cessation of finger to screen when she realises she is making the lines appear. She stills herself and tries again, dabbing with her finger. It would seem to us that she is testing her theory of: 'I did that, did I? Yes, I did.' She makes delicate taps, lifting her finger slowly, then adds long swirling lines, testing her theory again. She turns, wordlessly asking her adult companion, who smiles and nods. She returns to her marks, adding longer lines, creating loops. These marks have an element of gesture about them and as Ingold says: 'The line to which [this flourish] gives rise is, therefore, intrinsically dynamic and temporal' (2007, p.72).

Satisfied, Grace moves away. A week later she again works in this digital mode, now armed with the knowledge that her finger makes the mark. She covers a quarter of the page with swift moves, the marks betraying her haste and her knowledge.

Adian, at two years old, is used to the screen, knowing his finger is the agent for the marks. When he encounters the colour bar and the opportunity to change colours, he understands its role immediately. While selecting yellow, his finger accidently taps orange and he experiments with it, framing the rest of his work with an orange line. This 'accidental analogy' (Machón, 2013) will become one of his future techniques as he accommodates occasional random elements in his mark-making.

Loved companions

I had been working with a group of two-year-old children on their relationships with 'loved companions' (attachment objects), those teddies, blankets and soft toys which are an essential part of some children's body and being. Never far from the child, these sometimes-ragged entities were silent supporters, witnesses, confidants and emotional backers. I was researching each child's relationship with this companion, wanting to understand the depth and nuances, ultimately discovering these creatures had names, were gendered and were 'alive', responding to the child's advances and needs. To enable us to talk and think together, I gave the children an opportunity to make marks about their companions. I took photos on the iPad and asked the children to add drawings. Nui Nui (two years and two months), was immediately animated, and framed her teddy's photo with a blue line, chanting his (yes, he was a he) name and calling to others to look. With an interested small crowd, she moved her fingers over the image, eventually obscuring him with a mass of blue lines. She chooses the Erase tool – it only erases the line, not the photo – and slowly revealed teddy again, shouting in a mix of thrill and delight, 'Teddy!' I think for a moment he really had 'gone' for Nui Nui, a sort of virtual peek-a-boo. I ask if I can record it. She nods and then repeats this sequence. The final result, a 31-second movie of Teddy's disappearance and reappearance, elicited the same thrilled response each time it was replayed. A collection of these loved-companion movies was made, with other children appropriating Nui Nui's idea and method. If making marks is a tool for making meaning out of lived lives and loves, this media certainly helped.

Eventually, at the end of the year, a book was 'published' which featured loved companions, including digital drawings, photographs and text, emulating a photographic book we had discovered called *Much Loved* by Mark Nixon (2013), an essay of nostalgia.

The children's familiarity with the digital medium made the task of collating the book easier than it might otherwise have been.

Projection

During the 1990s, before data projectors and iPads, I had used overhead projectors to create a space in which drawing acquired another dimension. With clear overhead sheets, white-board pens and a 'drawer' plus 'audience' it was possible to move the drawing from the page to the wall. More often than not, the game that ensued was derived from the presence of shadow, colour and light. This was *drawing with the 'other'*, an engagement with live projected drawings where children created a dialogue and discourse with the live projected image, the drawing and the mark-maker. These games, where a child 'takes a line for a walk' (Ingold, 2007), generate a discursive discourse linking the elements to make a drawn landscape co-constructed by action, words, ideas and serendipity.

In 2017, in order to make digital drawing a collective experience rather than an individual one, and to help children learn new ways of thinking together, I project the ongoing drawing onto any surface nearby, making it visible for others. I use a portable data projector linked to the iPad, but knowing how quickly technology hardware is changing, the reader might have other easier solutions. At the time of writing, large interactive screens are available; however, they're expensive and relatively cumbersome. I like the portability of the data projector. I've used it to project children's ongoing work in different rooms and spaces, on ceilings, walls or floors, the shed door, shade sails, or the veranda when we are undertaking work outside. I like the convenience of iPads, a part of our everyday portable equipment. Price is always a factor, and 'throwing money' at technology without thought for its physical flexibility is problematic.

Furthermore, the projection of drawn images onto other surfaces, including people and furniture, and the subsequent bending of the 'rules' of light and colour creates another layer of understanding about colour and image. This added dimension makes room for other children besides drawers to enter into the experience.

I found digital-drawing-projecting and playing-in-the-image was more successful outside than indoors, as the thrill and excitement generated by the experience was often loud and physical. Children dashed in and out of the image, needing space to retreat to when this play became overwhelming. An eventual space in which all this work took place was the shed door, at the end of a covered veranda. This roller-shutter door became the screen with the iPad and drawer located 2 metres away, tethered to the data projector and seated on a stool facing the shutter. This left room for players in front of the roller door on what became a makeshift stage playing within the image, but still within proximity of the drawer who was creating the image.

Often it would seem that the two, the child within the image and the drawer, were unconnected. The children *within* the image navigated the cognitive dissonance when confronted with new information that contradicted their existing theories and knowledge. They peered at colour on the skin, at the transformation of bodies and the ability to manipulate that image by moving within it. One child confronted with purple skin ran to the bathroom to wash it off. Understanding the temporality of the image and its effect gave rise to experimentation with bodies within colours.

It was then that the relationship between drawers and explorers became more interactive, with requests from performers to the child drawing at the iPad to 'make me green'. For several weeks, we watched drawers respond to such requests and observed the growing entanglement of image, drawing and makers. The entangled process became clear when I overheard a three-year-old call to her companions 'go in, go in', inviting them to dance and move within her image as she drew. The children's recognition that they were inside the colours and lines and integral to the emerging image was thrilling, like dipping into water. Over time, children's confidence had grown. In the beginning, they had appeared overwhelmed by the transformative immersion in colour and would retreat, shrieking and running, to watch from *without* the image, at times checking they were still themselves. This image play was still a noisy and physical affair, and I delighted in the outdoor location, where constant reminders to be quiet and not run were unnecessary. I know that the veranda gave the experience opportunities to be playful as the restrictions of being indoors did not dampen the children's behaviour. Initial thrill soon changed to intention. For some time, the younger drawers were unaware the image on the shed door was the one they were working on at the iPad. 'It's copying me,' said Alice. Time to discover they were the agent making the images was essential in the evolution of the work. Eventually the children understood the projection was linked to the drawer, and was not permanent, or fixed in time.

Teachers alongside children

Our pedagogical ability to listen, observe and reflect gave us the insight to glimpse the complexity of playful thinking, to respect, facilitate and marvel in their abilities. It would have been easy to 'take over' and plan ahead. But this organic and wild play, now transformed into joyful problem solving and togetherness, was, I felt, something that should remain in children's realm and control. Our presence as admirers, companions and occasional software technicians supported the child-led trajectory. Our knowledge that drawing and representation was essential for children to communicate ideas, that they had an innate drive, and our understanding of the media, and belief in children's skills, coalesced into a dance between children, images, their ideas and our ideas. At the end of play each day, I would ask children to reflect and recall what had happened, using my notes and photos and the drawn artefacts as memory scaffolds. During the course of these chats, new intentions for drawings and narratives would emerge, and before the resumption of digital drawing play the next day I would recap on these reflections: 'Are you still thinking you'd like to … ?' My role as a reliable memory or prompt, as well as my awareness that children may have been contemplating the game overnight, meant that in the morning they were able to resume their image play with agency and flexibility.

The fluidity of image and play soon determined a new genre, one in which the drawer and player/performer created a virtual landscape to play and draw within. The three following narratives illustrate the task-scape children created.

The aeroplane

The first of these games we saw was when Chen (five years old), finding the iPad unused, quietly drew a series of aeroplanes. Three children playing nearby glanced over and saw the shed door covered with aircraft. James and Eric ran over and began to talk about flying, clambering 'into' the craft, squatting down to indicate they were seated, putting on

> seatbelts and "flying", embroidering the game with engine sounds. Chen at first continued his plane drawing work, however, seeing the flying play, he began adding details, with more planes to different destinations. A third player, Megan, entered the image, adding detailed knowledge of the role of passenger. 'Where is the food?' she enquired, the play-scape of image and imagination expanding further. The stimulus for the play, Chen's plane images, became the virtual world in which players created pivots to sustain the game for a further 20 minutes. Requests for detail, responses to play and language, movements through, away, from and returning to the door were intentional, as was the addition of pilot 'controls' on the door added by the players, to make the plane ascend and descend, often with dizzying speed and sound effects. This work was yet another clear indication that *"Children actively construct their own understandings and contribute to others' learning."*
>
> (DEEWR, 2009, p.9).

As we were able to see their thinking 'made visible', a clear link was made with an intended outcome.

The chocolates

Clara, from a family of jokers, was drawing on demand for two younger players. She had invented a meme of 'eating' as an interactive game. She would ask players what they wanted to 'eat', draw the food (her work was recognisable) and then, as children jumped toward the images, pretending to eat with wide open mouths making loud munching and swallowing sounds, Clara would use the Erase tool to take small bite-sized chunks out of the 'food'. Each bite corresponded with a jump by a player. Well versed in the limitations of games with little verbal communication, the players and Clara would call out instructions before moving, so they could coordinate the bites. 'Eat the strawberries now – they are delicious,' Clara would call, so the players knew which part of the image to jump towards. The rattle of the shed shutter and their shouts made a rousing addition to the game.

Over time, Clara, unasked by the players and desiring to complicate the game, drew round brown shapes, 'chocolates', interspersed among the requested foods. Naturally a hit, these chocolates were 'eaten' voraciously. Clara laughed merrily each time, happy to draw more chocolates. The racket attracted others and the game continued for 30 minutes. Once it was over, Clara confided to me, 'They weren't really chocolates … it was poo.' The ethics of humorous tricks was something we talked about later.

Basketball

Chen and Marlon took the physicality of the children's image-playing games to new heights with the first intentional co-construction of a virtual 'within-scape'. Planned the day before, following morning play, they discussed and worked out their plans during lunch. Marlon, a keen and competent basketballer, wanted Chen to draw a basketball hoop for Marlon to jump to and throw the ball into. So the next morning Chen, settling down at the iPad, drew a hoop at the top of the screen, knowing it would appear projected high up on the roller door, above Marlon's head. This technical knowledge was only acquired by frequent use of the media in that space and over time. Marlon made heroic leaps to get the ball into the hoop. The ball was imaginary and not represented by lines, but only by Marlon's cupped hands. After each leap, a declaration was made, 'In or out?', and judged by whether Marlon's hands had reached the drawing. After several 'successful' shots, Chen began a tally at the bottom of the page, adding a line for each goal. Newer hoops were drawn and the game continued until Marlon could no longer jump. In this instance the drawer became referee, co-constructing the outcome of the 'within-scape'.

These task-scapes – the aeroplane, chocolates and basketball court – are complex, socially constructed spaces of child thinking, constantly under construction and perpetually in process, also becoming playful arenas for ideas evidenced in spatial distance and plurality. The examples show that the 'we' rather than the 'I' 'create[d] shared and negotiable ways of thinking within the group' (Bruner, 1996, p.23) that supported young children's abilities to think together. By taking on the mantle and skills of interdependent thinking (Costa & Kallick, 2009) through playful encounters with digital drawing, children created environments where the complex task of learning to think with others was supported and fostered. The affordances, the many attributes bundled within a medium of digital drawing, enabled children to explore, reveal, externalise, construct and convey meaning.

The technological landscape is in flux with the current speed of invention and innovation, so it behoves early childhood teachers to pause and consider which of these new attributes will be helpful in the construction of curriculum which honours the principles of early childhood education. As in choosing any equipment or curriculum resource, critical reflection is required to see if the technology is fit for purpose.

- Does it match your educational philosophy?
- Is the child in charge?
- Can children think with it?
- Does it offer possibilities for rich complex play?
- Does the media promote individual or interdependent play – is it better with two (or more) children?
- Does it foster creative thinking and problem solving?
- Has it an elegance of design enriching the users' experience?
- What is the role of the teacher?

These are a few questions, and as with any critical reflection are only the beginning.

As Hockney (2018) has pointed out, 'People tend to forget that play is serious.' In playing through digital drawing with the processes, affordances and complexities of mark-making, the children in the examples presented in this chapter are, to paraphrase Kress, co-shapers of meaning and knowledge. Play is serious, and children's agency to engage in playful thinking, playful representation and play-filled relationships, with teachers alongside, is central to early childhood pedagogy.

As has been demonstrated here, digital drawing is another vehicle for children to become familiar with and utilise digital techniques to share the meaning(s) they are making of the world. This 'interactive agency' (Lenz Taguchi, 2009), with teachers being alongside children, broadens children's abilities to connect with others and to thus be more completely themselves.

References

Bruner, J. (1996). *The culture of education.* Harvard University Press: Cambridge, MA.

Costa, A., & Kallick, B. (2009). *Habits of mind across the curriculum: Practical and creative strategies for teachers*. Association for Supervision and Curriculum Development: Alexandria, VA.

Department of Education, Employment and Workplace Relations (DEEWR). (2009). *Belonging, being and becoming: The early years learning framework*. Commonwealth of Australia: Canberra.

Eisner, E. (2001). *The arts and the creation of mind*. Yale University Press: New Haven, CT.

Gayford, M. (2011). *A bigger message: Conversations with David Hockney*. Thames and Hudson: London.

Hockney, D. (2018, May 4). Retrieved from www.art-quotes.com/getquotes.php?catid=230#.WupX8rZL0SI.

Ingold, T. (1993). The temporality of the landscape. *World Archaeology*, 25(2), pp.152–174.

Ingold, T. (2007). *Lines: A brief history*. Routledge: London.

Kolbe, U. (2014). *Children's imagination: Creativity under our noses*. Peppinot Press: Byron Bay.

Kress, G. (2010). *Multimodality: A social semiotic approach to contemporary communication*. Taylor and Francis: London.

Lenz Taguchi, H. (2009). *Going beyond the theory/practice divide in early childhood education*. Taylor and Francis: London.

Machón, A. (2013). *Children's drawing: The genesis and nature of graphic representation*. Fibulas: Madrid.

Nixon, M. (2013). *Much loved*. Abrams Image: New York, NY

Vecchi, V., & Ruozzi, M. (Eds). (2015). *Mosaic of marks, words, materials*. Reggio Children: Reggio Emilia.

2

PRESCHOOL TEACHERS BEING ALONGSIDE YOUNG CHILDREN

The development of adults' relational competence in playworlds

Beth Ferholt, Monica Nilsson and Robert Lecusay

To many preschool teachers, it is nothing new that heartfelt, joint play with children keeps them human and so makes them better teachers. However, this topic is rarely discussed in pedagogical research, or even explicitly included in teacher education and professional development.[1] One of the productive challenges of working in the field of early childhood education and care is combining researchers' and teachers' knowledge and ways of knowing (Ferholt & Schuck, forthcoming; Nilsson et al., 2018). This chapter presents findings from studies that combine researchers' perspectives and teacher's insights. We suggest that a certain type of adult–child joint play, called playworld (Lindqvist, 1995), can be a means for preschool teachers to bring their personal selves, not just their professional, teacher selves, into their work with young children (Ferholt & Schuck, forthcoming; Nilsson et al., 2018). Furthermore, we argue that this dynamic can, in turn, allow these teachers to develop relational competence.

Playworlds are interactive activities in which children and adults can be simultaneously creatively engaged (Lindqvist, 1995). In playworlds, adults actively enter into fantasy play with young children as a means of promoting the development and quality of life of *both* adults and children. In the two playworlds discussed herein, children and adults transform their preschools and classrooms into worlds inspired by books using joint scripted and improvisational acting, as well as play writing and set design. Through this process the children are able to work with their teachers such that their teachers' relational competence develops.

Nelson Mandela's famous quotation helps convey the import of looking to playworlds to develop adults' relational competence:

> No one is born hating another person because of the color of his skin, or his background, or his religion. People must learn to hate, and if they can learn to hate, they can be taught to love, for love comes more naturally to the human heart than its opposite.
>
> (1994, p. 384)

We have found that young children can teach adults in the area of relational competence, if adults join young children in one of their primary modes of being, play, as fellow human beings, not just as teachers. In our playworld research we have seen that children help adults relate to others in ways that are responsive and characterized by dialogue.

We are three professors of early childhood education and care who have been studying playworlds together and with children, teachers, and fellow researchers for 15 years. Beth and Monica each worked with young children for a decade or more before becoming researchers and teachers of teachers: Beth was a preschool teacher in New York City and Monica was a preschool teacher in Stockholm. The materials in this chapter were ethically obtained following appropriate procedures.

Relational competence

Relational competence is "the skill of entering into and building relationships" (Aspelin, 2015, p. 35). It is considered an important part of teacher professionalism. Studies indicate that responsive and dialogic relations between teachers and children are one of the most important aspects of quality in preschool activities (Persson, 2015). As Aspelin states: "Questions about what teachers' relational competence means, how it promotes students' learning and how it can be developed in teacher education, further education of teachers and in pedagogical practices [are] largely unexplored" (2015, p. 35). We believe that playworlds are a fruitful place to start remedying this lack.

Our analysis of playworlds, described in this chapter, begins from a relational pedagogical perspective (Aspelin & Persson, 2011). We apply this conceptual framework to our analysis of transcripts and fieldnotes in two case studies of early childhood teachers creating playworlds for the first time. Our findings lead us to believe that when preschool teachers bring their personal selves, not just their teacher selves, into their adult–child joint play with young children, these adults develop in ways that are undervalued but essential in early childhood education and care. Our conceptual framework allows us to make this hypothesis plausible to you, our reader.

Aspelin (2015) describes two forms of relational competence. Teachers in "attitude *to* relationships" are focused on handling social relations in educational settings and influencing students' relations concerning, for example, teachers, friends, and people in society. In other words, these teachers are acting "from outside," while teachers in "attitude *in* relationships" encounter the student "from inside" the relationship, without preconceptions of what will happen. For instance, when there is a child who has not been responding to our efforts to help them navigate relationships successfully, over a long period of time, we reach the end of our known approaches and go out on a limb, creating a new approach *with* the struggling child, as we simply do not know what else to do.

We can describe "attitude *to* relationships" as co-operation and "attitude *in* relationships" as co-existence, if we apply the following definitions from Aspelin and Persson (2011) to Aspelin's ideas about relational competence:

> Co-existence signifies a personal encounter between two persons ... Co-existence cannot be defined using conventional behavioral concepts ... Co-existence is characterized by unpredictability and it lacks elements of planning and calculation. Co-existence is a goal in itself; i.e. meaning is inherent in the relationship.
>
> (2011, p. 10)

Aspelin and Persson go on to contrast co-operation with co-existence: "Co-operation represents a process in which individuals coordinate their actions. The process is mediated by social patterns ... Co-operation is created by purposeful action, i.e. it includes goals outside of the relationship" (2011, p. 10).

It can be useful to think of oneself as a person in the world, as well as a teacher, in order to start to make sense of these concepts (Ferholt

& Schuck, forthcoming). For example, if a teacher wants to work with a reading specialist to ensure that a child learns to read (perhaps an activity that should not be a part of early childhood education and care but something with which many teachers of young children are familiar) the two teachers might jointly, delicately negotiate the day's schedule to include the required remediation with other necessary activities (co-operation). If a teacher and child are laughing together over a good book, neither one caring if anything concrete is accomplished, both adult and child might simply be enjoying the experience of laughing with another person they care about (as they would with, for instance, a family member) (co-existence).

Playworlds

Lindqvist's creative pedagogy of play (1995, 2001) was designed to investigate how aesthetic activities can influence children's play, and the nature of the connections between play and the aesthetic forms of drama and literature. The basis for the pedagogy is Lindqvist's (1995, 2001) reinterpretation of L. S. Vygotsky's (1978, 1987, 2004) theories of play and imagination in conjunction with his writings on the psychology of art (1971). Lindqvist (1995) uses the creative pedagogy of play to find a "common denominator" of play and aesthetic forms, a denominator that she calls "the aesthetics of play." She considers one of the most important conclusions of her investigation to be that the development of adult–child joint play is made possible through the creation of a common fiction, which she calls a "playworld" (1995).[2] (For a detailed discussion of playworld theory see Nilsson & Ferholt, 2014.)

Playworlds first spread from Sweden to Finland (Hakkarainen, 2008). In 2003–2004, a first U.S. playworld was organized (Baumer et al., 2005) and there are playworlds taking place in the U.S. today, with data currently under analysis; new forms of playworlds that are partially inspired by these U.S. playworlds and partially inspired by pedagogies developed in Reggio Emilia, Italy (Reggio Children and Project Zero, 2001), are now taking place in Sweden (Nilsson et al., 2018); and playworlds are also taking place elsewhere (Marjanovic-Shane et al., 2011). (For a detailed survey of playworld research see https://quote.ucsd.edu/lchcautobio/polyphonic-autobiography/section-5/chapter-14-adultchild-play-emotion-cognition-and-development-in-playworlds/.)

Through international collaboration among playworld researchers in Sweden, Finland, and the U.S., we have identified three conditions that we believe are essential in the creation of the shared responsibility for directing the adult–child joint play that is at the heart of the types of playworlds described in this chapter (Ferholt et al., 2015; Ferholt & Lecusay, 2010). First, adults in a playworld enter fully into children's play by taking on play roles, putting on costumes and entering character. In doing so, they are required to partially step outside their role as teacher and join the children in the role of fellow actor. Second, children as well as adults co-construct the environment in which play takes place: The children do not play in an environment that has been designed for them by adults alone. And third, Lindqvist's pedagogy grounds play in works of children's literature that address epistemological and ethical dilemmas that are of great interest to people in a variety of life stages. Because of this grounding, the teacher is personally invested in the topics, and therefore in the process and outcomes of a playworld.

Playworlds can be described as combinations of adult forms of creative imagination, which require extensive experience (e.g. art, science), with children's forms of creative imagination (e.g. play), which require the embodiment of ideas and emotions in the material world. The development of both children and adults in this intergenerational, hybrid form of play has been of central interest to playworld researchers in part because, unlike many intergenerational activities, playworlds allow children as well as adults to take the position of expert. (See Paananen and Rainio's chapter in this book for an example of a study that takes for granted the benefits of adult–child play activities, such as playworlds.)

- Have you felt yourself developing your own relational competence while working with young children?
- What do you understand play to be? Is play different in early childhood; for older children; in adulthood?

The development of adults' relational competence in playworlds

In both of the playworlds discussed below, participating teachers described experiencing changes in their engagement with others at their preschool and schools, and indicated that these changes were related to the integration of their professional and personal selves. These changes included a greater understanding of children's perspectives leading to a deepened connection with the children, and concomitant positive effects on collaboration between children and teachers, as well as between teachers and between researchers and teachers. The teachers attributed these changes, in part, to the ways in which role-play with the children in the playworlds had helped them to step outside of their traditional roles as teachers.

Lindqvist describes the creation of opportunities for teachers to "step out of their 'teacher roles'" in playworlds thus:

> During the course of the theme, I have seen the teachers become someone in the eyes of the children. They have turned into interesting and exciting people. I have often had the feeling that staff members at a day-care center are perceived as rather anonymous grown-ups. Sometimes, the children will not even notice if a teacher is ill and has been replaced. In a way, assuming roles has liberated the adults – it has enabled them to step out of their 'teacher roles' and leave behind the institutional language which is part of the teacher role in pre-schools and schools. By virtue of the fictitious role, the teachers have dared to try new attitudes and ways of acting.
> (Lindqvist, 1995, pp. 210–211)

We argue that Lindqvist's observation that "teachers become someone in the eyes of the children" can be understood in terms of co-existence and attitude *in* relations. Specifically, we see Lindqvist's observations that "(a)ssuming roles has liberated the adults – it has enabled them to step out of their 'teacher roles'" (p. 210) as a way in which co-existence and relational competence, understood as "attitude *in* relationships," can potentially emerge in playworlds.[3]

Methods: Participants and context

The first case study is based on observations from a two-year ethnographic research project that took place in three Swedish preschools, all following a Reggio-inspired *pedagogy of listening* and *exploratory learning* approach (Reggio Children and Project Zero, 2001). The children who created this playworld with their teachers were two and three years old. The research project was originally designed to examine if and how the teachers in these three preschools adopted the playworld activity into their own practices.

The second case study is analyzed in less depth than the first, but supports related findings. It is based on observations from a two-year ethnographic research project that took place in a U.S. public elementary school. The children who created this playworld with their teacher, and also with researchers, ranged in age from five to seven years. This project was originally designed to see what a playworld would look like in a U.S. early childhood education setting.

Data collection and analysis: Playworld as formative intervention

Although Lindqvist did not use the term, many playworld studies, including Lindqvist's, can be described as "formative interventions" (Engeström, 2008). In a formative intervention "the subjects construct a novel solution or novel concept, the contents of which are not known ahead of time to the researchers," and "the contents and course of the intervention are subject to negotiation and the shape of the intervention is eventually up to the subjects," while "the aim is to generate intermediate concepts and solutions that can be used in other settings as tools in the design on locally appropriate new solutions" (Engeström, 2008, pp. 15–16).

In both playworld studies discussed in this chapter, data was gathered through participant observation using a variety of documentation methods, including interviews, fieldnotes from observations, and audio-recorded reflection-and-planning meetings. In the Swedish playworld data also included teachers' pedagogical documentation. Analysis took place both among researchers and in collaboration with participating teachers. Important in both playworlds were the facts that artists were employed to document the playworld at certain points in the process and, to different degrees in the different playworlds, that art methods were incorporated into the social scientific analysis (see Ferholt, 2010).

Developing adults' relational competence in playworlds: Example #1

The event that we present from the Swedish playworld is a discussion that took place among three preschool teachers who participated in that study (we will call them Marie, Elisabeth, and Charlotte). The discussion took place during a teaching reflection and planning meeting. This meeting constituted an important turning point in the teachers' incorporation of the playworld activity into their own practice, as it involved the transposition by these teachers of modes of interaction and conflicts, which had taken place in the classroom playworld, into the reflection meeting itself.

Chronologically, at the point in the project during which this discussion took place a picture book had been read to the children several times. The book depicted a story about a princess who awoke to a strange noise. As part of the playworld activity, Marie had recently appeared outside the preschool window as the princess, sleeping outside and then being awakened by the noise. The children then rushed outside to join the princess on their own initiative. On this first day of role-play, the children joined the princess in all sorts of stories and in "hearing" many noises, and this joint play continued over the course of many weeks. After just a few weeks, Elisabeth joined Marie and the children in the playworld as a "basement troll." The basement troll was the source of the noise in the book and was quite scary in the book, and Elisabeth also behaved in scary ways during the joint play. Although the princess was brave in the book, in the classroom Marie played a variety of roles in a variety of stories, some of which required more bravery than others.

The teachers' meeting begins with Marie being upset because she feels lonely. She observes that no one wants to play with her when she is in her princess character. The following is the transcript of the meeting with interpretation and analysis inserted.

MARIE: They [the children] want to play with me because I am a princess, but I want to play with them because they are a ... actually, the same need as they have, I have a need to be with them. It might not be their needs but for me it is easier to play if, I have a need to play with someone that is not Tim [name of a child]. ... Do you understand what I mean? But it might be my needs, it might have nothing to do with the children's needs?

After discussing this quote with Marie, we understand her to be expressing discomfort at not having co-players. The children are too interested in the princess, which makes Marie feel lonely. She wants the children to be her playmates and enter the playworld in role with her. Marie is engaging in an exploration of her own emotional dilemma, without preconceptions of this exploration's outcome, and as such she is not solely in a professional role with a "*to* attitude," but is also accessing her personal self with an "*in* attitude."

ELISABETH: But I believe you are so obsessed with being, that it should be more theatre. I don't understand how to explain it but I think you are more obsessed because you have demands on yourself, aiming for something …

Here Elisabeth is pointing out that Marie is confusing play with theatre, and that Marie is in need of too much control.

MARIE: But you don't play with me (*inaudible*) … Because, that is what I feel. I tried to play with you! And you don't really want to.
ELISABETH: (*Laughter*) I don't really feel like it. Yes.
MARIE: When I came there with my princess it was like this, you'd actually rather play with the children.
ELISABETH: Yes.
MARIE: Because when I came into the kitchen and tried like this, then it was like this: "Oh, yes, but" – admit that it was a little bit like that.
ELISABETH: Yes, a little bit like that. But I don't feel … I don't know entirely, I don't trust you (…) the play.
CHARLOTTE: (*Laughter*)
MARIE: No, I felt that!
ELISABETH: Yes, you felt that.
MARIE: We have to do this again.
ELISABETH: Yes, and then I was thinking that whom could I think of playing with? But then I was thinking like this. This is what it might be like for the children.

The teachers now speak as they might to friends or family, about how they feel hurt or vulnerable playing together. Marie is expressing her feeling that the children became a shield, in that they were being used to prevent Elisabeth and her from playing together. They talk about working together, as their work includes play, but it is a discussion about how they are relating to each other's selves that encompasses several areas of their lives.

THE SUBSTITUTE TEACHER THEN ADDS: Yes, we want the children to be able to play together with everybody and here we can see that that is not so easy all the time.

ELISABETH: No!

MARIE: No, and we are good at working together but we can't play together.

Soon after this point in the conversation, Marie says to the researchers: "[We] ... have never been so honest and open with each other and that is good!" And after this discussion, Marie was eager to write a book to show that they, the teachers, had been a part of something that others don't entirely understand. We believe that this *something* is all three teachers bringing to the fore their non-teacher selves, and in this way entering "attitude *in* relationships" with each other such that they encounter each other "from inside" the relationship, without preconceptions of what will happen. Furthermore, we suspect that it was the play with children in playworlds that led these teachers to be able to do this.

From this data we tentatively conclude that due to the fact that in playworlds adults enter into imagining with people (children) who cannot imagine without the material (play), meaning that they (children) always play, and the adults must play, or they have no one to imagine with; and, as a result of this impetus, adults do enter into and sustain roles beyond their teacher selves in playworlds, and have the potential to continue to practice this skill with their coworkers when out of playworlds, in this way developing new forms of relational competence with their coworkers.

Example #2

The two-part event that we will present from the first U. S. playworld study is an extended statement made by the elementary school teacher who participated in the study (we will call him Michael) to one of the researchers who had been in role in the playworld. The statement began in a fieldnote by Michael and then continued in a spontaneous and informal post-playworld analysis that took place between the teacher and several of the researchers via email.

Chronologically, the playworld sessions described below had just been completed before the fieldnote was recorded. This playworld was based on C. S. Lewis's *The Lion, the Witch and the Wardrobe* (1950). Over the one-year period during which the playworld took place, there were 14 playworld sessions, each of which lasted approximately two hours. Most of these sessions included reflection upon the enactments in the form of discussion, which was followed by free play or art activities.

Most of these 14 sessions included all four researchers, who played the child heroes of the playworld. The teacher joined in role playing for the first time during the seventh of these sessions, playing the evil White Witch, and the children joined in role for the first time during the eighth of these sessions, as themselves. For the final sessions the children were the primary planners of the adult–child joint play. All 14 playworld sessions involved set pieces and props created by both the adults and children, including props that were designed to appeal to the participants' sense of touch, smell, and sound. The classroom activities were conducted in and around these props: a cardboard dam, cave, castle, and so on.

In the following excerpt transcribed from a video fieldnote, Michael explains bringing his personal self into the Narnia playworld through discussing his favorite moment in that playworld:

> But I think for me personally, my favorite moment, you know, just me personally – not being altruistic – was, the day that Beth walked in.
>
> ["The day that Beth walked in" refers to the day that Beth, the researcher who was sent to meet Michael, walked into Michael's classroom to visit and then invite him to join the project.]
>
> Yeah. If it can't be the one – because ultimately B. [student] being nice to N. [student] is my ultimate goal. So that kind of signifies my favorite moment, also.
>
> It's tough. Those three.
>
> But I'd have to say, as a teacher … (*He points in front of himself, down at the floor, then raises his hand to the height of his neck and draws a circle with his hand.*) Uh, for what I do in the classroom B. being nice to N. was the ultimate time.
>
> As a teacher involved in *this* [he means the Narnia playworld, as he points to the cardboard sets of the playworld that are around him], it was (*his hand is now drawing a slightly larger circle in front of his neck*), it was the box on the head [referring to when he as the White Witch was trapped in the Narnia playworld]. (*He points to his head.*)

And as me personally, as a teacher as well but as me personally (*the circle he is drawing with his hand becomes larger still*), is was when Beth walked in the door.

Does that clarify things?

I know it sounds like I'm choosing three but it's actually one for each of my ... three narratives: teacher, teacher involved in how I ... (*He was pointing with a finger for each of these three "narratives," but then he starts the list again while making a small circle with his left hand by his left ear each time he names one of the three narratives.*)

Person – being a human in the world. Teacher in the classroom. And then teacher involved in this Narnia.

So those are my three moments for each of those... narratives.

So that's three for you, Beth.

The underlined portions of this fieldnote state that Beth walking in the door was from Michael's "person – being a human in the world" narrative. Four years after recording this fieldnote, Michael provides a useful description of Beth's entering his "teacher in the classroom" narrative, thus describing his person narrative being included in his teacher narrative through his participation in the Narnia playworld. He does so using a term from his own and Beth's joint analysis of the television show *Lost*, and the episode titled "The Constant" (March, 2010). As Michael explains (in an email sent March 15, 2009), a "constant is someone who helps you reflect back on what you yourself did ... (a) constant helps you remember your own experience (and this person may/may not have experienced anything you did)." Michael adds: "A constant is sort of like a beacon ... guiding you back on course. But, also giving you hope." Michael then argues that, through the Narnia playworld, Beth became his "constant for when I am teaching": "When all is chaotic (in my classroom) and I need something to 'right my ship' I think of [Beth]. I do not have to consciously think about you: you just appear in my brain."

This description by Michael of Beth's role for him is closely related to "attitude *in* relations" in the sense of an existential meeting, as in co-existence, in which one person is immediately present vis-à-vis another. One of our tentative conclusions from this data is, again, that adults enter into and sustain roles beyond their teacher selves in playworlds, and continue to practice this skill with their coworkers when out of playworlds, in this way developing new forms of relational competence with their coworkers. Michael was the White Witch in the playworld and this allowed Beth to become, eventually, Michael's "constant."

- What questions do you have about the methods described, the case studies themselves, and the conclusions that we have drawn?
- Do you find that the case studies support our claims? Why, or why not?

Culmination

In this chapter we have discussed being alongside children in playworlds, learning from children in playworlds because children are expert players, and specifically thinking of playworlds as a play pedagogy in which adults develop their relational competence. Children in a playworld benefit from adult expertise and experience in the arts and sciences, while adults in a playworld benefit from playing with children because children refuse to play with adults (at least in playworlds) if these adults do not become interesting and exciting people to the children, rather than anonymous grown-ups, by leaving their institutional "teacher roles" behind. As Michael, the teacher in the second example, explained: "(H)ere is an analogy ... I have on my football helmet ... and everyone else is playing basketball. The kids are playing basketball ... and if we want to play, we need to get rid of the helmet" (from an email cited in Ferholt, 2009, p. 17).

Furthermore, these case studies have led us to believe not only that, for these early childhood teachers, their relational competence developed through co-existence, in which "attitude *in* relationships" had a potential to emerge; and that "attitude *in* relationships" occurred in their playworlds; but also that, while their relational competence developed through the fostering of trust and authentic/honest communication, this communication was often difficult for some of these teachers (Ferholt et al., 2018). In this chapter we have been thinking of the work of caring for, raising, and educating young children, using the metaphor of the counter-intuitive and uncomfortable instructions that are given to adults traveling with small children on a plane: "In case of emergency, put on your own mask first." First we must let children remind us, while we are princesses, witches, and trolls, how to relate in ways that are characterized by responsiveness and dialogue, as it is only after making sure that we are receiving this relational oxygen that we can consistently demonstrate such forms of relational competence with the people, both large and small, with whom we live in our preschools and elementary schools.

Notes

1 The exception that proves this rule is the well-known work of teacher and author Vivian Paley. However, even Paley (1986) maintains, and describes adults in, the roles of transcriber of and audience for children's play.
2 Lindqvist gives rich and concrete examples in her publications of implementations of her creative pedagogy of play (1995, 2001, etc.).
3 See Ferholt et al. (2018), Ferholt (2009), and Ferholt and Schuck (forthcoming) for related analyses of the two playworlds discussed in this chapter.

References

Aspelin, J. (2015). Lärares relationskompetens. Begreppsdiskussion med stöd i Martin Bubers begrepp "det sociala" och "det mellanmänskliga" (Teacher's relational competence. A concept discussion, supported by Martin Buber's concepts of "the social" and "the inter-human"). *Utbildning Och Demokrati*, 24(3), 49–64.

Aspelin, J., & Persson, S. (2011). Co-existence and co-operation: The two-dimensional conception of education. *Education*, 1(1), 6–11.

Baumer, S., Ferholt, B., & Lecusay, R. (2005). Promoting narrative competence through adult–child joint pretense: Lessons from the Scandinavian educational practice of playworld. *Cognitive Development*, 20, 576–590.

Engeström, Y. (2008). *The Future of Activity Theory*. Paper presented at the Second Congress of the International Society for Cultural and Activity Research, San Diego, CA.

Ferholt, B. (2009). *Adult and Child Development in Adult–Child Joint Play: The Development of Cognition, Emotion, Imagination and Creativity in Playworlds*. Unpublished dissertation. San Diego, CA: University of California.

Ferholt, B. (2010). A multiperspectival analysis of creative imagining: Applying Vygotsky's method of literary analysis to a playworld. In C. Connery, V. John-Steiner & A. Marjanovic-Shane (Eds), *Vygotsky and Creativity: A Cultural Historical Approach to Play, Meaning-Making and the Arts* (pp. 163–180). New York, NY: Peter Lang.

Ferholt, B., & Lecusay, R. (2010). Adult and child development in the zone of proximal development: Socratic dialogue in a playworld. *Mind Culture and Activity*, 17(1), 59–83.

Ferholt, B., Lecusay, R., & Nilsson, M. (2018). Adult and child learning in playworlds. In P. Smith (Ed.), *The Cambridge Handbook of Play: Developmental and Disciplinary Perspectives* (pp. 511–527). Cambridge: Cambridge University Press.

Ferholt, B., Nilsson, M., Jansson, A., & Alnervik, K. (2015). Creativity in education: Play and exploratory learning. In T. Hansson (Ed.), *Contemporary Approaches to Activity Theory* (pp. 264–284). Hershey, PA: IGI Global.

Ferholt, B., & Schuck, C. (forthcoming). Research-life or a method of creating aesthetic form: The playworld activity and the development of a method for the study of individual behavior and consciousness. In P. Dionne & A. Jornet (Eds), *Doing CHAT in the Wild: From-the-field Challenges of a Non Dualist Methodology*. Rotterdam: Sense Publishers.

Hakkarainen, P. (2008). The challenges and possibilities of a narrative learning approach in the Finnish early childhood education system. *International Journal of Educational Research*, 47, 292–300.

Lewis, C. S. (1950). *The Lion, the Witch and the Wardrobe*. New York, NY: Macmillan Publishing.

Lindqvist, G. (1995). *Lekens estetik. En didaktisk studie om lek och kultur i förskolan*. Forskningsrapport 95: 12, SKOBA, Högskolan i Karlstad. (The Aesthetics of Play. A Didactic Study of Play and Culture in Preschools). Acta Universitatis Upsaliensis. Uppsala Studies in Education 62. Stockholm/Sweden: Almqvist & Wiksell International.

Lindqvist, G. (2001). When small children play: How adults dramatize and children create meaning. *Early Years*, 21(1), 7–14.

Mandela, Nelson. (1994). *Long Walk to Freedom*. New York, NY: Little, Brown and Company.

Marjanovic-Shane, A., Ferholt, B., Nilsson, M., Rainio, A. P., & Miyazaki, K. (2011). Playworlds: An art of development. In C. Lobman & B. O'Neill (Eds), *Play and Culture Studies, Vol. 11* (pp. 3–31). Lanham, MD: University Press of America.

Nilsson, M., & Ferholt, B. (2014). Vygotsky's theories of play, imagination and creativity in current practice: Gunilla Lindqvist's "creative pedagogy of play" in U.S. kindergartens and Swedish Reggio-Emilia inspired preschools. *Perspectiva*, 32(1), 919–950.

Nilsson, M., Granqvist, A. K., Johansson, E., Thure, J., & Ferholt, B. (2018). *Lek, lärande och lycka: lekande och utforskande i förskolan* (Play, Learning and Happiness: Play and Exploration in Preschool). Stockholm: Gleerups.

Paley, V. G. (1986). *Mollie Is Three: Growing Up in School*. Chicago, IL: University of Chicago Press.

Persson, S. (2015). *Delstudie 4: Pedagogiska relationer i förskolan. Förskola tidigintervention* (Pedagogical Relations in Preschool. Preschool Early Intervention). *Delrapport från SKOLFORSK-projektet.* Stockholm: Vetenskapsrådet.

Reggio Children and Project Zero. (2001). *Making learning visible: Children as individual and group learners.* Reggio Emilia, Italy: Reggio Children and Project Zero.

Vygotsky, L. S. (1971). *The Psychology of Art.* Cambridge, MA: MIT Press.

Vygotsky, L. S. (1978). *Mind in Society: The Development of Higher Psychological Processes.* Cambridge, MA: Harvard University Press.

Vygotsky, L. S. (1987). Imagination and its development in childhood. In R. W. Rieber & A. S. Carton (Eds), *The Collected Works of L. S. Vygotsky, Vol. 1* (pp. 339–350). New York, NY: Plenum Press.

Vygotsky, L. S. (2004). Imagination and creativity in childhood. *Journal of Russian and East European Psychology,* 42(1), 7–97.

3

PLAYING IN AND THROUGH THE MUSICAL WORLDS OF CHILDREN

Margaret S. Barrett

Research has demonstrated that children experience and respond to music in the womb and retain memory of these early experiences for some time after birth. For children music is a ubiquitous part of their world as they experience, respond to, and playfully engage with the sound worlds of their mother initially and then to those of their broader social and cultural environments. Researchers working in diverse environments globally have identified common elements in children's early music experience including the use of song in infant–carer relationships. Australian studies exploring the use of musical parenting and care through a cultural psychology lens have demonstrated the importance of shared playful music-making in early learning and development, including children's identity work.

This chapter outlines the range and complexities of children's musical worlds, the nature of their engagement in these worlds in and through musical play, and the life and learning outcomes that may accrue from such engagement. Topics addressed include: musical parenting as play, communicative musicality, children's invented singing, song-making, and music-making, intersecting worlds of musical play, technology-mediated musical play for young children, and life and learning outcomes of engaging in musical play.

Infants and children's early sound worlds

At birth we emerge into the world with functional sensory systems – some more developed than others. Hearing, smell, and touch are more mature than vision as infants have been drawing on and using these sensory systems throughout early life in the womb. The ability to hear emerges around 18 weeks of life and continues to develop throughout gestation (Lecanuet, 1996). Whilst the infant's initial sound world is the rhythmic thrumming of the mother's body, it is not long before the capacity to hear sound external to the womb is formed. Perhaps the first external stimulus to which the infant responds is that of the mother's voice (Voegtline et al., 2013). Infants in utero become a partner in the musical activities and engagement of the mother, at times demonstrating through strategically-timed kicks or settlings the nature of their responses to these experiences. Research studies have demonstrated that exposure to music "prenatally has a significant and favourable influence on neonatal behaviour" (Arya et al., 2012) with infants aged 6–8 weeks responding with signs of recognition and familiarity to music which had only been heard previously in the womb. In short, we seem to be programmed to engage with music from the earliest moments of life and learning.

Researchers in a range of fields argue that song is the earliest form of music-making in human existence and that it played a vital role in the survival of the species (Mithen, 2007). Singing and song-making appear to be a universal feature of human culture and a common element in the early life experiences of infants. Songs are used to soothe and calm through infant-directed lullabies, to arouse and engage through lap-songs and finger plays, to bond through musically-imbued conversational turn-taking, and as a means to teach children about elements of their world (Barrett, 2009). Infant-directed singing and song-making also serve to strengthen emotional and social bonds between infant and carer and establish a safe, supportive, and secure environment for the infant's health and well-being. And through all of this musical engagement, infants are also learning the musical vocabulary of their culture and the generative and performance practices that embody this vocabulary. Such work begins early. A longitudinal study of maternal singing interactions with infants aged 3–4 months and subsequently at 7–8 months of age demonstrates that the infants were alert to and responsive to their mothers' expressive emphasis in the temporal organisation of the song. The infant participants learned their mothers' dynamic temporal modelling of the song (which beats are emphasised), demonstrating this through increased synchronous behaviours on those beats emphasised by the mother (Longhi, 2009).

Whilst much of the singing and song-making described here is adult-led, children are not just passive recipients of the music-making of others. From birth, vocal sound-making is perhaps the infant's most effective means of communication. Infants are skilled in attracting our attention and ensuring that their needs are met through the cries of discomfort, hunger, and uncertainty that provoke parents and care-givers into action to change, feed, or comfort them. Similarly, the contented gurglings and cooings that accompany their happier moments prompt parents and carers to engage in playful vocal interplay. During these exchanges parents and carers draw on a musico-linguistic strategy known variously as *motherese* or *parentese* (Papoušek, 1996) in which the prosodic features of language (the rhythms, stresses, and intonation) are exaggerated.

These early dialogues between infant and care-giver have been described as instances of communicative musicality (Malloch & Trevarthen, 2009a), forms of cooperative and co-dependent interaction characterised by the musical elements of pulse, quality (expressive), and narrative (Trevarthen & Malloch, 2002). Through such communicative musicality infants "practise the gestures of song and ceremonial movements, and show them off with pride to people they trust" (Trevarthen, 2002, in Malloch & Trevarthen, 2009b, p. 7). Ellen Dissanayake suggests that these communicative activities are strategic on the part of the infant, serving evolutionary purposes to ensure that the helpless infant is cared for and protected from the immanent dangers of the environment (Dissanayake, 2009, 2012).

Beyond this strategic use, early vocalisations provide opportunity for the infant to explore the musical qualities of pitch, dynamics, and timbre as they use their cries and cooings for a range of emotional, practical, and social purposes. Such vocal exploration draws on the vowels, consonants, and musical prosody of the language/s to which they are exposed, thereby playing a crucial role in young children's early language development (Chen-Hafteck & Mang, 2012; Mang, 2001). In summary, infants' early vocalisations and musical play, undertaken alone, in dialogue or in synchrony with others, are powerful learning tools for social and emotional attachment and engagement, for language development, for music development, and for cultural identity and location. I shall expand on these issues below.

Musical play in family and community

Infants' and children's early sound worlds are those of the community in which they live. Within the family home, this includes not only those music experiences that are directed to the infant such as infant-directed song and speech, and music listening experiences designed for child listening; it also includes the musical preferences and music-making of parents, siblings, and that music heard incidentally across the day. Through the processes of musical parenting, music marks key events of the day for many children as song is used by parents and carers to accompany daily tasks such as getting up, bathing, getting dressed, and brushing teeth (Barrett, 2009, 2011). Music is also an important component of many rituals with songs and music-making designed to mark family celebrations such as birthdays, to support religious observances such as the singing of "Grace" before eating, and to demonstrate support for favourite sports teams.

On leaving the home, infants and young children continue to encounter music. Music accompanies journeys in the car and other forms of transport (for example, the music encountered in taxi journeys to and from care) and is a prominent feature of shopping experiences in malls, supermarkets, and department stores. In some settings, music is used to signal changes in the timetable of early learning and care settings and is a central aspect of religious observances in most practices. Bedtime rituals may involve stories and songs, and the playing of favourite music tracks. Infants and young children engage in these musical practices by themselves, with carers, and with siblings.

Curating children's music engagement has become a major focus of the music industry with a plethora of companies providing music experiences and products across a range of media. As an example, a brief Google search for "make your baby smarter by listening to music" unearths in excess of 2,260,000 sites, many drawing on the much-disputed "Mozart Effect" (Campbell, 1997/2001). Children's entertainers such as The Wiggles have created a global industry presenting concerts and selling CDs, DVDs, and associated clothing, toys, books, and home items such as lunch boxes, drink bottles, and cutlery sets. Kinderling Radio, an Australian digital radio station, provides "family-friendly kids'" radio for children and adults that aims to map the musical contours of the day with music programs such as "I'm Awake" at 6am, "Together Time" at 9am, "Settle Petal" at 5pm and "Sleepy Soundtrack" at 8pm (www.kinderling.com.au). Many children's toys and interactive books now incorporate music and sound effects, providing yet another source through which children engage with music. Increasingly, digital devices are being used in families as a means of mediating children's engagement with the world.

Children's exposure to this plethora of experiences and ways of engaging with music (as audience, as participant, as creator) provide them with models of music in action and lay the foundations for the repertoire on which they will draw in life and the learning. Nevertheless, research is demonstrating that for the benefits of music engagement to be realised in early learning and development, continuing joint interaction through shared music-making, a parallel to shared reading, is needed (Williams et al., 2015).

Learning in and through musical play

The interactions described in the first section of this chapter (infant-directed lullabies and songs, lap-songs and finger plays, and musically-imbued conversational turn-taking) are playful in nature and intent and may be viewed as the child's first experiences of play. Play is a learned cultural practice (Goncu & Gaskins, 2007) with parents, care-givers, siblings, and the family circle in which the child lives acting as the first teachers of this activity. Importantly, musical play is a rich medium for learning across a range of dimensions. What does such play look like and what is its function?

> 'You ready for "Eency Weency"?' Joseph's mum asks in a dramatically rising tone. Joseph, who is lying on his back on the carpet, drums both heels on the floor, watching his mother with a big grin. She kneels over him on the floor and starts to sing. As she sings her fingers 'spider' the full length of his body to his evident enjoyment. 'Down came the rain and flushed poor Eency out.' With hands raised into the air she flutters her fingers down towards Joseph to hold his raised hands. She continues 'Ooooo – out came the sun and dried up all the rain,' her arms describing an arc over and around Joseph before 'spidering' her fingers up his body once more to tap him gently on the nose. Throughout, Joseph continues to thrust his whole body in response to her singing and laughs with enjoyment as his mum finishes the performance with a joyful 'Wheeeeee!', rocking him gently from side to side.
>
> The song is repeated with no less enjoyment from either Joseph or his mother. This time she finishes with a bout of exaggerated kisses on his cheek before asking 'Are you ready?' She launches into another song, 'I'm Gonna Shake, Rattle and Roll', holding Joseph by his sides and rocking and

rolling him in time to the song. This song finishes with an extended 'YEEAAAHHH' and clapping from Mum to which Joseph responds with a falling vocalisation. His mum responds by imitating his vocalisation and settling herself more comfortably on the floor beside him.

Joseph's mum begins to sing 'Twinkle, Twinkle', raising her arms to the sky, forming a star shape, and twinkling her fingers at the relevant moments. Joseph watches the movements of her arms and fingers, his gaze returning to her face throughout the song, again thrusting his legs to his own beat as she sings. As she reaches the last line, twinkling her fingers over him, he reaches up to grasp her hands, pulling them towards him as the song finishes. Again he laughs as the song ends. 'Yeeaahhh! So exciting,' comments his mother, leaning down towards him and bringing his hands together with hers whilst making loud kissing sounds. 'Do you want to do "Twinkle, Twinkle" again?' Taking his continued movement and fixed gaze as a 'yes' she starts to sing again. Throughout the song Joseph reaches continually towards his mother's gesturing hands, following their movement with his eyes.

'What now?' she whispers. 'What now?' After a pause she whispers, 'Shall we do "The Grand Old Duke of York"?' She repeats the question with rising tone and volume. Joseph increases his thrusting, raising his legs and arms in the air and accompanying all with vocalisations of delight. 'I think we should … Huh … I do … U-uh,' she confirms, grabbing his feet and kissing the 'beautiful feet'. 'Are you ready?' she asks as she grasps him with both hands. 'Are you ready?' she repeats as she lifts him into the air and settles him on her knee facing her. She begins to sing, holding Joseph and bouncing him gently in time to the song, raising him into the air as the Duke's troops march to the top of the hill and settling him back on her knee as they descend. He cries with delight as he is whooshed through the air, up, down, and side to side, all movements marked by the marching beat of the song. All is repeated, this time with the camera focused on Joseph's face – he has a broad grin on his face throughout and gurgles appreciatively at the end.

The episode finishes as his mum rests him back down on her raised knees to sing 'Row, Row, Row Your Boat'. Joseph lies back against his mother's knees as she slides her legs up and down across the floor to the rocking beat of the song, quietened by her calm singing and the gentle movement of the 'boat'.

This video episode was recorded by a family participating in a longitudinal study of young children's musical engagement, learning, and development in family and community.[1] Data were generated by parents and care-givers maintaining a video diary recording their child's musical engagements and interactions. Interview data provided further insights into the nature and extent of music participation in the lives of the families and their children, and a brief weekly overview diary maintained (written) by the family provided insights into the range of repertoire and activity encountered from day-to-day.

Joseph was just six months of age and the first-born for his parents at the time of this recording. Music in this family is a central component of play and interaction. Both parents sing with and to Joseph; the home soundtrack consists of the jazz, classical, and folk music that his parents love; and there is a range of child and adult musical instruments available for him to play with. In this short musical play episode (less than five minutes) Joseph and his mum sing four different children's songs, each with actions that build on the song's musical qualities (the beat and rhythm, and pitch direction) and textual qualities (actions that match the words), each repeated. Joseph is no passive audience member to his mother's performances. Rather he watches her intently throughout, moves to her singing, and responds vocally at the end of each song.

The functions of this musical play episode are multiple. First, for Joseph and his mum their joint engagement in music-making is a means of bonding, of deepening and strengthening the emotional connections that bind them together. This playful engagement is enjoyable, meaningful, and fulfilling for both as evidenced in the synchronicity of their movements, joint gaze, joint touching, smiles, and laughter. Second, these songs are traditional songs of Joseph's parents' musical culture. They are songs that both parents knew as children and had sung to them by parents and care-givers in turn. They are songs that visiting grandparents and family friends hold in their musical memories and as such are a means of playfully engaging with Joseph whilst maintaining and sustaining the cultural heritage of children's musical worlds. Whilst learning these songs in the home, they are part of a shared repertoire that Joseph may encounter in future early education and care settings, providing him with a vocabulary of song and gesture with which he may engage and socialise with other children and care-givers. In turn Joseph may well sing these songs to and with his children. Third, each song contains within it numerous symbols, signs, and references to how the world operates: stars twinkle in the night sky; rain comes down and washes things away; and sun dries up rain. Information about directions is provided (up, down, and neither up nor down) with physical gestures that demonstrate and reinforce what these terms mean. Fourth, Joseph is learning the structures of song through feeling the underlying beat, the rhythmic patterns and variations, the contour of melodies across phrase structures, and the cadential structures that signal the end of a song. It is not by accident I suggest that Joseph's vocalisations fall at the end of the songs. Fifth, Joseph is building a vocabulary of musical possibilities, a vocabulary that he will draw on in his own playful music-making in the coming months and years. Finally, through this musical play episode Joseph is learning the performance practices of his culture as he is being prepared to move to the beat, to sing, and to gesture as modelled by his mother in her engagement with him. And each performance ends with a delighted acknowledgement as befits an engaged audience member. In his future playful music-making Joseph will draw on these performance practices, incorporating these into his own unique performance practices.

Working through a Cultural-Historical Activity Theory (CHAT) lens, Van Oers (2013) proposes a definition of play as a mode of activity that incorporates three parameters, those of: rules, degrees of freedom, and involvement. He suggests that play

> is an activity that is accomplished by highly involved actors, who follow some rules (either implicitly or explicitly), and who have some freedom with regard to the interpretation of the rules, and to the choice of other constituents of an activity (like tools, goals, etc.).
>
> (2013, p. 191)

Examining the vignette above through a CHAT lens that draws on the work of Vygotsky in particular, we see Joseph and his mother highly involved in an interpersonal interaction in which they use the cultural tools of song to establish mutuality and practice musical conventions, language, and performance practices. They sing and interact within the "rules" of the song structure and accompanying finger plays, yet with sufficient freedom to improvise on these in successive performances of the songs. Theirs is a form of cognitive cultural play drawing on Joseph's developing understanding of the meaning of words and their relationship to ways of behaving. Joseph is making "sense" of the cultural practice of singing an action song through his rapt attention and observance of the rules of such songs, including careful listening through the performance and vocalisation at its end. Theirs is a cultural practice playfully accomplished (Van Oers, 2013, 2014).

Structuring musical play and expanding on musical play

As children become more independent, in addition to the joint music-making described above, they begin to develop their own independent music-making. Researchers have noted the emergence of "out-line" songs (Hargreaves, 1986) in which children sing the general contours of a known song, "pot-pourri" songs (Moog, 1976) in which they "mash-up" short fragmentary elements of known songs, and "crib" songs (Barrett, 2018, 2016; Nelson, 1989; Sole, 2017). Sole describes the latter as "solitary spontaneous singing at bedtime" whose function is to "practice musical skills, reflect, experiment, self-soothe, and understand their own worlds" (2017, p. 1). A common phenomenon in the lives of children emerging around 16 months is that of invented song-making. Invented song-making may be traced to those early proto-musical interactions between parent and infant described as turn-taking exchanges of motherese or parentese. It has been defined "as a *genre of children's early song-making that is generative in intention, draws on the musical materials of the child's cultural experience, and is used as a means to engage with and make sense of their worlds*" (Barrett, 2018, original italics). Extended investigations of children's invented song-making have demonstrated the ways in which children draw on this practice as an accompaniment to play (Barrett, 2016), as a means to investigate possibilities of identity in and through music (2011, 2017), and as a generative practice (Barrett, 2012).

> It is a bright winter's day in Southern Tasmania. As Jay's mother steps quietly around the side of the house, video camera rolling, Jay can be heard well before he is seen. Over the sounds of the birds he can be heard rhythmically chanting, 'A te – te – here, a te – te … Eeehhh,' the latter on a falling

tone. He comes into sight standing on the raised stone steps that lead up to a lawn surrounded by ferns. He is gazing down at the ground as he begins slowly and thoughtfully, 'Oooohhhh Mac – Dooonald.' He turns to face the other direction and swings his arms alternatively in front of him as he sings 'Called … de bum-bum-bum.' He continues, 'Old Mac-Donald, called him to come. Oh, oh, oh (*falling tone*) um, um, um (*rising tone*). Bum, bum, bum; hee, a bum; Bum, bum, bum, bum, bum, bum, bum.' Jay is now conducting his performance with both arms swinging with such vigour he is in danger of toppling off the steps. He sings with increasing volume and emphasis, 'Bum, bum, BUM.' He steadies himself, now conducting just with his right arm and singing, 'Gonna, gonna jump, place I know.' He stops and begins to step carefully down from the edge of the lawn before turning back to proclaim loudly, 'And so, my, yard!', this last on a rising phrase, both arms raised in the air.[2]

Jay's mother has captured on video one of his many solitary musical play episodes (59 seconds). In this episode Jay draws on one of his favourite songs (Old MacDonald) to shape his own musical narrative. The singing traces some of the rhythmic and vocal contours of the model, but he has made it his own through interpolating his own phrases into the traditional song structure. When we examine the text, Jay's song consists largely of vocalisations of his current favourite word ("bum" – sanctioned when placed in an artistic context), with some references to his current setting, a "place I know" and his "yard". Jay is embodied with full physical engagement throughout as he conducts his performance – and we may speculate that his triumphant finish with arms raised is directed at an appreciative, if invisible, audience. At age three, Jay is inventing song as a component of his outdoor play; through this musical play he locates himself in his world, trials an identity as a performer to his own audience, and elaborates on a known song to structure his own.[3]

When we begin to listen to children's play, invented song is often an accompanying component. Such songs have been noted by numerous researchers; for example, by composer Donald Pond in the Pilsbury School studies in Santa Barbara in the early 1940s (Moorhead & Pond, 1978) and researcher Jon Bjørkvold in Norway in the 1980s (Bjørkvold, 1989). Whilst some may hear these songs as incomplete or inaccurate attempts at adult models of singing, I suggest an alternative view. Children have little interest in this song-making in replicating adult models, or indeed repeating an invented song in an identical version. As one five-year-old child remarked to me following multiple performances of a song about fairies, they differed "because I use my imagination" and she wished them to be different every time (Barrett, 2006). Adults can participate in such song-making by inventing songs to accompany everyday activity. As children model so effectively, there is no need to labour over the creation of something everlasting. Rather than the product, it is the engagement in the generative activity as an accompaniment to or means to reflect on that activity that is the prime function. Joining in with children's invented song-making is a means of extending that musical play (see Barrett et al., in press, for one example), of engaging in shared music-making, and elaborating on the musical repertoires that children bring to learning and care settings.

Concluding remarks

Whilst some views of play have emphasised that such activity is child-directed and marked by enjoyment and freedom from adult involvement (Pellegrini, 2011), there is a growing body of research that recognises that adults are present in all play, either explicitly as co-partners or implicitly through the cultural tools and activities that children draw on in their play (Fleer, 2015; Van Oers, 2013). Engagement of adults in children's play, particularly in education settings, is shaped by three modes of play: child-initiated, adult-guided, and technicist/policy-driven (Wood, 2014). Wood argues that contemporary policy practices in relation to early learning and development shape play as pedagogy, instrumental in nature with a focus "on planned and purposeful play, (where) forms of learning that are privileged reflect developmental levels and learning goals" (Wood, 2014, p. 152). Drawing on this work, Fleer argues for a more expanded understanding of the pedagogy of play, one which seeks to build play replete with social and symbolic complexity (2015, p. 1812).

Children's performances of known and invented song in their musical play constitutes, I suggest, a form of play that *is* replete with social and symbolic complexity. Such play emerges from the earliest interactions between infants and carers. Importantly, such play is mutually constitutive with both adult-directed and child-initiated activity working in concert to establish joint knowledge and learning. The challenge is for us as carers and educators to re-engage with our own early singing and invented song-making in order to share in musical play with children.

Notes

1 Barrett, M. S., & Welch, G. F. (2013–2015). *Being and becoming musical: Towards a cultural ecological model of early music development.* Funded by the Australian Research Council Discovery Program, grant no. DP130102488.
2 This video data was generated in the following project: Barrett, M. S. (2005–2007). *Young children's world-making through music: Young children's identity construction in and through music.* Funded by the Australian Research Council Discovery Program, Grant No. DP0559050.
3 A full account of Jay's musical output is provided in Barrett (2012).

References

Arya, R., Chansoria, M., Konanki, R., & Tiwari, D. K. (2012). Maternal music exposure during pregnancy influences neonatal behaviour: An open-label randomized controlled trial. *International Journal of Pediatrics.* Online first. www.ncbi.nlm.nih.gov/pmc/articles/PMC3299264/. doi: 10.1155/2012/901812.

Barrett, M. S. (2006). Inventing songs, inventing worlds: The "genesis" of creative thought and activating in young children's lives. *International Journal of Early Years Education*, 14(3), 201–220.

Barrett, M. S. (2009). Sounding lives in and through music: A narrative inquiry of the "everyday" musical engagement of a young child. *Journal of Early Childhood Research*, 7(2), 115–134.

Barrett, M. S. (2011). Musical narratives: A study of a young child's identity work in and through music-making. *Psychology of Music*, 39(4), 403–423.

Barrett, M. S. (2012). Mutuality, belonging and meaning-making: Pathways to developing young boys' competence and creativity in singing and song-making. In S. Harrison, G. F. Welch & A. Adler (Eds), *Perspectives on males and singing* (pp. 167–187). Dordrecht, the Netherlands: Springer.

Barrett, M. S. (2016). Attending to "culture in the small": A narrative analysis of the role of play, thought, and music in young children's world-making. *Research Studies in Music Education*, 38(1), 41–54.

Barrett, M. S. (2017). From small stories: Laying the foundations for narrative identities in and through music. In R. MacDonald, D. Hargreaves & D. Miell (Eds), *Handbook of musical identities* (pp. 63–78). Oxford: Oxford University Press.

Barrett, M. S. (in press). Singing and invented song-making in infants and young children's early learning and development: From shared to independent song-making. In G. F. Welch, D. M. Howard & J. Nix (Eds), *The Oxford handbook of singing*. Oxford: Oxford University Press.

Barrett, M. S., Flynn, L., & Welch, G. F. (in press). Music value and participation: An Australian case study of music provision and support in early childhood education. *Research Studies in Music Education*.

Bjørkvold, J. (1989). *The muse within: Creativity and communication, song and play from childhood through maturity* (W. H. Halverson, Trans.). New York, NY: HarperCollins.

Campbell, D. (1997/2001). *The Mozart effect: Tapping the power of music to heal the body, strengthen the mind, and unlock the creative spirit*. New York, NY: HarperCollins.

Chen-Hafteck, L., & Mang, E. (2012). Music and language in early childhood development and learning. In G. E. McPherson & G. F. Welch (Eds), *The Oxford handbook of music education, Vol. 1* (pp. 261–278). Oxford: Oxford University Press.

Dissanayake, E. (2009). Root, leaf, blossom or bole: Concerning the origin and adaptive function of music. In S. Malloch & C. Trevarthen (Eds), *Communicative musicality* (pp. 17–29). New York, NY: Oxford University Press.

Dissanayake, E. (2012). The earliest narratives are musical. *Research Studies in Music Education*, 34(1), 3–14.

Fleer, M. (2015). Pedagogical positioning in play: Teachers being inside and outside children's imaginary play. *Early Child Development and Care*, 185(11–12), 1801–1814.

Goncu, A., & Gaskins, S. (Eds). (2007). *Play and development: Evolutionary, sociocultural, and functional perspectives*. New York, NY: Lawrence Erlbaum Associates.

Hargreaves, D. (1986). *The developmental psychology of music*. Oxford: Oxford University Press.

Hedegaard, M., & Fleer, M. (2013). *Play, learning and children's development: Everyday life in families and transition to school*. Cambridge: Cambridge University Press.

Lecanuet, J. P. (1996). Prenatal auditory experience. In I. Deliege & J. Sloboda (Eds), *Musical beginnings: Origins and development of musical competence* (pp. 3–34). Oxford: Oxford University Press.

Longhi, E. (2009). "Songese": Maternal structuring of musical interaction with infants. *Psychology of Music*, 37(2), 195–213.

Malloch, S., & Trevarthen, C. (Eds). (2009a). *Communicative musicality: Exploring the basis of human companionship*. Oxford: Oxford University Press.

Malloch, S., & Trevarthen, C. (2009b). Musicality: Communicating the vitality and interests of life. In S. Malloch & C. Treverthen (Eds),

Communicative musicality: Exploring the basis of human companionship (pp. 1–12). Oxford: Oxford University Press.

Mang, E. (2001). Intermediate vocalisations: An investigation of the boundaries between speech and song in young children's vocalisations. *Bulletin of the Council for Research in Music Education*, 147, 116–121.

Mithen, S. (2007). *The singing Neanderthals: The origin of music, language, mind and body*. Cambridge, MA: Harvard University Press.

Moog, H. (1976). *The musical experience of the pre-school child* (C. Clark, Trans.). London: Schott.

Moorhead, G. E., & Pond, D. (1978). *Music of young children*. Santa Barbara, CA: Pillsbury Foundation for Advancement of Music Education. (Reprinted from works published in 1941, 1942, 1944, and 1951).

Nelson, K. (Ed.). (1989). *Narratives from the crib*. Cambridge, MA: Harvard University Press.

Papoušek, M. (1996). Intuitive parenting: A hidden source of musical stimulation in infancy. In I. Deliege & J. Sloboda (Eds), *Musical beginnings* (pp. 88–112). Oxford: Oxford University Press.

Pellegrini, A. D. (Ed.). (2011). *The Oxford handbook of the development of play*. Oxford: Oxford University Press.

Sole, M. (2017). Crib song: Insights into functions of toddlers' private spontaneous singing. *Psychology of Music*, 45(2), 172–192.

Trevarthen, C., & Malloch, S. (2002). Musicality and music before three: Human vitality and invention shared with pride. *Zero to Three*, September, 10–18.

Van Oers, B. (2013). Is it play? Towards a reconceptualization of role play from an activity theory perspective. *European Early Childhood Education Research Journal*, 21(2), 185–198.

Van Oers, B. (2014). Cultural-historical perspectives on play: Central ideas. In L. Brooker, M. Blaise, & S. Edwards (Eds), *The SAGE handbook of play and learning in early childhood* (pp. 56–66). Los Angeles, CA: Sage.

Voegtline, K. M., Costigan, K. A., Pater, H. A., & DiPietro, J. A. (2013). Near-term fetal response to maternal spoken voice. *Infant Behavioural Development*, 36(4), 526–533.

Vygotsky, L. (1978). *Mind in society*. Cambridge, MA: Harvard University Press.

Williams, K. E., Barrett, M. S., Welch, G. F., Abad, V., & Broughton, M. (2015). Associations between early shared music activities in the home and later child outcomes: Findings from the longitudinal study of Australian children. *Early Childhood Research Quarterly*, 31, 113–124.

Wood, E. (2014). The play-pedagogy interface in contemporary debates. In L. Brooker, M. Blaise, & S. Edwards (Eds), *The SAGE handbook of play and learning in early childhood* (pp. 145–156). Los Angeles, CA: Sage.

EDITORIAL PROVOCATIONS
Engaging readers and extending thinking

Sophie Alcock

Children and adults living and playing alongside each other through worlds and languages of drama, drawing and music are themes in these three chapters. We read about children (and adults) playing with creating socio-dramatic fantasy scenes, with creating drawing and with creating music.

- Does creativity always involve some play?

In Chapter 1, Robertson describes the excitement and the meaning-making possibilities for children engaged in seriously playful digital drawing. Children in these vignettes playfully explore and imaginatively extend mark-making possibilities through using screen technology to create complexly-layered imaginative stories. Teachers support by empowering children to experiment and learn the technology that supports these narrative co-creations. Teachers teach without disrupting the flow of shared experience. This style recalls the learning that can happen when children have the freedom to explore and play with stuff. In this case "stuff" is the technology associated with other ways of imaginatively and creatively making meaningful marks.

- How might educators integrate freedom with play-based pedagogy?

Imaginary worlds created through play are central to the playworld work referred to by Ferholt, Nilsson and Lecusay in Chapter 2. These researchers explore the complex relational dynamics that can emerge within the adult–child joint fantasy play of playworlds. They courageously interrogate intimate nuances that teachers disclose when bringing their personal selves into their actor roles within playworlds, making links to teachers and children learning relational competence through play.

- What do readers think and feel about teachers playing and feeling, like children?
- Do – or should – teachers play like children? Why?
- Perhaps child-attuned teachers are also attuned with their own inner child?

The metaphor of *attunement* leads nicely into musical worlds explored by Barrett in Chapter 3, where she skilfully maps musical landscapes to extend adults' musical ways of being alongside. These include "shared playful music-making". As Barrett points out, "Singing and song-making appear to be a universal feature of human culture and a common element in the early life experiences of infants" (Chapter 3). Movement, rhythm and play underpin musicality across cultures. While researching the role of indigenous music in the promotion of children's cognitive development in Zambia, Reuben Mukela (2013, p. 1) points out: "In Africa the term 'music' … pervades many social activities that include "dance, songs, and play. African words for music sometimes also refer to play." Similarly, the ancient Greek word for music – *mousike* – encompasses the temporal arts: music, dance, drama, poetry. These are time-based arts that move when played into creation and in turn move us with feeling.

As Barrett explains, "There is a growing body of research that recognises that adults are present in all play, either explicitly as co-partners or implicitly through the cultural tools and activities that children draw on in their play" (Chapter 3).

- To whom does the play belong? is it just children's play?

Coming from three different subject disciplines the five authors of these three chapters expand our understandings of adult's roles in (children's) play. They challenge us to rethink the ways in which adults and children live, play and relate together and alongside each other in early childhood settings. As well as exploring roles of adults alongside children playing, these inspiring chapters highlight ways in which adults too can become players by responsively engaging with and alongside children.

Reference

Mukela, R. M. (2013). *The role of indigenous music and games in the promotion of cognitive development in Zambian children in Senanga and Shangombo districts of Western Province*. Unpublished MA dissertation. Lusaka: University of Zambia.

Section 2

THOSE WHO EDUCATE

4
OBSERVING AND INTERPRETING YOUNG CHILDREN PLAYING
Reflecting on feelings

Sophie Alcock

Being alongside children while observing them playing wildly can be emotionally challenging, particularly when teachers interact affectively with the children. Through the reflective interpretation of an observed event, this chapter introduces three related and relational metaphorical concepts: vitality affect, holding and interpersonal field. All three concepts highlight the emotional energy felt in play. The focus on vitality affects and interpersonal fields avoids an overly individualist observer focus by highlighting the group ethos and the relational spaces felt and observed in-between and amongst children and adults. Holding is a fundamentally relational concept; it is the intimate trust that accompanies feeling securely held by another person. The spaces in-between people come into focus when observing and interacting with children as interconnected beings. Just as observations implicitly include observing teachers, play can also include teachers in interpersonal fields that support diverse patterns of interconnectedness, together and apart. Working with these concepts of vitality affects, interpersonal fields and holding as tools offers ways into role-play for teachers observing, reflecting and participating with children in their play. This is a position I hope you will find interesting, stimulating further thinking when you consider the question at the end of the chapter.

This chapter presents several relational concepts as observation tools. I suggest these concepts can assist teachers' observing, interpreting and reflecting on the affect dimensions – emotions and feelings – in children's pretend play. The concepts include: vitality affect (D. Stern,

1985, 2010), interpersonal field (D. B. Stern, 2013a, 2013b) and holding (Winnicott, 1974). They allude in different yet complementary ways to the unconsciously and consciously felt vitality, the movement, intensity and tone of bodily-felt experience that underpins feelings and emotions and aligns with the energy in play.

My intention is for teachers to interpret beyond purely descriptive and superficially reflective observations of what is visible and seen, to further explore affective ways of being with and observing young children relationally, interactively, imaginatively and reflectively in the moment. As responsible educators, teachers are challenged to prioritise feelings and emotions and to value unconscious as well as conscious and visible dimensions of play, as well as exploring their own roles in playing and relating with children.

The freedom associated with playing can give voice to children's emotions and feelings. This ability to feel emotions, to be open to the feeling of feelings, is fundamental to living with awareness and aliveness. Emotions include relational and body-based sensations (Fogel et al., 2006). Young children playing spontaneously exude vitality in feelings while creating sense and meaning through playing with issues and materials that matter to them. In play, meanings may be hidden beneath the surface; things are not always what they seem. These invisible layers can make children's wild play particularly challenging for teachers observing, becoming involved and participating. Yet teachers' observations of children at play inform their pedagogical practices. Teacher participation in wild pretend play is, in my experience, not so common, hence that focus in this chapter.

Open-ended reflective questions to consider while reading include:

- What are the roles and responsibilities for teachers participating in children's play?
- Does the play belong just to children?
- How and why can teachers actively empower children to feel vitality affects in play?
- How and why can teachers value children expressing and playing with powerful emotions in pretend play?
- How and why can teachers actively empower children to feel feelings in pretend play?

The concepts of vitality affect, relational and interpersonal field (Lewin, 1943; D. B. Stern, 2013a; Tubert-Oklander, 2013), and holding (D. W. Winnicott, 1960, 1974) offer useful interpretive tools for teachers observing play in its spontaneous complexity (Alcock, 2016, 2017), by illuminating the energy and movement in connections and communication between, amongst and within children playing together and teachers participating in that play. Each of these constructs is explained briefly below.

Vitality affect (D. Stern, 1985, 2010) highlights the energy observed and felt in the non-verbal, body-based, ways in which children play, move and connect. Children playing together exude energy – vitality. The felt tone and messages conveyed in and between children's moving bodies, the shifting eye-gaze, word tone and other sounds, communicate more complexity than the literal meaning of spoken words alone. The energy that emerges amongst and between physical bodies as thinking-feeling moving subjects, expressing and perceiving pre-reflectively, intelligently and purposefully, is an obvious focus for teachers' observations. Daniel Stern (2010, p. 5) has further explained vitality affect as: 'a whole … It is a Gestalt that emerges from the theoretically separate experiences of movement, force, time, space and intention' (amongst children playing). Vitality affects contribute to the feelings and emotions that are generated and emerge amongst children playing. Vitality affects feature strongly in the subjectively and intersubjectively felt energy observed in and between the bodies of children and a teacher playing together in the event presented in this chapter. Vitality emerges within interpersonal fields in dynamic emergent processes that are integral to the relational processes in children's play.

Interpersonal field refers to the relational and dynamic context of everything that is present to an observed metaphorical field. The field concept is a process and a metaphor; it can allude to a playing field, a marked space and a magnetic or gravitational type of force. I am interested in the felt tone, force or energy between and amongst people and things in that space (D. B. Stern, 2013a, 2013b; Tubert-Oklander, 2013). Thus, the interpersonal field includes more than physical environment and social context; it also refers to feelings and thoughts, unconscious and conscious, that shift and change between and amongst the people and things that occupy the field, including observers.

Holding, as Winnicott (D. W. Winnicott, 1960, 1974) used the term, refers to the feeling of being safely held psychologically as well as physically, like a baby securely held by its trusted caregiver. Holding is not enough in itself. Feeling securely held enables children to relax, to let go, to play and explore by working with sense and meaning-making processes. This metaphor of holding can further inform teachers' interpretations of their active roles in supporting children's play through holding children, while also observing and participating in playing with them.

Observing young children playing is fascinating, particularly when the teacher is also a participant and the play is imaginative and surreal, as in the event presented later in this chapter. Sociodramatic play involving small groups of children, as is common in early childhood care and education (ECCE) settings, can seem like shared dreaming. The process and attitude of playing combines feeling, thinking, dreaming and acting. Thus, children playing together can appear to be acting out dreams as they co-create a third imagined space, an interpersonal playing field, where felt-time expands inwards and outwards.

Participant observation involves teachers in listening for qualities of vitality, including dullness, between children's playing bodies in this dream-like play, and noticing how these vitality affects (including low energy) shift. Observing by listening to vitality affects has been particularly insightful for me as an observer conditioned to notice head-minds, rather than body-minds, and to separate feeling from thinking. Yet, feelings of vitality are felt in bodies; without our bodies, we are no-body. With movement, bodies can speak, think, feel and relate with others.

Observation lenses that include vitality affect, holding and interpersonal field can enhance both the observation field and the ways in which teachers observe and reflect on children playing. Observing includes diverse ways of seeing, listening, reflecting and feeling the vitality within, between and amongst children and teachers in that moment. All these concepts – holding, vitality affect and interpersonal field – refer to relational understandings of feelings and emotions as emerging between and amongst as well as within people. They highlight the ever-changing interconnectedness of all phenomena, an obvious yet easily overlooked and complicating dimension of the observation process. Awareness of interconnectedness precludes any exclusively individualistic observer focus on children as separate subjects, or objects.

The teacher participating in the following event was attuned with the listening, seeing, feeling, playing process. Her participation within the play process seemed to expand the interpersonal field of play, increasing the feeling of time and the complexities in the narrative plot, though it was the children who introduced the mythical elements. Importantly, she knew these children and they trusted her.

Pretend play that includes mythical elements can support children in making sense of things including change, through trying out different perspectives, playing with roles, creating and breaking rules and exploring feelings of agency and altered power relationships. The uncertainties in change can be existentially challenging for children, as well as for adults (teachers). Myths use narrative to explore the big questions of change in life, such as birth, death and rebirth, by calling on powerful emotions, such as fear, anger, love and safety, evoked by these questions. Myth-users (including children) recreate narratives to provide emotional and intellectual security in the face of strong emotions (Bettelheim, 1976; Egan & Nadaner, 1988). Children playing out mythic themes represent their worlds and experience in dramatic narrative-like ways as stories with beginnings, middles and endings, though these stories are not always linear. Moreover, the stories we create and recreate throughout our lives embed knowledge, sense and meaning through these narrative ways of knowing (Bruner, 1986); drama has been described as the expressive art form of myth (Bruner, 1962).

Corsaro (2017) has observed that peer group resistance to adults is one of the ways in which young children interpret and recreate culture; children recreate community and culture in their peer play. Becoming members of peer groups with agentic group roles can also support children learning citizenship through experiencing the give and take of becoming actively-contributing citizens, collaborating as members of a community and even learning to challenge authority, with group support. They can play with the power of group feelings of agency and resistance, sometimes using teachers as objects in the play. The teacher becomes an object in the following event, provoking questions around her teacher role as a secure holding base supporting children's aggressive pretend play. In playing with peers, young children in early childhood group settings can also experience togetherness and feelings of belonging in groups other than their families.

The teacher herself plays a central participant role in the following dramatic event, becoming the target for children's group resistance. Like a 'good enough' caregiver (Alcock, 2017; Winnicott, 1974), she becomes a holding base, supporting children to safely let themselves go into experiencing the vitality of their wild play as it emerges and evolves, co-creating group interpersonal fields of play.

Research methods

Ethnographic methods were used in the study that informs this paper (Alcock, 2016). Observation data from that study was collated as a series of narrative-like events, framed by the emergence and flow of play with beginnings, middles and endings signalled by children announcing and framing each play event (Bateson, 1972; Goffman, 1974). Framed events are one way of representing diverse interpretations of play, while being true to observed experiences. This paper revisits that observation data, re-interpreting events with a focus on affect. The following event is one of several observations on a recurrent 'children chasing teacher' theme. It contains all the elements of a good story.

Fast action fills this five-minute-long observation, connecting past and future in the present and making the event feel much longer than its real-time length. As mentioned earlier, play changes how time feels.

Background

The event evolved after a special morning tea-time. Unusually, this eating together routine included all twenty-four four-year-old children as well as the three teachers, four parents and myself, as the researching observer. The children comprised boys and girls in fairly equal numbers with a mixture of ethnicities including Somali, Indonesian, Samoan, Rorotongan, Māori and Pākeha (New Zealand European).

My notes on the day describe the scene-setting interpersonal field of this particular tea-time:

> Three teachers, shared history, friends, all born in the seventies, within two months of each other, all wearing seventies clothes today, will jointly celebrate their birthdays, on Saturday night (tomorrow) in the early childhood centre; parents and friends are invited, me too. This is a "grown ups" party. However, the preparations and party-like atmosphere are pervading the children's programme. The teachers have been trying out hippy-like long seventies garb, as if they're children's dress-up

clothes. Children's collage materials are being transformed into streamers and other decorative accessories. And now the teachers are testing a fondue set, with the children as consumers of fruit pieces pierced onto shish kebab sticks and then dipped, by adults, into the communal hot chocolate fondue pot which a teacher holds over the portable gas fondue stove, on a low table. Twenty-four children and seven adults watch the process with interest. The adults joke and laugh while children watch, wait and eat with interest. Teacher J puts her arm fondly around Teacher C as she leans over her reaching for another stick. "How many kindies have fondue for morning tea? just as well we don't have cheese with wine ..."

Everyone is standing and the children don't have to be there, but are. Most seem to want more chocolate dipped fruit and the teachers too say "Yum."

This interpersonal field implicitly included objects such as the fondue set, the dress-ups, the words and actions as well as human bodies that together mediated the communication adding to the ethos – the vitality – felt between and amongst children and adults in this co-created, ever-changing relational field of morning tea-time. Years later I continue to feel awed and surprised by the lively playfulness of these three teachers. Like giant children imagining themselves in the seventies of their birth, pretending by wearing dress-ups in the form of colourful long dresses with jangly beads and flowing scarves, playing with a seventies cheese fondue set, laughing and joking with contagious vitality. These teachers playfully and imaginatively re-created their vision of seventies New Zealand as (birthday) party people, thirty years on.

Head teacher Sue had been most 'in control' during the fondue making; moving amongst the children who were crowded around a low table. She handed out chocolate buttons and fondue fruit sticks, explaining, directing and instructing. As this morning tea-time finished and the children began moving to other activities, the teacher–child power balance changed with several of the children seeming to catch the teachers' playfulness, as if on cue.

The chasing event

The 'teacher chasing' scene erupts suddenly, as about six children burst out of the building, chasing teacher Sue.

ALAN: We can just get a machine and it can crack the world.
BEN: And we'll eat you up.
JO: And we are going to make you fall down. If you run your fastest we'll run after you.
TEACHER SUE: Go on then, catch me.
TEACHER SUE (*CHANTING*): You can't get me.
(She stands facing her chasers and makes a teasing face at them, calmly twinkling her fingers in the air, beside her ears, in time with her chant. The children run after her, yelling.)
CHILDREN: Get her … Get her, get her, get her.
(The number of chasers increases to eight.)
TEACHER SUE: Oh, you've got me.

They pull her down to the ground, their movements matching screams of joy as children connect with teacher Sue in physical touching, their exuberance expressed in sounds and actions. Teacher Sue's body flops voluntarily and she lies on the ground. Three children climb on and lie over her, kicking and waving their legs in the air, laughing and screaming with glee, yet carefully avoiding any hurting. Others watch excitedly jumping. Gilda (who has no English) initially watches, then, seeing no danger, she becomes the fourth to lie gently on the teacher, playfully kicking her legs in the air and laughing.

JACKIE: Cut her, cut her. *(He waves two plastic knives.)*
(One child puts on teacher Sue's very large, black velvet, pointed sun hat that has fallen off her. The cone-shaped hat covers his entire head. He jumps lots of excited little hard bounces under a giant witch-like hat and giggles loudly; a jumping giggling black witch hat!)

Vitality affecting interpersonal fields

Together these children and the teacher exuded vitality in every dimension – movement, force, time, space and intention – while also simply playing, having fun and pretending. The teacher's teasing actions and tone encouraged the children's play with feelings of power, agency and control. The children used their whole bodies, four of them lying on top of her, energetically connecting as a peer group with the common intention of overpowering teacher Sue as their shared object of resistance. The children's movement matched their screams of joy as they ran after teacher Sue, connecting with her physically, touching, pulling her down. Their excitement was felt and expressed in physical action, and in sounds with and without words, controlling and overpowering the powerful giant by lying on and over this fallen teacher and playfully holding her body down with their bodies, smothering and devouring her. As the observer, I felt the force of intention in the relatively powerless children's playfully aggressive words and actions, directed towards the giant teacher.

This teacher-chasing erupted amidst the tensions of a routine transition time when children were moving from a seated and physically constrained inside routine to outside expansiveness with freedom to move their bodies. The transition interrupted the continuity of morning teatime and the dynamics of the interpersonal field shifted from children sitting inside to running outside, from being quietly controlled to spontaneously, playfully and relationally experiencing other physically exuberant ways of being and feeling agentically in control. Like the negative capability of 'cracks that let the light in' (Cohen, 1992), transitional tensions seemed to create cracks that enabled spontaneous play to expand into the program. The teacher responsively mediated and further empowered these children to physically act out their dramatic play, using her body as an object (D. W. Winnicott, 1960, 1974). Paradoxically the teacher became engaged in playing with and alongside children in two conflicting roles simultaneously. She became both a centrally supportive anchor – a secure holding base – and also an object of resistance, an object for children to attack, within their wildly challenging and subversively dramatic play.

The event continues:

TEACHER SUE: Lift me up. (*She offers up her hands.*)
ALAN: We can't lift you. Into the pond [sandpit].
(*Screams from children ... Three of them pull her gently. She walks where they lead her, towards and into the sandpit, and they begin putting sand on her.*)
TEACHER SUE (RUNNING OUT OF THE SANDPIT): I don't like it all over me.
BEN (HOLDING A SHOVEL FULL OF SAND): We'll put it on your feet so you'll die.
TEACHER SUE: Okay, if you just put it on my feet. I'll just roll these up. (*She rolls up her pants; the children bury her feet in wet sand.*)
TEACHER SUE: Oh it's cold. Oh, oh, it's freezing.

JO: You're dead now.
TEACHER SUE: Am I dead?
JO: Yeah.
TEACHER SUE: What do I do now then? I suppose I lie down.
ALAN (TO ANOTHER CHILD WHO'S LAUGHING): It's not funny.
(*She lies down in the sandpit; the children bury her feet again.*)

The power in myth: playing and acting

A mythic narrative unfolded with the teacher calmly play-acting her victim role. Like a 'good enough' (Winnicott, 1960) caregiver, the teacher showed sufficient emotional maturity to responsively join in the play and not reactively feel destroyed. In this way she held the children emotionally, thereby enabling them to symbolise destructive feeling-thoughts through acting out dramatic play. Together these children played with powerful feelings dramatically and with much vitality, drawing on mythical concepts around death, birth, growth and rebirth, and associated shared feelings of power, control, chaos, resistance, agency and subversion.

Boys dominated throughout this event in both number and vitality affect. Alan, Ben, Jo and Jackie initiated the teacher-chasing play, using words as well as actions to enthusiastically and rebelliously lead the chase. Perhaps they desired teacher Sue's level of power and control? They certainly challenged her teacher power by intently suggesting various child-empowering and aggressive ways to overthrow this giant adult female teacher. Ben wanted to eat her, Jackie to cut her up, while Jo wanted to trip her up and Alan suggested more broadly cracking the world. The teacher responsively allowed these challenges, holding the tension by playfully acting in the dramatic roles assigned to her by the children.

- How comfortable might you be in Sue's position? Why might that be?
- Why and how might teachers challenge these potential gender stereotypes from within play?

The event continues:

JO: Now you're going to grow into a tree.
TEACHER SUE: Am I growing into a tree?
JO: Yep.

BEN: Put her in the fire. Put her in the fire. Put her in the fire.
TEACHER SUE: Help, Jackie, save me.
   (*Jackie does so, while teacher Sue tells the children that Jackie is saving her.*)

The children 'destroyed' teacher Sue several times over. Following their earlier threat of eating her, teacher Sue was cut up. Together the children imagined lifting her up; they led teacher Sue to a pretend pond (sandpit) where she died again, her feet symbolically buried in cold sand as if it was water. Sue then grew into a tree and the children threatened to burn her, like wood in a fire. In asking Jackie to save her, teacher Sue subtly changed the plot of the play narrative. She contained and held the play narrative from her role within the play, actively shifting the narrative towards a safe conclusion, redirecting the play and altering the vitality affects within the interpersonal field. Through securely holding the children's wild play, teacher Sue supported the children in playing towards and accepting some sort of resolution to this mythic narrative. The interpersonal field began to feel calm.

The event continues:

TEACHER SUE: What about making some fondue on the fire, some chocolate fondue?
JO: Okay, and then we're going to put poisonous chocolate fondue all over your face.
TEACHER SUE: Now, what sort of fondue are we going to make?
JO: Chocolate, and then we'll put it all over your face.
TEACHER SUE: No, no, no, no.
OLLIE: No, we're going to eat it.
TEACHER SUE: We'll need some spoons ... Let's find some things to dip in it. What can we find?
   (*All play with the spoons in the pots, all standing and moving, none sitting.*)
OLLIE: I need a knife to cut you up.
TEACHER SUE: Oh no, you can't cut me up now, I'm dead ...
   (10.05–10.10am)

Endings and beginnings: Holding and processing in play

Teacher Sue redirected and transformed the narrative in the play towards a calm ending that almost cathartically reconnected with the themes of chocolate-fondue-making and eating, with which the play had begun. The sand and water of the pond and burial ground became transformed into a chocolate-fondue-making scene, involving about eight children in teacher-initiated pretend play. Children's movements, the force and the pace of the play – the vitality affects – slowed down noticeably in this scene where teacher Sue gently reasserted her caregiver-teacher role. Feeling safely held by a 'good enough' teacher enabled the children to process and resolve their wild play narrative towards an ending, which also resonated with the beginning. Endings are never final (Winnicott, 1974). Teacher chasing was a recurrent theme in children's (and adults') play in this ECCE centre, perhaps partly because the three teachers were very playful friends, a little like giant four-year-olds, even celebrating their thirtieth birthdays together in a Saturday night party in the kindergarten. Playfulness may be contagious!

The consuming power of making things and powerful people disappear through eating became an intriguing sub-theme re-appearing on several occasions in this event and others. It began with the 'real' chocolate-covered-fruit fondue-eating morning teatime and continued with Ben's threat to eat the teacher, while Jackie wanted to cut her up. Making and eating pretend chocolate fondue in the sandpit rounded out the narrative in this event.

Eating features strongly in the mythic children's picture book *Where the Wild Things Are* (Sendak, 1963/2013), which begins: 'The night Max wore his wolf suit and made mischief of one kind and another his mother called him "WILD THING!" and Max said "I'LL EAT YOU UP!"' Max is sent to his room without eating anything. Yet, on his return from visiting his wild things, Max finds his supper warmly waiting for him. Food both nurtures and disappears by being eaten up. Food also fuels energy, contributing to vitality, and teachers can tune into children through awareness of the complexities in children's 'food' play.

The peer group togetherness in the teacher-chasing play facilitated group collaboration. It also went beyond a simple chasing game by extending children's shared imaginations and challenging boundaries around accepted societal rules of behaviour. In playing with reality, these children were able to experience shared group feelings and emotions around belonging, power, responsibility and agency; existential essential imperatives for becoming individuals and citizens within communities. It helps to have teachers who can play. Being in touch with their own inner child might well mediate teachers becoming attuned and engaging playfully with the children they teach.

The flexibility in play reduces the tensions that can characterise individuals relating to others. In reversing roles and power relationships and in mimetically playing with and recreating mythic concepts, roles and relationships, children (and teachers) can experience diverse ways of feeling, thinking and being. We are alone yet, through the process of playing together, connected. In this sense, children playing together can experiment with forms of being and knowing that help them process and organise experiences, feelings, thoughts and emotions.

Does this play suggest to children that violent solutions to problems are acceptable or are they simply enjoying the sense of the ridiculous and the physicality of rough-and-tumble play?

The tone in this event was communicated primarily through the vitality affects in children's movement. Movement, with added words and imagination, mediated children connecting and communicating the narrative together in play. But it was the vitality affect in children's chasing, catching, jumping on, burying and jumping with glee types of movements that co-created and communicated the dynamic interpersonal field setting of this narrative-play. Physical movement patterns, in their extraordinarily coordinated dynamism, were the dominant narrative signals. The commanding words of a few children and the teacher supplemented these movements and added imaginative complexity, clarity and richness to the play. In such ways, narrative-play structures with plots and resolutions dramatically acted out can provide emotional security for children by supporting them to feel (Bruner, 1962, Egan & Nadaner, 1988). Birth, death, eating, killing and other big life questions with subtexts of security, power and control were addressed in this mythic dramatic play.

As in rough-and-tumble play, these children were aware of the pretence in their play and that real hurt was not part of the play, though the teacher was imaginatively destroyed. The physicality in the play resembled rough-and-tumble play with the addition of a complex narrative. Paradoxically, the teacher simply continued to support the children with trust and emotional holding, playing her role in their wild physical play. And she was reborn, twice.

Rough-and-tumble play with its aggressive tendencies is the type of play early childhood teachers find most difficult to support, according to Storli and Sandseter (2015), yet as they and other researchers argue, such play is important for children's development and learning, particularly in the realm of social competence and self-regulation (Narvaez et al., 2012).

Amazingly this event only lasted five minutes, yet as a narrative that offers multiple complex interpretations it felt closer to five hours long. This is an example of negative capability in action, expanding the play, like light in cracks alluded to earlier (Cohen, 1992). The feeling of time is a common element in holding, vitality affects, interpersonal fields and play, where time can become expansive and dream-like, unlike objectively linear logical time. Subjective time is also well illustrated in *Where the Wild Things Are* (Sendak, 2013), where Max 'sailed off through night and day and in and out of weeks and almost over a year to where the wild things are.' Importantly, time and the physical environment as dimensions of the interpersonal field add to the range of observational challenges for teachers, who are participants as well as observers, in the same interpersonal field.

When the flow of the day changes tempo, the tone of the interpersonal field also shifts, in this case shifting inwards and outwards. In such interactive ways time and place reciprocally affect the ever-changing dynamics of interpersonal fields. A related challenge for teachers interpreting and reflecting on child observations is to keep closely focused on what is both felt and observed, what is seen and heard in that moment. The teacher in this event was implicitly observing in the moment, sensing vitality affects and responding accordingly. The interconnecting categories of movement, force, space, time and intention that come together as vitality affects offer a complex and dynamic tool for teachers insightfully observing, interpreting and reflecting on social-emotional experiences in play. In a circular way, vitality affects also impact the vitality felt within wider interpersonal fields of play.

Concepts presented in this chapter challenge teachers to reflect and interpret the unseen layers of changing interpersonal fields by observing the dynamics of affect and vitality in children's group play processes rather than within individual children. Vitality emerges between – as well as within – players; the skin is permeable. The event presented in this chapter provokes readers to consider the value for children of playing physically with strong feelings, and the related role of teachers in supporting children's play by using concepts such as holding, while also engaging in play with and alongside children. When children feel securely held by teachers, they are free to process feelings and experiences within their interpersonal fields of play.

A question to ponder: What alternative strategies might another teacher have used that could also have empowered the children in physical (rough-and-tumble) play, in co-creating and playing towards experiencing narrative resolutions while working with sense and meaning-making processes?

References

Alcock, S. J. (2016). *Young children playing: Relational approaches to emotional learning in early childhood settings, Vol. 12*. Singapore: Springer.

Alcock, S. J. (2017). Interpersonal fields of play. *Early Child Development and Care*, 187(5–6), 924–934. doi:10.1080/03004430.2016.1210134.

Bateson, G. (1972). *Steps to an ecology of mind*. San Francisco, CA: Chandler.

Bettelheim, B. (1976). *The uses of enchantment: The meaning and importance of fairy tales*. London: Thames and Hudson.

Bruner, J. S. (1962). *On knowing: Essays for the left hand*. Cambridge, MA: Belknap Press of Harvard University Press.

Bruner, J. S. (1986). *Actual minds, possible worlds*. Cambridge, MA: Harvard University Press.

Cohen, L. (1992). Anthem. *The future* (Columbia COL 472498 1).

Corsaro, W. A. (2017). *The sociology of childhood* (5th ed.). Los Angeles, CA: Sage.

Egan, K., & Nadaner, D. (1988). *Imagination and education*. Milton Keynes: Open University Press.

Fogel, A., et al. (2006). *Change processes in relationships: A relational-historical research approach*. Cambridge and New York, NY: Cambridge University Press.

Goffman, E. (1974). *Frame analysis: An essay on the organization of experience*. Cambridge, MA: Harvard University Press.

Lewin, K. (1943). Defining the 'field at a given time'. *Psychological Review*, 50(3), 292–310. doi:10.1037/h0062738.

Narvaez, D., Panksepp, J., Schore, A., & Gleason, T. (2012). The value of using an evolutionary framework for gauging children's well-being. In *Evolution, early experience and human development: from research to practice and policy*. Oxford University Press. Retrieved 25 September 2018 from www.oxfordscholarship.com/view/10.1093/acprof:oso/9780199755059.001.0001/acprof-9780199755059-chapter-1.

Sendak, M. (1963/2013). *Where the wild things are* (50th anniversary edition). New York, NY: HarperCollins Publishers.

Stern, D. (1985). *The interpersonal world of the infant: A view from psychoanalysis and developmental psychology.* New York, NY: Basic Books.

Stern, D. (2010). *Forms of vitality: Exploring dynamic experience in psychology, the arts, psychotherapy, and development.* Oxford: Oxford University Press.

Stern, D. B. (2013a). Field theory in psychoanalysis, Part I: Harry Stack Sullivan and Madeleine and Willy Baranger. *Psychoanalytic Dialogues*, 23(5), 487–501. doi:10.1080/10481885.2013.832607.

Stern, D. B. (2013b). Field theory in psychoanalysis, Part 2: Bionian field theory and contemporary interpersonal/relational psychoanalysis. *Psychoanalytic Dialogues*, 23(6), 630–645. doi:10.1080/10481885.2013.851548.

Storli, R., & Sandseter, E. B. H. (2015). Preschool teachers' perceptions of children's rough-and-tumble play (R&T) in indoor and outdoor environments. *Early Child Development and Care*, 185(11–12), 1995–2009. doi:10.1080/03004430.2015.1028394.

Tubert-Oklander, J. (2013). Field, process, and metaphor. *Psychoanalytic Inquiry*, 33(3), 229–246. doi:10.1080/07351690.2013.779889.

Winnicott, D. W. (1960). The theory of the parent–infant relationship. *International Journal of Psychoanalysis*, 41, 585–595.

Winnicott, D. W. (1974). *Playing and reality.* Harmondsworth: Penguin.

5

GROWING PLAYFUL PEDAGOGIES

A case study of educational change

Alma Fleet and Mel Kemenyvary

This chapter is a study in three parts associated with a case study from two remote mining towns in South Australia. The study presents children's perspectives, excerpts from educator interviews and Mel's reflections. As a university-qualified primary school teacher, Mel has moved into and out of a preschool and the first years of school, working alongside others in a small school. Her participation in three years of professional development projects (facilitated by Sydney-based project team member Alma and her local colleague Angela) has encouraged Mel to embed play-based pedagogies in her teaching. Having discovered some resistance from those around her, and wanting to understand more about her positioning in this landscape, Mel interviewed former students, friends and colleagues to explore both the highlights and complexities of prioritising play when teaching and learning alongside young children. Analysis throughout identifies key elements in the data.

This story emerges from a community-engagement agenda developed by a major employer in a remote mining area. Following a tendering process, an external consultancy group (Semann & Slattery) was employed to assist in a 'ground-up' community capacity-building approach focused on improving educational outcomes in an area encompassing several small towns around a hub community. A regional education forum (a committee of the governing council) wanted a multi-faceted approach across all sectors. As part of the resulting initiative (named Mining Minds), and building on community-grounded consultative research, projects were launched to support the continuity of learning (including transition to school from prior-to-school settings) and leadership. Over three years, participation in the professional development opportunities was invited from across the area and supported by local mentorship (Angela – previously a principal in the small town where Mel lives and works) and consultancy facilitation (including Alma from the successful external tendering group). Ethics permissions were gained from those involved in the portions of the projects contributing to report-writing and publication. Ongoing community support enabled project adjustments to suit local interests and funding body goals.

As project facilitators understood the importance of effective infrastructure and cyclical facilitation, professional learning opportunities were provided to assist practitioner inquiry-based educational change (Fleet, DeGioia, & Patterson, 2016). As part of this professional development, Angela contributed both group and individual input (presentations, articles, conversations) relating to the role of play in young children's learning, particularly envisioned as hands-on investigation and agentic problem-solving by both children and adults. There were efforts to share engagement and pedagogies across the philosophical and geographical boundaries between local prior-to-school and school settings. Pre-existing challenges related to the differing minimal qualifications required in each sector and different governance, ranging from university-qualified teachers in the Department of Education (including schools and four-year-old kindergartens) and Catholic authorities to local community groups overseeing child care (long days for children from 6 months through school age) – with few university-qualified educators. Accountability pressures often shaped the practices of teachers in the schools (responsible to a national curriculum) while educators in the kindergartens/preschools/childcare centres (guided by the National Quality Framework, including the Early Years Learning Framework, or EYLF; Australian Government Department of Education Employment and Workplace Relations (DEEWR), 2009) were keen to suppor the continuity of learning through valuing play across the transition period into the first years of school.

Over time, Alma introduced practitioner inquiry and strategies to encourage an agenda of curiosity and data-based decision-making. Mel became involved as a teacher in the small isolated school where (previously) Angela had been principal. This chapter begins with children's perspectives, followed by those of educators across the early childhood age range from both Mel's town and a nearby larger centre, finishing with Mel's story, her perspectives and our analysis of the data presented.

Children's memories

In assisting the authors to understand the place of 'play' in education (broadly defined) in this area, a sensible place to start is with voices of children from local prior-to-school settings. Separate from the professional development projects, views of these children were sought to contribute to this study. Twenty-two children were interviewed, a comprehensive group considering that the preschool had only a few children in any given year, in a very small town with a transient population affected by local employment opportunities. Contributors included 13 boys and nine girls from seven years of preschool (kindergarten and child care) experience:

- 3 children from 2017 – now aged 5 (2 boys; 1 girl)
- 1 girl from 2016 – now aged 6
- 5 children from 2015 – now aged 6/7 (3 boys; 2 girls)
- 1 boy from 2014 – now aged 8
- 5 children from 2013 – now aged 9/10 (2 boys; 3 girls)
- 4 children from 2012 – now aged 10 (2 boys; 2 girls)
- 3 boys from 2011 – now aged 11

Mel reported:

> When I asked some of the past preschool students to reflect on their preschool memories, many spoke fondly of experiences with paint and craft materials, the array of dinosaur and animal/habitat play scenes and of their time outdoors, playing in the sand, riding bikes and playing in the cubby.

Singing, playing games and making things also figured highly. A nine-year-old regretted that 'school doesn't have as much fun as kindy because there's more learning and not as much time for fun', which was echoed by a six-year-old who said, 'The work has changed now and it's harder, like Maths.' Though another child from the same 2015 group commented that

> I made stuff all the time. I liked cutting and sticking with the boxes ... I really liked drawing with pencils and textas

and making books. Sometimes we played games about numbers. Now we have to do more work, but I like it.

Similar insight about connections between play and learning was in the 10-year-old's comment that

> We used to use the hammers and wood a lot to make things. We also used to make lots of craft and I liked playing with the other kids in the cubby and in the sandpit. I liked kindy because you didn't have to do work for learning. You just had to play.

The children had definite memories about particular activities or friends (pseudonyms) who they enjoyed, like the six-year-old who commented:

> Kindy was fun. I loved it because I could play with lots of toys and Johnny was there. Johnny was my bestest friend. He's actually still my bestest friend! I liked to make those insect things with the big eyes and we made see-saws for them out of wood. We did dressing-up and lots of making. I liked playing the games and playing with all the dinosaurs. I made a nest for dinosaurs and there was even some eggs in it.

and the 10-year-old who said:

> I remember playing Mobilo with the little connectors and making cars; especially ones with fenders. I liked playing in the sandpit, digging big holes, and I remember the first time we actually reached the bottom. That was with Greg, me and Ben, and Billy. It took a long time ... I think because we were small, it was bigger and seemed so good. Now I look at it, it's not such a big space, but it still is good. I loved being able to choose what I wanted to play with and that made me not bored.

Alongside the enthusiasm for 'playing chaseys' and riding bikes was warmth for inclusion. An eight-year-old happily remembered: 'I really liked making Play-Doh monsters with the arms and legs and faces ... Oh, and Greg used to let me ride in his wheelchair.'

And respect for feathered friends as well: 'Once there was a swallow flying around in the room and you got it outside for us. I really wanted to catch it and hold it, but we had to let it go.'

There were mixed comments about the transition to school, with some wistful pragmatism:

> We were always trying to build stuff, but we never actually got it ... but we still kept on trying. At my other kindy, lots of my friends left because the town was closing down. No-one ever got in trouble at kindy, but it's a bit different at school!

Another nine-year-old, thinking back, commented:

> [T]here was always lots of glittery beads and buttons and cool stuff to make with. I could do lots of making if I wanted to and we didn't have to stop like when it's time for Science ... I also did stuff like sewing and construction with the blocks and Mobilo and cooking. I loved cooking so much. I wish we could still play like that.

On the other hand, three of last year's preschoolers were enthusiastic about both sites, one saying: 'We do lots of reading now but I have to read it myself. Now I can do all the school work.' Another said, 'I had a birthday and then I was a school kid. I'm big now!', and a third noted cheerfully:

> I liked kindy because I like to make Play-Doh and mixing the glue. I liked to play with the birds and make a nest for them. At school I have to do work. School's better because I get prizes all the time and nobody else gets them. I must be the best reader!

Currently, Mel is sharing these perspectives with colleagues as part of ongoing conversations related to the goal of improving educational outcomes.

Educators' perspectives

Contributors included university-qualified teachers, both early childhood and primary-school-oriented, as well as TAFE (Technical and Further Education/Junior College) Diploma-qualified educators and those studying. Of the 19 participants, four had taught primarily in the first years of school, seven mainly worked with children aged three to five in a kindergarten/preschool setting and eight had worked across a range of settings including those with children from age three to 12. More than half had been directly involved in the practitioner inquiry projects with Mining Minds. As curiosity about how participants conceptualised 'play' was central to this investigation, we did not offer definitions in our conversations with educators or children. Strong opinions and deep emotions surfaced in their eagerness to explain their perspectives as evidenced below.

Respondents' comments (with pseudonyms) included perspectives foregrounding a positive image of the child, such as:

> I have strong beliefs that children learn through play. I learn so much from them each day and I am always impressed how capable they are in becoming masters of their own learning.
>
> (Alicia)

> Play is paramount, seeing children as strong individuals and trusting them to make decisions. Scaffolding their learning by learning with them is amazing.
>
> (Barb)

> Children need solid blocks of time throughout the school and preschool day where they can engage in this type of play where choice and autonomy is a strong motivator for task engagement and learning occurs through interacting with environments, peers and teachers, both spontaneously through experience and via teachers intentionally making the most of the "teachable moments".
>
> (Hannah)

And those who saw play as foundational in children's growth and development:

> Even if people say a child is ready for school, they are going to be even more ready if they have had that exposure to play. You can really tell which kids haven't had that

exposure through playgroup or different play environments. They have so much more trouble negotiating and dealing with conflict resolution.

(Cassie)

Working in kindy and childcare taught me that the children learn so much when they play. The relationships that children form with each other and their educators is a great foundation for any child ... It is very easy to see the children who should be playing still in the classroom, because they are the ones who have trouble with the work.

(Gaynor)

I feel confident that allowing children time for play-based learning can help them develop and scaffold all areas of their development. I am building upon my knowledge and use my knowledge to help children scaffold their learning through play.

(Kara)

I love play! Children have a chance to develop age-appropriately at an individual level. Further training in this area would help me to become more confident. In my opinion, this type of early education sets children up for success later.

(Sheila)

There were also those who, by positioning themselves as learners, strengthened their interpretations of 'play':

When I started [working in child care], it was a very naive version of play ... It wasn't until I'd been working there and writing learning stories that I realised the learning happening through play.

(Rosie)

It wasn't until we really started to investigate play, to look at playful situations and engage in these with the children, that our true understanding as a team began to gel.

(Moira)

> I would welcome the opportunity to teach in a kindergarten setting as I think this experience would shine the light on what play-based learning looks like in an early childhood setting, which would then assist in making informed decisions around my pedagogy in a junior primary setting, while meeting the numerous requirements and demands placed on us as teachers in a school setting.
>
> (Narelle)

It was also clear in our analysis that infrastructure and socio-political factors had a major impact on people's perceptions, both from the restrictive perspective ...

> I don't feel like play is a priority, because there is so much pressure to get the kids to a certain level. Like the Reception kids need to be at a certain reading level by the end of first term but some of them don't even know their letters, so how can they reach that level?
>
> (Bree)

> I feel our current system and those in leadership – from head office through to the [regional] partnership – [are] completely out of touch with the reality of education. They are so obsessed with data, standardised models of assessment and assigning levels and benchmarks to children, that they have forgotten the reality that everyone is different. I think the quote "Everybody is a genius, but if you judge a fish by its ability to climb a tree, it will live its whole life believing that it is stupid" needs to become the daily mantra for all leaders.
>
> (Kirsty)

... and from the facilitative perspective:

> I was trained in quite traditional ways in the [1990s] and play was very planned and observed and developmental-based; we used checklist after checklist. It seemed we categorised children. Then I moved to another area and first started to hear about Reggio philosophies ... The introduction of the Early Years Learning Framework to our sector has been amazing and the further we immerse into the meanings

behind it the more worth and focus I see. And the last couple of years learning here with Mining Minds projects has grown my positivity for the future of our sector.

(Barb)

We delved into research on the stages of play and began familiarising ourselves with the play types and the approximate age groups we would expect to see these occur in … Our learning came from the conversations that we had about the play taking place, both with the children as it was unfolding and as a team afterwards, and [we] had to decide on a way to effectively document the learning.

(Mel)

Pedagogical leadership plays an important part in these scenarios (see Cheeseman & Walker, in press), as reflected in comments relating to context:

I noticed that if the leadership part of the school doesn't come from an early years background, how can they help the educators better themselves if they don't have an understanding of the early years?

(Norma)

My thinking is we have to be accountable regardless of the methodology used; that's a given – we have to be able to show what children are learning from the environments we have provided and also note any unintended learning that may occur, as well as ensuring we are aligning our programs with the ACARA curriculum.[1] It is, in my view, concerning when teachers are blaming leadership for the lack of action on their own part with regard to play.

(Andrea)

There's also a strong thread about the importance of the culture of the site. For example, as Alicia notes:

I think we are on the right track as a centre. We are wanting our service to be Reggio Emilia-inspired. The philosophy is to have the right image of the child in our daily practice. The environment is the third teacher. It is a process that may take some time in building up strong educators with the same passion, and same values, but I am sure we will get there.

Other aspects of site culture are more problematic, as Roslyn reported from a conversation with her sister:

> She is a teacher in a 3/4 class now but usually teaches 1/2s. She was worried about her children "playing" too much in Reception classes ... It made me realise how undervalued play is even by other teachers ... if school teachers undervalue play, it is no wonder that children have less access to play experiences in school settings.

Personal perceptions frame professional practice. This is highlighted in the continuum of comments from Kara's strong advocacy:

> I feel that play means many things. It is a "medium" for developing social/emotional skills, gross motor and fine motor skills and cognitive skills. It is about being in a safe environment, learning collaboratively. It is about learning in an enjoyable, relaxing way.

And from Norma's understanding of potential ...

> Different people at different levels may not have that understanding, thinking that play is "just play", but you can incorporate so many different things and the kids can learn as well. You can have meaningful play where the kids are learning literacy and numeracy and different things against not-meaningful play.

... to the prior-to-school person:

> There was a time not long ago when I had a conversation with a Reception teacher. She was telling me about her expectations of preschoolers before starting school. She wants them to start school with skills already mastered in cutting with scissors or holding a pencil. In her talk, there was no mention of learning dispositions or questions related to how children play in our sector.

And a school person:

> Play and the way it is viewed has ultimately remained the same. Parents have always questioned its value and teachers have always struggled to justify its place in the curriculum or in fact as the curriculum. This is in part due to the constraints placed on us by [the Department] and the ACARA curriculum but mostly it is our own perceptions and creativity. It is difficult to maintain.

Andrea, an experienced teacher in the first years of school ('junior primary') commented that:

> A key factor affecting the confidence to implement play is the ratio of supervising staff ... It's difficult for us to provide a program that reflects the kindergarten environment when ratios are vastly different. One teacher to up to 24 students in a school setting is vastly different from kindergartens. [Also] often teachers want to have a program to follow so they can be sure they are doing the right thing or have that accountability.

Findings

In investigating the attitudes of child and adult participants towards 'play', it became clear that there were different definitions of the term. The more formal the setting, the more likely it was that 'play' was seen as an optional 'extra' – desirable in principle but inappropriate for the educational space. On the other hand, some participants could see that 'teaching through play', in what we are referring to as 'playful pedagogies', enabled the inclusion of child-initiated investigations, and hands-on exploration that would generally be recognised by early childhood educators, as 'play'. The degree of adult control and/or engagement in these circumstances was widely divergent.

In this small study, sector of employment (prior-to-school or formal schooling) was a clearer indicator of attitude towards play and playful pedagogies than qualifications, age or amount of experience. Those who had worked primarily in prior-to-school settings (seven) and those who had worked in both sectors (eight) had greater understanding of play and playful pedagogies than most of those who had worked primarily in the school sector (four). Overall, 11 people were positive with strong understandings of play and seven were reasonably confident with some caveats, while one person was not engaging with the concept productively. While the most sceptical attitudes were expressed by two people with degrees (currently working in schools, though one had child care experience), advocacy and scepticism seemed to be more related to mentorship and facilitation in understanding the potentials of play than to qualifications. In terms of implementation: of the 10 degreed teachers, four are very strong advocates of playful pedagogies, seeing potential for embedding these approaches across the curriculum (in either sector); three feel constrained by the curriculum or their leaderships' approach to accountability/assessment; while the other three are confident that they could (or could learn to) incorporate playful pedagogies in their teaching.

Mel's story

Establishment of our children's centre after a devastating school fire gave opportunities to start afresh and implement play-based pedagogy as standard practice. Educators, parents and our wider school community shared a desire to establish a quality service for local children and families. With Angela as principal, learning together about play, we fuelled interest in exploring dispositions for learning. Could we use dispositions to inform learning and convince the doubters of the value of play? How could we use this to document growth? Was this enough to appease data-hungry line managers?

Our journey has led us to develop strengths-based practices, where individual children's learning experiences are seen through a positive mindset, focusing on what they 'know, can do and understand' – as advocated by the national Early Years Learning Framework (DEEWR, 2009, p. 17) – and are recorded as learning stories, an analytical record of what an educator has seen a child doing within the early years setting. Continual changes to the structure of our site, staffing, qualifications and fluctuating student enrolments have resulted in an ever-evolving service for our educators, children and families.

As Mel reflects, I've had the opportunity to work between the two settings both separately and at the same time (combining preschoolers and junior primary children in the same class). It's not easy, but with a bit of creativity both curriculum frameworks can marry up nicely. It is important that educators provide learning opportunities and resources that complement the knowledge, skills and understandings of individual children, in order to respond to and nurture their dispositions for learning. It's about finding a respectful balance between the two frameworks, fostering engagement and customising the learning to suit individual children. With a little more support from a site level in terms of curriculum, timetabling flexibility and support staff, and a greater focus on the documentation of programming reflection and assessment, I'm confident that other educators could embrace playfulness.

We had something truly wonderful in our small school. When a whole site embraces playful pedagogy, educators become more cohesive and confident, as do students and their families. When a school can work collaboratively to share the journey and develop dispositions for learning in all children (and educators), regardless of age, everyone benefits. This can only happen, though, when all levels of education are equally valued, staffing and funding is adequate, training opportunities abound and educators are prepared to be brave advocates for children, coming up with creative responses to challenges. Considering and reflecting on this chapter also highlighted how quickly hard work, relationships and strengths-based documentation come undone, when this balance is altered.

Our combined participation in the Mining Minds projects has contributed to the growth of playful pedagogies amongst educators and foregrounded a collective voice, a desire to be part of change. Although the degree to which it has been embraced differs amongst educators, our participation in the projects has enabled us to agree that we want to reshape the perception of accepted expectations of early years schooling in our local area. Many educators already have – and those that don't yet desire to have – the knowledge, skills, resourcing and confidence to implement pedagogies of play through the early years and beyond, because we value playful engagement where choice and autonomy are paramount. We see the success, wonder, motivation and awe that playfulness evokes, and want this to be commonplace in all learning environments. We want our schools, our non-early-years colleagues and parents to not only understand and respect our philosophies and pedagogy, but value and support our efforts to engage learners through playfulness, to develop their individual dispositions for learning. We want opportunities to have 'lived-teaching experiences'.

There is consensus between educators in the area that we are on the right track. Despite constant challenges, we remain upbeat and dedicated to improving outcomes and finding alternatives. More than ever before, we are networking and sharing in important discussions around play. We are consistently seeking and sharing professional development opportunities, striving to make our learning provocations and spaces more enticing, and actively fostering children's appreciation of and connection to the natural environment through nature play (see www.natureplay.org.au/). Most educators are members of various online groups who share their success stories locally of learning through play. Reflective practice is big on our agendas as the projects have fostered networking and online communication.

We have all tried to implement playfulness in some form, yet, on the whole, most early-schooling educators do not feel that their efforts have been successful or valued by their non-early-years colleagues. In my discussions with educators, all were familiar with their primary curriculum, but most admitted that they were not as familiar with the EYLF. Interestingly, those who had the most success with implementing playfulness were those educators who had worked, or currently do work, between the prior-to-school and school frameworks.

It seems that further opportunities must be given for educators to spend quality time networking, with emphasis on exploring both frameworks and their connectedness in the nurturing of playful pedagogy. If we could implement this as standard practice, educators would be more confident in their ability to turn ideas into actions. There would be less reliance on the structure and time-tabling of traditional schooling to deliver curriculum content, and greater flexibility for educators to better match the individual learning styles of children in their care.

For me personally, in our tiny site, I feel the effect of these constraints more so as time goes on. In recent years, it has often been a lonely, long, hard road to follow. Staff turnover, their (sometimes) lack of understanding of playful pedagogy, low student enrolments and the break-down of our once strong and vibrant early years integrated service have seen a shift in philosophy in our site.

I need to let go of the fact that I can't control what happens at a departmental, regional or site level, but I can control what happens on the days I work and what the learning looks like. My philosophy remains the same; I will continue to implement reflective practice to build on what's working well and change what's not. Low enrolments for next year again present me with a unique opportunity to explore combining our preschool and Reception– Year 2 children and really challenge pedagogies of play. Now, more than ever, I just need to be brave!

Challenges

Natalie, another experienced junior primary teacher, lamented:

> The idea of assessments and my need for control holds me back from letting students have choice and variety in play experiences. I want to do more but there is so much to assess. If there is more play, then it gets even harder to get the assessment information. There isn't always physical evidence of the learning.

Mel noted that this perspective reinforces the importance of meaningful documentation valuing playful engagement (see, for example, Fleet et al., 2012, 2017).

Another challenge which became apparent between educators is the lack of conversation and collaboration between/across settings and across frameworks. Successful transitions can only be facilitated when communication between educators from both sectors and parents occurs; prior learning is respected and valued; and their strengths, interests and progress are shared.

Hannah stated:

> Teachers need to be flexible, confident and empathic to effectively support, challenge and assess student learning. I feel that many teachers lack the confidence to approach teaching in this fashion, particularly in the school environment where it seems as though the pressure of the required curriculum bares down on such important pedagogical choices and in the interest of "fitting everything in". Play is then often only used as either a reward for finishing work, compliant behaviour or an occasional "special treat".

Yet some educators believe that it needs to move beyond communication. Kirsty, also a very experienced junior primary teacher, suggested, 'I strongly believe schools and kindys need to build in extra non-contact time, to give teachers from school and kindy a chance to work together to meet the needs of the children.'

Kirsty's model suggests students work between the kindergarten (preschool) and the school for their first week of school, with school teachers working at the kindergarten for some of the times when students are not attending school and possibly kindergarten teachers observing to see what happens in Reception (the first year of school). From weeks two to six, students should attend four times per week, allowing them time to adapt and adjust to the rigors and change that comes with attending school. Teachers could use the extra day for collaborating with the kindergarten, meeting families of students and so on.

Further supporting Kirsty's model, Narelle reflected:

> I believe that when you have a lived-teaching experience of the "where are they going" (i.e. Year One) and the "where have they come from" (i.e. Reception), you have a true appreciation of how to cater for the individuals in your care, both academically and emotionally. The "where have they come from" is something that I knew I wanted to explore further as I knew that I could be making the transition between kindy and school much smoother and not as "jarring".

Nevertheless, perhaps our focus has moved beyond sole educators rethinking pedagogy. Conversations such as Narelle's are evident that it is time for sites and systems to rethink in order to make these 'lived experiences' a reality. Individuals can't move beyond the here and now if they don't have opportunities to experience and implement; nor do they have the capacity to execute such initiatives.

Across this study of 19 educators, the eight who were keen advocates/particularly enthusiastic were all influenced by experience with a relative (child/sister/parent). The personalising of theory cannot be ignored in landscapes of professional learning! Related to this finding was the fact that those who were particularly positive all acknowledged the role of mentorship – either from a centre director, school principal or project facilitator, often while stating that a change in leadership had been a major factor in highlighting or diminishing perceptions of the value of play. It can be surmised, however, that in addition to systemic factors, personal inclinations, attitude, knowledge and openness to possibility are key factors in embracing playful pedagogies in early childhood education.

Finally

While the Australian Early Years Framework (DEEWR, 2009) advocates play-based pedagogies, embedding the philosophy across the early childhood age range can be problematic. This investigation enabled the sharing of voices from people most affected by this pedagogical intention. From children's reflections, clear themes included nostalgia for play and its association with friends and having fun as well as agency for choice and fewer constraints on time: 'We sometimes made bridges with the soft building block things. It was easy back then, because we had fun.'

Adult attitudes ranged from 'happy to learn' to 'why won't they understand', coming from both sides of the playground fence. Hearing these perspectives may provide provocations for considering how pedagogical provocations filter through to lived experience, and perhaps offer ways forward in offering children playful pedagogies across their early childhood years.

Note

1 ACARA is an independent statutory authority responsible for school-based curriculum. 'ACARA's strategic directions are set by its Charter and any other written instructions from the Council of Australian Governments (COAG) Education Council' (www.acara.edu.au/about-us).

References

Australian Government Department of Education Employment and Workplace Relations (DEEWR). (2009). *Belonging, Being and Becoming – The Early Years Learning Framework*. Canberra, ACT: DEEWR.

Cheeseman, S., & Walker, R. (in press). *Thinking about Pedagogy in Early Education: Pedagogies for Leading Practice*. London: Routledge.

Fleet, A., DeGioia, K., & Patterson, C. (2016). *Engaging with Eduational Change: Voices of Practitioner Inquiry*. London: Bloomsbury.

Fleet, A., Patterson, C., & Robertson, J. (Eds). (2012). *Conversations: Behind Early Childhood Pedagogical Documentation*. Mt Victoria, NSW: Pademelon Press.

Fleet, A., Patterson, C., & Robertson, J. (Eds). (2017). *Pedagogical Documentation in Early Years Practice*. London: SAGE.

6

THE ROLE OF CONTEXT WITHIN EARLY CHILDHOOD EDUCATION IN IRELAND

Margaret O'Donoghue

How policies are enacted is contingent on the context in which they are translated. This chapter will look at the role of context in the enactment of early childhood education (ECE) curriculum change. ECE in Ireland operates under a split model system in which the childcare and education sectors function independently. In practice, there are two separate systems. ECE in pre-schools for children aged between three and four years is the responsibility of the Department of Children and Youth Affairs, while the responsibility of children in early years primary school (age four to six years) rests with the Department of Education and Science (DES). Throughout this chapter, the term "ECE" refers to children aged between four and six years who attend junior infants (the first year) in primary school.

Internationally, pre-schools and primary schools have developed very much as separate entities and vary in several ways in terms of their objectives and approaches to ECE, resulting in differences in pedagogy and curricula (Einarsdottir, 2013; Fabian, 2013; Ministry of Education New Zealand, 2013; Perry, Dockett & Harley, 2012). The compulsory age at which children must attend primary school in Ireland is six years; however, children can attend from the age of four. Statistics show that 65 per cent of all four-year-olds and most five-year-olds are enrolled in primary school, entering at junior infant level and progressing to senior infant level at six years of age (Education in Ireland, 2011).

In 2009, the National Council for Curriculum Assessment (NCCA) launched Ireland's first early childhood curriculum framework, called Aistear (pronounced *Ash-ter*). Aistear is the curriculum framework for all children from birth to six years in Ireland. Aistear sought to complement and extend the primary school curriculum (Department of Education & Skills, 1999; DES, 2016) and promotes a curriculum that builds on children's interests. It supports the concept that curiosity, wonder, resilience and playfulness should be at the centre of what and how children learn (NCCA, 2012).

As an early childhood curriculum framework, Aistear encompasses the junior and senior infant curriculum and promotes continuity of learning from pre-school to primary school. In 2016 the Irish DES launched the language strand of a new primary school curriculum (PSC). While Aistear focuses on the development of attitudes, values and learning dispositions and is neither statutory nor inspected, the PSC centres on the acquisition of subject-based knowledge and the development of age-appropriate skills and is subject to external inspection (Gray & Ryan, 2016). Therefore, an important issue emerges in terms of how educators perceive the relationship between the new primary curriculum and the recommendations contained in Aistear, particularly because of a potential tension for educators having to follow the statutory primary curriculum and the non-statutory Aistear curriculum framework.

A report in 2017 (Urban, Robson & Scacchi) exploring professional practice in the pre-school sector noted that ECE remained fragmented in Ireland. In perhaps acknowledging the implicit barriers erected between early years pre-school practice and early years primary school practice, the report emphasised that "The foundation for all professional practice in early childhood, regardless of the setting or occupational role is sound knowledge relating to working with children ... families ... other professionals and the wider local, national and international context" (p. 6). The report aimed to bring together the factions of Irish ECE into a "competent system" (p. 5), emphasising that a "critical understanding of one's own role as a professional, team worker, critically reflective practitioner, and continuous learner (regardless of one's level of formal qualification, experience, or occupational role)" (p. 6) was fundamental to realising this aim.

Context

The Aistear framework supports a socio-cultural view of learning and development. As a curriculum framework it promotes the child as a competent learner from birth and as an active agent in their own learning and development through their interactions with the world

(NCCA, 2009). This view recognises the period of early childhood as a time in and of itself and is underpinned by theories that recognise children as social actors who actively participate in and co-construct their knowledge, identity and culture with peers and adults (James & James, 2004). Aistear can be used as an assessment tool to support teachers to build a picture over time of a child's learning progress across the primary curriculum; this information can then be used to celebrate the child's learning and to help make decisions about the next steps for future learning (NCCA, 2009). Indeed, as an early childhood framework, Aistear promotes a child-led and play-based approach in tandem with the learning outcomes encapsulated in the new PSC. However, research from a study by Hunter and Walsh (2014, p. 33) identified that while teachers appear to recognise the value of this emphasis on play, they may lack the skills needed to provide quality play experiences and that their efforts are mainly "tokenistic" in nature. Additionally, they found that there was little evidence that play was linked to the aims and learning goals of Aistear or the underlying principle of the PSC in relation to the child being an active agent in their own learning.

Building on these findings, Gray and Ryan's study (2016), which looked at Aistear in relation to the primary curriculum (DES, 1999), highlighted that 43 per cent of ECE teachers reported being unfamiliar with their role in implementing Aistear in the PSC. In addition, 64 per cent of teachers responded that they did not feel confident about organising play-based learning activities. A further study by O'Donoghue (2016) found that while there was a consensus among the teachers on the important role of play in ECE, the language they used suggested a mainly didactic approach with an emphasis on the curriculum learning objectives. As one teacher said, "I would say most of the time it is probably coming from me ... you have to be very definite in your objectives, you know what you have to cover. You have to stay on track."

The study further highlighted that teachers work in different environments with different constraints and pressures that impose on their day-to-day practice. Findings from the study found that the teachers felt the need to prioritise the learning objectives set down by the curriculum rather than providing time for play. Moreover, they did not identify that the children were learning during their play. Burgess and Fleet (2009, p. 47) caution that in the absence of external pressure for mandatory enactment regarding curricula reform, "there is the risk of day-to-day issues taking priority over non-mandated curriculum documents and so, the status quo remains". This view is reflected by teachers in O'Donoghue's study (2016):

TEACHER 1: For child-initiated I do try to go with it when it happens but it doesn't happen, I mean it can't happen when you have so much to do – you have such a short day and you are trying to get everything done.
TEACHER 2: I always kind of struggle with Aistear with the playtime aspect of it ... I would love to do more of it but I just feel that we don't have the time to facilitate it.
TEACHER 3: I find it hard to get the curriculum covered, I only do art at playtime so if they don't go to the creative station how are they doing art? I know the idea is they choose for themselves where they play and if they don't like something they can go somewhere else ... but I find that hard.

These findings draw attention to the need for those who educate to make a mental shift in their thinking and move away from a pedagogical approach that sees children learn through a Developmentally Appropriate Practice lens (Bredekamp & Copple, 1997) where the adult is the sole reproducer of knowledge.

Hurst and Joseph (1998) suggest that a key task for the early years teacher is to create a balance between giving children time and space to learn through their self-initiated play and providing learning which is more formally negotiated between the child and the adult. One teacher in O'Donoghue's study (2016) described how she planned out each day, but one day the children observed a rainbow in the sky. Guided by the children's interest the lesson became all about the rainbow.

TEACHER 2: They did a great job on drawing their rainbows, I think it was because they were so excited ... . I think if I had gone home and planned to do a lesson on rainbows it would not have turned out like that. There was no template, no colouring exercise. They drew their own rainbows and they were brilliant.

Considerations

Crucial to effective pedagogy is how those working in ECE understand children's learning and developmental theories and how that knowledge is applied in practice (Moyles, Adams & Musgrove, 2002). Supporting and empowering teachers to change how they transmit curricula content should begin from a point that "affirms them as knowledgeable practitioners" (Fleet, DeGioia & Patterson, 2016, p. 91). A change in pedagogical approach "may also require the development of documents to initiate and support change" within ECE (Burgess & Fleet, 2009, p. 45). Dunphy (2008) suggests that the practices of primary school teachers have been shaped by the primary curriculum (DES, 1999), and as part of that curriculum they have been enculturated into what constitutes appropriate ways of being within that context. Teachers enact new curricula policies as the "silent partners in educational change" (Burgess & Fleet, 2009, p. 47). A study by Gallant (2009) of kindergarten teachers' experiences reported that many teachers felt frustrated by new requirements, disempowered and pushed by administrators to implement new policies that were not compatible with their beliefs or their practical context. In light of these empirical findings, researchers have emphasised the need to listen to and support the teachers as they undergo curricular reforms (Gallant, 2009; Zembylas, 2010).

Evidence suggests that providing quality play experiences for children in the early years will require those who educate to reconceptualise ECE and move from a predominately didactic approach to how the curriculum is enacted to a socio-cultural model. Such a model views children as being active participants in their learning and the classroom as a place where knowledge is co-constructed between the adult and the child (OECD, 2006; Gray & Ryan, 2016; Hunter & Walsh, 2014; O'Donoghue, 2016). This approach provides children with a sense of belonging and connectedness to their world and creates an environment where the child and adult co-exist in interdependent relations (Dahlberg, Moss & Pence, 1999; Dunne, 2005; Moss & Petrie, 2002).

The need for change in pedagogical practices in infant classes in Ireland has been indicated by a number of research studies and reports. The Organisation for Economic Co-operation and Development Thematic Review of Early Childhood Education and Care Policy in Ireland (OECD, 2004) described infant classes as one of whole-class teaching, with children sitting quietly at tables. The approach they suggested was directive and formal compared to practices observed and theoretically underpinned in other countries, where more emphasis is placed on exploratory learning and self-initiated, hands-on (as opposed to table-top) activities (OECD, 2004). The report highlighted that a "predominately didactic approach" towards early learning was observed (OECD, 2004, p. 84). The report concluded that the impetus driving the teachers' pedagogical approach was a prescribed curriculum, with little account being taken of children's interests or concerns. The findings resonate with a study by Murphy (2004) which looked at curriculum implementation in 15 Irish junior infant classes. The findings highlight that "patterns of interaction and activity in the observed classrooms generally remain teacher focused rather than child centred" (p. 256). The significance and concern in relation to these findings are that research suggests that over a decade on, a predominately didactic approach persists within the infant classroom (Eivers et al., 2010). Further, O'Donoghue's study (2016) found that teachers' expectations of the junior infant class are for children to sit quietly in large groups for long periods of time rather than allow for playful, child-led experiences away from their desks.

Teachers' values and beliefs

Urban, Robson and Scacchi (2017) highlight the need to look at how Aistear as a policy framework is interpreted within different contexts and how it translates into practice. Critical to understanding how the new primary language curriculum might be enacted and managed in relation to Aistear within the early years primary school classroom is an exploration of how teachers' values and belief systems influence their pedagogical approach. Edwards and Nuttall (2009) highlight that changing educational practice is notoriously difficult and that sustained changes must be reinforced by re-alignments in teachers' knowledge and beliefs. Supporting teachers to implement a play-based curriculum requires the development of policies that are sensitive to the different approaches to play as well as considering developmental and learning objectives (Pylea, Delucaband & Dannielsaa, 2017).

The role of those who educate in a socio-cultural model of ECE is central since it is the educator who enables the learning to take place by actively engaging with the children, the curriculum and the learning context. Such views challenge the concept of children as passive objects who are properties of their families to be shaped and socialised by adult teaching (Smart, Neale & Wade, 2001).

Adopting a socio-cultural pedagogy recognises children's agency and inherent capacities (James & James, 2004; Mayall, 2002; Moss & Dahlberg, 2005). Moreover, it promotes a rights-based approach to early years teaching and is in line with the United Nations Convention on the Rights of the Child (1989).

Aistear as a policy text promotes a child-centred rights-based approach to ECE and advocates for children to have opportunities to make choices about what, how and with whom they want to play. Children have the capacity to contribute to society as competent social actors and can contribute to shaping their own experiences (Brooker, 2002; Garrick et al., 2010). Lansdown (2011) posits that a child-centred approach promotes a structured, child-centred curriculum that includes teaching-learning methods appropriate to the child's developmental level, abilities and learning style; and considers the needs of children over the needs of the other actors in the system. In addition, she argues that a child-centred curriculum encourages participation, creativity, self-esteem and psychosocial wellbeing. Adopting such a pedagogical approach enables children to initiate and direct their play with the support of interested and responsive adults.

The classroom environment is a complex mix of interrelationships between teachers and children, context and pedagogy. Professional cultures (Ball, Maguire & Braun, 2012) refer to teachers' values, belief systems and commitments within schools and include teachers' understandings of curriculum policy, how children learn and develop and the school ethos. Similarly, Artzt and Armour-Thomas (1996, p. 8) suggest that teachers' belief systems and decisions represent "implicit assumptions about curricula, knowledge, teaching and learning and act as cognitive and affective filters through which new knowledge is interpreted and enacted". Moreover, Loizou (2017) draws attention to the fact that while teachers discuss the benefits of play in ECE they are mainly trained in the organisation of the classroom space and materials and that their personal involvement is often neglected.

Research on teaching effectiveness by Bowman, Donovan and Burns (2001) showed that teachers have implicit beliefs about the subject matter, their students and their roles and responsibilities. These elements collectively and individually influence the way teachers' practice. Fenwick (2008), underlining the importance of the individual and their beliefs, argues that individual differences in perspectives, dispositions, position, social and cultural capital and forms of participation are often unaccounted for. Research has shown that personal beliefs about the effectiveness and the appropriateness of the curriculum and teachers' personality characteristics are contextual factors that need to be considered when introducing curriculum change (Li & Baldauf, 2011; Lieber et al., 2009; Tobin, 2007). Moreover, Hunter and Walsh (2014, p. 33) argue that teachers cannot rely on a policy document to act as an infallible blueprint for practice and that a change in policy statements alone will not ensure a change in pedagogy. They propose that teachers need to be upskilled, so that they develop a more "nuanced and sophisticated" understanding of the meaning of play as pedagogy in the early year's classroom. This resonates with Hedges and Cullen (2012), who suggest that policy statements be accompanied by policy strategies and appropriate funding to ensure the continuing professional development that early years teachers require.

A study by Unwin et al. (2007) offers important insights regarding the enactment of the new PSC in relation to Aistear. Unwin et al. (2007) underline the importance of the need to identify and take serious account of the contextual factors that affect all organisations, as these are central to developing our understanding of the nature of pedagogical practice. Furthermore, they give a note of caution that in the absence of explicit guidelines that intentionally cultivate the transfer of desired skills to practice, tacit behaviours that perpetuate undesirable practices may persist. In a similar vein Cohen (2006) argues that the extent of pedagogical variety and the nature of the learning opportunities available to and created by workers exist within a set of contextual relationships. Moreover, they demonstrate that although an early childhood curriculum framework exists (Aistear) along with the rhetoric of promoting a child-centred and rights-based approach, it does not in itself ensure its implementation.

These findings underline the need to understand why there is such a gap between what those who educate think and say and how that relates to their pedagogical practice and the ECE experiences of the children. Effectively these findings suggest that, without identifying the current pedagogical practices of ECE teachers and how they understand Aistear, current policy will continue to promote and possibly assume that Aistear is implicit within the enactment of the new PLC. This is not the case.

These issues are not confined to Ireland. A study by Einarsdottir, Dockett and Perry (2009) highlights that in almost every case, more teachers reported naming practices that they believed were very useful than reported using those practices. Their study found that in Iceland, although not many of the primary school teachers reported that they held shared meetings to discuss education and continuity in children's education, 61 per cent of primary school teachers reported it to be a good idea. Furthermore, Colmer (2013), in a study of how Australian early childhood centre directors understood and lead professional development and learning during a major reform of curriculum, found that although they articulated belief in the value of collaborative professional learning, individualised, one-off, external professional development events remained a common strategy.

A study conducted in Israel (Sverdlov, Aram & Levin, 2014) explored the impact of a new pre-school literacy curriculum on kindergarten teachers' beliefs and perceptions and of the literacy promoting the practices in the new curriculum. The findings highlight that six years after the new curriculum programme was introduced 78 per cent of kindergarten teachers used the literacy curriculum only once per week and 19 per cent less than once per week, ranging from once a month to several times a year. Sverdlov et al.'s (2014) study is significant as it underlines the fact that the introduction of a new curriculum does not automatically ensure its enactment.

Ball, Maguire and Braun (2012) argue that individual policies and policymakers do not usually take into consideration the complexity of institutional policy enactment environments, but rather work on the assumption that schools can and will respond, and respond quickly, to multiple policy demands and other expectations. The authors suggest that a framework for policy enactment needs to consider a set of objective conditions in relation to a set of subjective "interpretational dynamics" (2012, p. 21). Moreover, they argue that the material, structural and relational elements need to be incorporated into policy analysis to understand policy enactments at institutional level.

Ball et al.'s (2012, p. 43) conceptualisation of policy enactment draws upon and brings together "three constituent aspects of the messy reality of school life". These aspects, material, interpretive and discursive, taken together make up a version of what Ball et al. (2012, p. 43) describe as "material semiotics" which Law (2007, p. 2) suggests "are better understood as a toolkit for telling interesting stories about and interfering in the complex webs of social relations and relations of power that produce and circumscribe policy and practice in schools". Schools operate in different contexts and will have different capacities, potentials and limits (Lauder, Jamieson & Whikeley, 1998). These, they suggest, constitute a material context of interpretation and create different practical possibilities and constraints for policy enactment and frameworks of expectation within which responses to policy are constructed. Policy enactments also depend to some extent on the degree to which particular policies will "fit" or can be fitted within the existing ethos and culture of the school or can change ethos and culture (Ball, Maguire & Braun, 2012, p. 10). Building on this, they argue that policy enactment should not be understood as a "moment" but rather as a "process of interpretation that is framed by institutional factors involving a range of actors" (Ball, Maguire & Braun, 2012, p. 15). As signalled earlier, what happens inside a school in terms of how policies are interpreted and enacted will be mediated by institutional factors which include the ethos of the school and the leadership role adopted by the principal.

Conclusion

Curriculum reform is complex; it requires taking into consideration a number of factors. These include the availability of support from colleagues, administrators and principals, the availability of effective professional development programmes and the reform's cultural and contextual fit (Lieber et al., 2009; Li & Baldauf, 2011).

Cultures vary and change over time; thus, notions of childhood and how children learn change correspondingly. How curriculum policy is written is closely linked to the current discourse on how children learn; however, as this chapter points out, policies are not enacted by those who govern but rather by those who educate. Those who educate bring their own experiences, beliefs and understandings to bear on what they see or read and therefore the enactment of the new PSC in relation to Aistear will be understood and implemented from positions of the subjectiveness of those who educate. Supporting those who educate to develop a pedagogical approach that adopts a child-centred, rights-based approach to ECE similar to Aistear requires school principals to understand the interaction between the different contextual elements which include the teachers, their practices, their values, attitudes, ideas and beliefs (Rodd, 2015). Moreover, it requires the provision of a space where those who educate are supported to work collaboratively and reflect on how they can engage in a pedagogical approach that supports a child-centred rights-based-approach curriculum. This would be a curriculum where children construct their knowledge from their experiences and interactions with the world around them and where the ECE teacher can foster their growth and development by building on their interests, needs and strengths within a safe and caring environment.

References

Artzt, A., & Armour-Thomas, E. (1996). Evaluation of instructional practice in the secondary school mathematics classroom: A cognitive perspective. Paper presented at the Annual Meeting of the American Educational Research Association. ERIC Document Reproduction Service No. ED397131.

Ball, S., Maguire, M., & Braun, A. (2012). *How Schools Do Policy: Policy Enactments in Secondary Schools*. New York, NY: Routledge.

Bowman, B.T., Donovan, M.S., & Burns, M.S. (2001). *Eager to Learn: Educating Our Pre-Schoolers*. Washington, DC: National Academic Press.

Bredekamp, S., & Copple, C. (1997). *Developmentally Appropriate Practice in Early Childhood Programs*. Washington, DC: NAEYC.

Brooker, L. (2002). *Starting School: Young Children Learning Cultures*. Buckingham: Open University Press.

Burgess, J., & Fleet, A. (2009). Frameworks for change: Four recurrent themes for quality in early childhood curriculum initiatives. *Asia-Pacific Journal of Teacher Education*, 37(1), 45–61. DOI: 10.1080/13598660802534489.

Cohen, J. (2006). Social, emotional, ethical and academic education: Creating a climate for learning, participation in democracy and well-being. *Harvard Educational Review*, 76(2), 201–237.

Colmer, K. (2013). Leading for professional development and learning. Presentation at the Leadership Perspectives from Near and Far – From Australia and Europe, An International Leadership Research Symposium. 13 December, Sydney.

Dahlberg, G., Moss, P., & Pence, A. (1999). *Beyond Quality in Early Childhood Education and Care: Postmodern Perspectives*. London: Falmer Press.

Department of Education & Science. (1999). *Primary School Curriculum: Introduction*. Dublin: Government Publications. Retrieved from www.ncca.ie/uploadedfiles/Curriculum/Intro_Eng.pdf.

Department of Education & Science. (2016). *Primary School Curriculum*. Dublin: National Council for Curriculum and Assessment.

Dunne, J. (2005). Childhood and citizenship: A crossed conversation. Keynote presentation at 15th Annual European Early Childhood Research Association Annual Conference, 31 August to 3 September 2005, published as "Childhood and citizenship: A crossed conversation" in *European Early Childhood Education Research Journal*, 14(1), 2006, 5–19.

Dunphy, E. (2008). *Developing Pedagogy in Infant Classes in Primary Schools in Ireland: Learning from Research*. St Patrick's College, Drumcondra: Education in Ireland. Retrieved from www.educationinireland.ie/index.

Education in Ireland (2011). Retrieved from www.educationinireland.ie/index.

Edwards, S., & Nuttall J. (2009). *Professional Learning in Early Childhood Settings*. Rotterdam: Sense Publishers.

Einarsdottir, J. (2013). Transition from preschool to primary school in Iceland from the perspectives of children. In Margetts, K., & Keinig, A. (Eds). *International Perspectives on Transition to School: Reconceptualising Beliefs, Policy and Practice* (pp. 69–78). NY: Routledge.

Einarsdottir, J., Dockett, S., & Perry, B. (2009). Making meaning: Children's perspectives expressed through drawings. *Early Child Development and Care*, 179(2), 217–232.

Eivers, E., Clerkin, A., Millar, D., & Close, S. (2010). The 2009 national assessments of mathematics and reading. Retrieved www.erc.ie/documents/na2009_report.pdf.

Fabian, H. (2013). Towards successful transitions. In Margetts, K., & Keinig, A. (Eds). *International Perspectives on Transition to School: Reconceptualising Beliefs, Policy and Practice* (pp. 45–55). NY: Routledge.

Fenwick, T. (2008). Understanding relations of individual–collective learning in work. *Management Learning*, 29, 3.

Fleet, A., De Gioia, K., & Patterson, C. (2016). *Engaging with Educational Change: Voices of Practitioner Inquiry*. London: Bloomsbury.

Gallant, P.A. (2009). Kindergarten teachers speak out: Too much, too soon, too fast. *Reading Horizons*, 49(3). Retrieved from https://scholarworks.wmich.edu/reading_horizons/vol49/iss3/3/.

Garrick, R., Bath, C., Dunn, K., Maconochie, H., Willis, B., & Wolstenholme, C. (2010). *Children's Experiences of the Early Years Foundation Stage*. Research Report RR071. London: Department of Education.

Gray, C., & Ryan, A. (2016). Aistear vis-à-vis the primary curriculum: The experiences of early years' teachers in Ireland. *International Journal of Early Years Education*, 24(2), 188–205.

Hedges, H., & Cullen, J. (2012). Participatory learning theories: A framework for early childhood pedagogy. *Early Child Development and Care*, 182(7), 921–940. Retrieved from www.-tandfonline-com.lcproxy.shu.ac.uk/doi/abs/10.1080/03004430.2011.597504.

Hunter, T., & Walsh, G. (2014). From policy to practice? The reality of play in primary school classes in Northern Ireland. *International Journal of Early Years Education*, 22(1), 19–36.

Hurst, V., & Joseph, J. (1998). *Supporting Early Learning: The Way Forward*. Buckingham: Open University Press.

James, A.L., & James, A. (2004). *Constructing Childhood: Theory, Policy and Social Practice*. Basingstoke: Palgrave Macmillan.

Lansdown, G. (2011). *Every Child's Right to be Heard: A Resource Guide on the UN Rights of the Child General Committee*. General Comment No. 12. London: Save the Children Fund.

Lauder, H., Jamieson, I., & Whikeley, F. (1998). Models of effective schools: Limits and capabilities. In Slee, R., Tomlinson, S., & Weiner, G. (Eds). *School Effectiveness for Whom?* (pp. 51–69). London and Bristol, PA: Falmer.

Law, J. (2007). *Actor-Network Theory & Material Semiotics*. Retrieved from www.heterogeneities.net/publications/Law2007ANTandMaterialSemiotics.pdf.

Li, M., & Baldauf, R. (2011). Beyond the curriculum: A Chinese example of issues constraining effective English language teaching. *Tesol*, 45(4), 793–803.

Lieber, J., Butera, G., Hanson, M., Palmer, S., Horn, E., Czaja, C., & Odom, S. (2009). Factors that influence the implementation of a new preschool curriculum: Implications for professional development. *Early Education and Development*, 20, 456–481.

Loizou, E. (2017). Towards play pedagogy: Supporting teacher play practices with a teacher guide about socio-dramatic and imaginative play. *European Early Childhood Education Research Journal*, 25(5), 784–795. Retrieved from www.-tandfonline-com.lcproxy.shu.ac.uk/doi/abs/10.1080/1350293X.2017.1356574.

Mayall, B. (2002). *Towards a Sociology for Childhood Thinking from Children's Lives*. London: Open University Press.

Ministry of Education, New Zealand. (2013). *Transitions: Collaborative Relationships and Sharing Responsibility*. Retrieved from www.educate.ece.govt.nz/learning/exploringPractice/Transitions/TransitionsInEarlyChildhood/CollaborativeRelationships/LocalInitiatives.aspx?p=2.

Moss, P., & Dahlberg, G. (2005). Beyond quality in early childhood education and care: Languages of evaluation. *New Zealand Journal of Teachers' Work*, 5(1), 3–12.

Moss, P., & Petrie, P. (2002). *From Children's Services to Children's Spaces*. London: RoutledgeFalmer.

Moyles, J., Adams, S., & Musgrove, A. (2002). *SPEEL: Study of Pedagogical Effectiveness in Early Learning*. Research Report No. 363. London: Department for Education and Skills.

Murphy, B. (2004). Practice in Irish infant classrooms in the context of the Irish primary school curriculum (1999): Insights from a study of curriculum implementation. *International Journal of Early Years Education*, 12 (3), 245–257.

National Council for Curriculum and Assessment. (2009). *Aistear, the Framework for Early Learning*. Dublin: NCCA.

National Council for Curriculum and Assessment. (2012). *Executive Summaries: A Compendium from Commissioned Research on Primary Language*. Dublin: NCCA. Retrieved from www.ncca.ie/en/Curriculum_and_Assessment/Early_Childhood_and_Primary_Education/PrimaryEducation/Primary_Developments/Language/Review-and-Research/c1.pdf.

O'Donoghue, M. (2016). Exploring how primary school teachers understand Aistear: A pilot study. Children's research digest. *Children's Research Network*, 3(2), 14–17.

Organisation for Economic and Community Development. (2006). *Starting Strong II in Early Childhood Education and Care*. Paris: OECD Publishing.

Organisation for Economic Co-operation and Development. (2004). *Thematic Review of Early Childhood Education and Care*: Background Report. Paris: OECD Publishing.

Perry, B., Dockett, S., & Harley, E. (2012). The early years learning framework and the Australian curriculum: Linking educators' practice through pedagogical inquiry questions. In Atweh, B., Goos, M., Jorgensen, R., & Siemon, D. (Eds). *National Curriculum: Mathematics – Perspectives from the Field* (pp. 155–174). Mathematics Education Research Group of Australasia. Retrieved from www.merga.net.au/sites/default/files/editor/books/1/Chapter percent208percent20Perry.pdf.

Pylea, A., Delucaband, C., & Dannielsaa, E. (2017). A scoping review of research on play-based pedagogies in kindergarten education. *Review of Education*, 5(3), 311–351. Retrieved from https://onlinelibrary-wiley-com.lcproxy.shu.ac.uk/doi/epdf/10.1002/rev3.3097.

Rodd, J. (2015). *Leading Change in Early Years Principles and Practice*. London: Open University Press/McGraw-Hill Education.

Smart, C., Neale, B., & Wade, A. (2001). *The Changing Experience of Childhood: Children and Divorce*. Cambridge: Polity.

Sverdlov, A., Aram, D., & Levin, I. (2014). Kindergarten teachers' literacy beliefs and self-reported practices: On the heels of a new national literacy curriculum. *Teaching and Teacher Education*, 39, 44–55.

Tobin, J. (2007). An ethnographic perspective on quality in early childhood education. In Zhu, J.X. (Ed). *Global Perspectives on Early Childhood Education* (pp. 131–143). Shanghai, China: East China Normal University Press.

United Nations Convention on the Rights of the Child (UNHCR). (1989). Geneva: Office of the High Commissioner for Human Rights. Retrieved from www.ohchr.org/EN/ProfessionalInterest/Pages/CRC.aspx.

Unwin, L., Felstead, A., Fuller, A., Bishop, D., Jewson, N., Kakavelakis, K., & Lee, T. (2007). Looking inside the Russian doll: The interconnections between context, learning and pedagogy in the workplace. *Pedagogy, Culture & Society*, 3(15), 333–348.

Urban, M., Robson, S., & Scacchi, V. (2017). *Review of Occupational Role Profiles in Ireland in Early Childhood Education and Care*. London: University of Roehampton Early Childhood Research Centre.

Zembylas, M. (2010). Teachers' emotional experiences of growing diversity and multiculturalism in schools and the prospects of an ethic of discomfort. *Teachers and Teaching*, 16(6), 703–716.

EDITORIAL PROVOCATIONS
Engaging readers and extending thinking

Sophie Alcock

Adults' diverse understandings and curiosity towards rethinking and exploring different views of play are connecting threads running through the chapters in Section 2 of this volume. The three chapters highlight the different ways in which personal experience and social and cultural contexts shape educators' diverse understandings and practices around play, playfulness and play-based curriculum, from both macro and micro perspectives. It is perhaps not surprising that educators – despite working with children playing – understand and practice play in different ways. Not only are understandings of play shaped by experience but also play is notoriously impossible to define in any one way. The very act of pinning down play by attempting to define complex processes and ways of being involved in playing is contradictory. These chapters challenge educators to reflect openly, positively and critically on their pedagogical and personal understandings and practice of play.

In Chapter 4, Alcock, writing from Aotearoa-New Zealand, invites readers to be critically reflective in rethinking both the 'aggressive' nature of children's physical rough-and-tumble narrative play and the role of educators in such play. She suggests several conceptual tools to re-focus ways in which teachers observe and connect with children playing in groups. Interpersonal field theory, vitality affects and psychological holding all emphasise teachers being open to feelings and tone in the vitality felt amongst children playing, and in teachers observing. This self–other awareness resonates with relational competence described by Ferholt et al. in Chapter 2 of this volume.

- How do educators come to shift and change their views and practices of play and play-based curriculum?

The above question is particularly pertinent for Chapter 5, where Fleet and Kemenyvary explore early school and early childhood teachers' understandings of and resistances to play-based curriculum. This research was associated with long-term teacher professional development situated in two remote mining towns in South Australia. Participants included Mel, a teacher who crosses over both education sectors and is the co-author of this chapter. School-age children were also interviewed about their memories of play in early childhood, prior-to-school settings; this mix of different voices makes for a stimulating array of values and understandings around play and play-based curriculum. Interestingly, findings highlighted that not only was play defined in different ways, but also views of play were largely based on personal experiences. The authors point out that those adults in the study who were keen advocates of play-based learning 'were all influenced by experience with a relative (child/sister/parent). The personalising of theory cannot be ignored in landscapes of professional learning!'

This important point gives weight to arguments for valuing experiential learning and raises further questions about effective pedagogy for adults.

- What types of strategies might support professional development programmes to impact educators' personal pedagogical play practices?

Pedagogical interpretations of play, playfulness and play-based curriculum seem to confound educators and researchers across cultures and countries. Issues around the personalising of curriculum are also echoed in Chapter 6, where O'Donoghue describes the enactment of Aister, Ireland's first early childhood curriculum framework. As she points out, curriculum policies are not enacted by government and policy-makers, but by those who educate. While enactment refers here to the process of passing legislation, enactment can also refer to acting something out physically. In acting out Aister, educators subjectively 'bring their experiences, beliefs and understandings to bear on what they see or read.' O'Donoghue suggests that the different ways in which Aister has and hasn't been acted out reflects issues around making curriculum personally meaningful in complex contexts, which in turn requires effective professional development to support teachers working reflectively and reflexively with new policy.

Reflection is important in the world of education and play. As part of the conversations surrounding the chapters, Michael Reed suggested: 'Reflection enables us to consider how we act and might act. ... [R]eflection means looking critically at what goes on in order that educators can formulate questions about the situations they find themselves' (Reed & Canning, 2010, p. 2). Reflection can create space for educators to be open, questioning and curious.

Threads addressed in Section 2 come full circle when educators are positioned as also being curious, alive and open to learning from children's play through critically reflexive and relational ways of reflecting on, in and, as is sometimes the case, with play, playfully.

Reference

Reed, M., & Canning, N. (2010). Introduction. In M. Reed & N. Canning (Eds). *Reflective Practice in the Early Years* (pp. 1–4). London: Sage.

Section 3

EMBEDDING FAMILIES AND COMMUNITIES

7

RECOGNISING AND RESPONDING TO FAMILY FUNDS OF KNOWLEDGE

Helen Hedges, Maria Cooper and Tamar Weisz-Koves

In New Zealand, a range of early childhood services is available for children from birth to school entry. Some services are teacher-led *(e.g., education and care centres, preschools, kindergartens, home-based services) and some are* parent-led *(e.g., Playcentre; Kōhanga Reo, where pre-school children and their families are immersed in the Māori language and culture; Pasifika initiatives, i.e. Pacific-centred education). The Ministry of Education partially funds all services, which are evaluated regularly by the Education Review Office.*

The vignettes in this chapter draw from research in a full-day, mixed-age (birth to 5) education and care centre. The project was a collaboration between academics (Helen and Maria) and teacher-researchers (Daniel and Trish) that positioned children and families as experts in relation to their own lives. Tamar was a parent participant in the project. Ethical principles of informed consent (and the ongoing assent of children), social and cultural sensitivity, and benefits for participants were paramount. The study was reviewed and approved by the University of Auckland Participant Human Ethics Committee.

This chapter explores how the concept of funds of knowledge can deepen and extend understandings of play, learning, and pedagogy through embedding practice with families and communities. We argue that positioning funds of knowledge centrally in the play-pedagogy arena enhances partnerships between families and teachers and encourages authenticity in children's educational experiences.

Debates about the play and pedagogy interface

In New Zealand/Aotearoa (NZ), there is a single, national curriculum framework that integrates both care and education, called Te Whāriki, a Māori term which means "woven mat". The metaphor of a mat refers to the ways in which the curriculum is woven from different strands and principles to provide a place for all (children, families, communities, and teachers) to stand on. This curriculum document has been recognised internationally as the first bicultural curriculum. Underpinned by indigenous Māori concepts and values, it is an inclusive, play-based, and non-prescriptive curriculum. Its vision of children as competent and confident guides teachers' responses to children's interests and abilities and decision-making about curriculum opportunities.

Te Whāriki has four principles: empowerment, relationships, holistic development, and family and community. The latter principle is our connection to this chapter, which invites a rethinking of play as pedagogy in relation to children's family knowledge and valued experiences. We provoke thought around the importance of teachers building relationships with families in order to provide meaningful play environments that enable children to express, represent, and connect their family lives, and explore identities as they grow in capability as learners, communicators, and citizens.

Play is an integral feature of early years learning environments. Debates about how play and pedagogy interrelate have often centred around the relative positioning of teachers, children, and families. Our chapter contributes to this debate by outlining ways children's play in early childhood settings originates in their family funds of knowledge. Family practices are often so embedded that parents may not think to articulate them as part of what they value and do. Yet, children frequently re-enact real-life experiences that represent their funds of knowledge in play-based environments. To recognise children's funds of knowledge teachers must learn about everyday family culture and practices. Engaging with children and families through funds-of-knowledge-focused home visits can be an effective way for teachers to learn about children's real-life experiences. When teachers understand these experiences are embedded in family funds of knowledge, they can rethink and adapt their pedagogical approaches to include supporting and providing play experiences that give children opportunities to re-enact and represent what their families value. In this way, learning environments and interactions can be deepened, partnership relationships between teachers and families enhanced, and children's identity development supported in meaningful ways.

"Children learn through play" is a pedagogical philosophy commonly expressed in early childhood education (ECE). Provision of richly resourced play environments continues to be an emphasis in early ECE in NZ. An associated principle is that children have "free choice" and long periods of uninterrupted play. However, as has been recognised through recent research, children are not always free to choose; for example, the environment has already been selected by adults (Wood, 2014). Whether educational environments represent children's family lives, or serve to send powerful messages that exacerbate differences between children's family and community lives and their educational experiences (Brooker, 2002), has yet to be fully debated. We propose that the concept of funds of knowledge is useful for connecting children's family and educational experiences and ensuring that environments reflect children's experiences from home.

Over the past 20 years, policy debates about professionalism and increased pressure for teachers to provide evidence of children's learning have led many countries to develop early childhood curriculum documents. Some of these have explicit goals for children's learning that reflect academic outcomes. Other goals have been developed around the importance of language and culture in response to global immigration. In this chapter we argue that the concept of funds of knowledge is useful for recognising and responding to children's cultural knowledge and experiences. We illustrate the potential of a funds-of-knowledge approach to provide new thinking about play as pedagogy in both centre and family contexts through vignettes of children from a project led by Helen and Maria. Tamar brings value having been a parent in our project. Her contributions have enriched and strengthened understandings of the concept of funds of knowledge and appropriate pedagogy for embedding family and community knowledge in early childhood practices.

Funds of knowledge

As a concept, funds of knowledge acknowledges the intuitive and implicit cultural knowledge families possess and is based on the idea that all households are rich in cultural knowledge and practices. It arose from early efforts at culturally responsive pedagogy that adopted a positive view of what families value and do (González, Moll, & Amanti, 2005). González et al. (2005) defined funds of knowledge as the bodies of knowledge—including information, skills, strategies, ways of thinking and learning, approaches to learning, and practical skills—which support household functioning, development, and well-being. For example, children might observe a parent writing a shopping list or reading a recipe, and participate in activities such as meal preparation and caring for younger siblings. In such ways, children develop knowledge embedded in specific family routines and practices.

The concept of funds of knowledge has been applied recently in ECE to deepen teachers' understandings of children's interests (Chesworth, 2016; Hedges & Cooper, 2016; Hedges, Cullen, & Jordan, 2011). When teachers are aware of children's funds of knowledge, they can draw on it to create responsive relationships and curriculum. This aligns with a statement in *Te Whāriki* (Ministry of Education, 2017) that the teacher's role is to "support children by affirming their identity and culture, connecting with and building on their funds of knowledge and having positive expectations for their learning" (p. 51).

Funds-of-knowledge-focused home visits are a useful way teachers can learn about the specific cultural knowledge of families. In the original project (González et al., 2005), primary school teachers visited selected family homes, and sometimes related community settings, up to three times. These teacher-researchers talked with family members about their lives, languages, cultures, and experiences. They observed cultural practices and artefacts in the home and asked questions about these. They needed to be keen observers and communicators because family practices tended to be informal and implicit, and therefore easily overlooked.

An important point to note is that these visits did not take place early in the teacher–family relationship; they occurred after a child had attended school for some time and teachers thought they already had some good knowledge of the child and parents. The visits were then less daunting for parents who may otherwise have worried about being judged by teachers. Visiting homes—rather than having parents come to events at educational institutions—shifted the balance of power by positioning the family as expert and the visiting teacher-researchers as learners, and enabled teachers to learn things that might otherwise be invisible to them (Lovatt, Cooper, & Hedges, 2017).

The pedagogical goal of a funds-of-knowledge approach is to recognise and incorporate family-based knowledge and expertise in educational settings in order to improve outcomes for all children. To do so, teachers met after their visits to share what they had learned, to reflect on beliefs that have been challenged, and to consider ways to use the knowledge in their classrooms.

We adopted the funds-of-knowledge approach in a Teaching and Learning Research Initiative project we undertook within the context of ECE in NZ (Hedges & Cooper, 2014). In our project, teachers visited family homes once in pairs, as we were mindful of time restraints on early childhood teachers' opportunities to learn together (Cooper et al., 2014).

Framing of the vignettes

We now offer three vignettes of children designed to give insights into how children's play interests related to their funds of knowledge. We describe how teachers were able to identify family funds of knowledge through home visits, ways the visits enabled teachers to make connections with what they had observed of children's play in the centre setting, and how funds of knowledge might be incorporated in pedagogy. Description of how the visits deepened understandings of children's real-life experiences at home and raised teachers' awareness of how children re-enacted these in the centre through their play is also provided. These insights into the benefits of a funds-of-knowledge approach lead into a rethinking of play and pedagogy.

Vignette 1: Zoe

Zoe was aged 3 years and 9 months at the time the teacher-researchers visited her family home. Zoe lived with her parents Tamar (chapter author) and Paul, and their cat Harry. During the visit, Trish and Daniel commented on a 1,000-piece puzzle that they noticed Zoe and her mum working on. This led to a conversation about how Zoe enjoyed puzzles and was good at seeing patterns. Daniel shared that he had noticed this the previous day reviewing a video taken at the centre of her hammering coloured shapes onto a board. Tamar responded that it was probably because the hammering experience involved two things Zoe really enjoyed: hammering and making sense of patterns. Trish and

Daniel agreed that Zoe seemed to really like hammering in the centre and asked if her parents were good at home maintenance tasks. Tamar laughed and said no.

Later, Daniel revisited the topic of home maintenance. Tamar shared her view that Zoe probably spent a lot of time doing carpentry at the centre because of her close relationship with Daniel, and reiterated that she and Paul did not see themselves as "do-it-yourself" people. While Daniel did enjoy undertaking carpentry projects with the children in the centre, such as making a large treehouse and bird feeders—two projects Zoe had been part of—Daniel indicated that Zoe's home life was likely to have had a significant influence on her play interests too. Daniel commented on the curtains Tamar had hung up in Zoe's bedroom and shared his impression that Tamar and Paul encouraged a "do-it-yourself" approach in the home by giving Zoe access to household resources and tools. As a result of Daniel sharing his insights, Tamar rethought her position and was able to identify multiple examples of jobs she and Paul had completed around the house, often with Zoe's input. For example, Zoe had helped to paint the fence in the driveway and put together flat-packed furniture, such as the TV cabinet and bookshelves. Tamar also talked about the time Zoe's grandmother (Nanny) from Ireland came to visit, describing Nanny as a practical person who did a lot of jobs around the house with Zoe while she was there.

The examples in this vignette demonstrate how funds of knowledge are embedded in families' everyday lives and are often so implicit that families may not be aware of these until someone else observes and comments on them. Daniel's insights into the connection between Zoe's interest in hammering and family home maintenance projects revealed an aspect of family practice that Tamar and Paul had not previously been aware of, and showed a connection between family life and the educational setting. Furthermore, Tamar gained a view of herself as someone who role modelled and included her daughter in home practices; this led to her being more conscious of when and how she did this.

This vignette illustrates how engaging in dialogue with families about their funds of knowledge is valuable in that it has the potential to lead to new insights and understandings for parents, as well as teachers. These, in turn, can positively influence parents and teachers' practices. The rich sharing that occurred between Zoe's family and teachers led to deeper insights into Zoe's play interests in the centre and how these connected with her experiences at home. Daniel later reflected on how his awareness of Zoe's funds of knowledge had deepened as a result of the home visit, and that he was able to draw from this awareness to enhance his practice with Zoe and other children in the centre (Lovatt et al., 2017).

From a parent's perspective, Tamar felt that the home visit had been a positive and affirming experience that facilitated positive insights about herself as a parent. She also felt it reinforced her decision to send Zoe to a centre where teachers clearly paid close attention to children and families. Both the teacher-researchers and Zoe's family expressed that the home visit and accompanying documentation had deepened teacher–family relationships. Discussions during and after the home visit enhanced communication about Zoe's learning at home and in the centre, and generated greater awareness of the connections between these contexts. Zoe is also likely to have benefited from the deeper relationships and enhanced communication between her family and teachers, including the understandings and practices generated by a focus on her funds of knowledge.

> Reflective questions:
>
> - How might children, families, and teachers benefit from funds-of-knowledge home visits?
> - How can time for home visits be factored into teachers' practices?
> - What additional strategies could teachers use to engage in meaningful discussions with children and families about their funds of knowledge?

Vignette 2: Hunter

During the consent process, parents had the choice to meet either in the centre or at home. Hunter's father initially selected the centre. Later, after seeing video footage of how teachers had extended Hunter's interest in drum play at the centre, his mother invited the teacher-researchers to come to their house. This is a positive example of home visits occurring after trust and relationships have been established.

Hunter, who was 4 at the time of the visit, lived with his parents, his 8-year-old sister, and 11-year-old twin aunts. His father was NZ-born but identified as Samoan, and his mother, who was Rarotongan, had moved to NZ when she was 14. English was their first language. This discovery led Trish to later reflect and challenge her assumption that the family spoke their heritage languages at home.

During the visit, Hunter showed Daniel and Trish the drum set he had been given for his birthday and kept at the end of his bed. While they were in the room, Dad commented, "The bed is only there for decoration!" Trish asked, "Why do you say that?", to which Dad replied, "Because we all sleep together on mattresses in the lounge." He and Mum explained that the whole family slept in the lounge. This cultural insight of co-sleeping was interesting for Trish to learn as Hunter had never mentioned it at the centre.

Daniel and Trish also learned of the importance of family and community activities in the weekends. For example, the family often watched his sister's netball game on a Saturday, and were at his grandparents' house "hanging out" and watching movies. On Sundays, they sometimes attended church, after which they would go to the park or spend more time at his grandparents' house. Hunter's mother and father said he loved church and often requested to go.

As the home visit progressed, the teacher-researchers learned of how proud both parents were of Hunter's developing competence in a number of areas, and how they supported this. His father had had a strict upbringing and so always made a point to tell his children to take up every opportunity that came their way; he was keen for his children to excel in what they did. Dad was particularly amazed about Hunter's knowledge and skill with technology (phones, iPad, laptops) and believed it was important that he and Mum give Hunter time to explore these.

Daniel and Trish learned that Hunter was often the first one up in the morning, and with Dad's help he could make his own breakfast—porridge, cereal, or toast, and a chocolate drink. He would pick out his clothes and watch the clock to ensure nobody was running late. He also enjoyed baking with Mum.

The teacher-researchers' insights built on what Mum had documented in Hunter's portfolio a few weeks before the home visit.

She had noted that Hunter was good at: picking out his own clothes, getting himself dressed, asking questions, keeping his room tidy, putting his seat belt on, cooking scrambled eggs, knowing his way around a laptop and iPhone, helping his mother bake, and reminding her when she forgot something. Hunter's thoughts about his developing competence were also captured in this documentation, such as his willingness to organise lunches for other children at the centre, dress himself, and write his name.

The home visit enabled the teachers to become more familiar with the home environment in which Hunter was keen to participate in these real-life tasks. It also provided further insights into Hunter's knowledge, skills, and attitudes towards other tasks. For example, Mum reflected on Hunter's interest in using carpentry tools at home and how he had been keen to help Mum hammer some wire in their backyard to stop their pet rabbit from escaping. Daniel and Trish noted that Hunter spent a lot of time hammering and sawing in the centre and enjoyed real construction tasks. For instance, once, Hunter had approached Trish about making a climbing frame because the centre one was broken.

Hunter's vignette, like Zoe's, demonstrates how funds of knowledge were naturally embedded in his everyday family life. When these were recognised during the home visit, his parents and teachers were able to consolidate their understandings of Hunter's experiences with the potential to further extend on them at home and in the centre. Having the opportunity to see the family environment in which Hunter demonstrated his competence afforded teacher-researchers fresh insights into his home experiences. As a result, they were able to make connections between his home experiences and his centre play-based experiences. Daniel and Trish then reflected on similar opportunities teachers had provided him in the centre, and potential opportunities they could provide to better reflect his funds of knowledge.

Reflective questions:

- How might teachers rethink their assumptions about children's home cultures and languages?
- What opportunities do children have to take increased responsibility for themselves and others in ways that reflect their participation in family and community life?

- What opportunities do children have to apply and build on their funds of knowledge through having access to real tools and participating in authentic tasks in play-based early childhood settings?
- What are the benefits of children learning about other children's family values and practices?

Vignette 3: Chloe

Chloe was aged 18 months at the time the teacher-researchers visited the family home she shared with her parents. During the home visit, Chloe's interest in doll and family play was discussed. Teachers learned that while Chloe had dolls at home, she appeared more interested in dolls at the centre which she put into pushchairs and took for walks. Chloe's grandmother (who was the owner of the centre) had told Mum that Chloe spent a lot of time playing in the family area. Chloe had asked her mother if she could buy a doll at a local gala, but quickly lost interest in it. However, when Mum told Chloe that she was pregnant, Chloe found the doll and put it under her mother's shirt as an expression of her understanding. Mum further shared that Chloe attended an ultrasound, which gave Chloe another insight into what having a baby means.

Like Zoe and Hunter, Chloe's interest in real tasks became apparent during the home visit. The teacher-researchers learned that Chloe's mum involved her in all the household tasks, and that Chloe was keen to engage with these. For example, Chloe often helped her parents to put the washing and powder in the machine, hang out the washing and sort pegs, and put dishes in the dishwasher. She also contributed to cooking meals through tasks such as rolling out pasta. Mum expressed that it was easy to involve her because she liked to help and was interested in knowing what was going on. Mum reiterated that Chloe wanted to do what the grown-ups were doing.

Daniel and Trish discovered that Chloe had a real hammer and tape measure at home. When her mother shared this, she recalled a time Chloe was given a choice of a water wheel or hammer and tape measure. Chloe had responded by throwing the water wheel down and taking the hammer and tape measure instead. This interest in real tools was expressed at home in a range of ways. For example, she had spent time watching landscaping work in the backyard. Chloe's intrigue with the landscaping work led her parents to give her some real tools to play with. On learning this, Daniel reflected that he had noticed Chloe's involvement when they were building raised garden boxes in the centre and shared his thought that she seemed keen to build something real.

By entering the family home as learners, the teacher-researchers were able to learn about Chloe's funds of knowledge, based on her participation in the real-life experiences with her family. These extended insights helped the teacher-researchers to make links between what Mum shared and what they had noticed about Chloe's play in the centre. As a result of the home visit, teachers supported Chloe's play by fostering her interest in cooking in the play kitchen. In one play episode, Trish observed Chloe feeding a baby. Rather than stepping in to guide her, Trish chose to support Chloe's agenda with time and space. The video captured of this play showed Chloe orchestrating the centre environment by shifting chairs around, positioning dolls on the chairs, and using a real baby's bottle filled with water to feed the dolls.

> Reflective questions:
>
> - How are children's experiences in real-life tasks in the home appreciated and valued as a source of curriculum in the centre?
> - What opportunities do children have to orchestrate, reshape, and change their play-based environments to represent their real-life experiences? And why is this important?
> - What real tools (rather than replicas) do teachers provide to foster children's competence at real-life tasks?
> - What opportunities do children have to access real tools, in spaces teachers do not always allow children to enter for health and safety reasons (e.g., kitchens, bathrooms, and storage areas)?

Rethinking play and pedagogy through funds of knowledge

Children's play is often grounded in their real-life experiences. Teachers' deepening understandings of children's family lives can positively influence their provision of play experiences and the pedagogies they use to support play. In addition, trust and reciprocity are deepened as families see that teachers care about getting to know their child and family at a deeper level. The sharing that occurs between teacher-researchers and children's families fosters shared understandings and a sense of community, enabling adults to enhance the ways they support children's play-based experiences at home and in the centre.

The funds-of-knowledge-based home visits in our project gave the teacher-researchers insights into children's play that deepened their understandings and connections in relation to what families value and do. As the vignettes of Zoe, Hunter, and Chloe illustrate, children's funds of knowledge were recognised through talking with parents about children's activities in and outside the home. This included their involvement in family life and adult activities such as household chores, home maintenance, family outings, and community participation. Children's use of real tools, engagement in real-life experiences, and taking responsibility for themselves and others were key insights illustrated in the vignettes.

The home visits highlighted families' everyday implicit knowledge as a significant influence on what children chose to recreate and re-enact in their play experiences. Knowing these children and families on a deeper level brought new awareness of children's competence and capabilities. The home visits and funds-of-knowledge lens helped to illuminate "aha" moments in the reciprocity between families and parents. As parents and teachers shared understandings of children and their experiences, it became evident that Zoe, Hunter, and Chloe all demonstrated strong interest in the adult world and making sense of adult roles and responsibilities. Teachers came to better understand the children's desire and intention to engage with real tools and be involved in real tasks with adults.

It seems then that an important function of play is to afford children opportunities to practise participation in real-life activities; to deepen their understandings and learning of the knowledge and skills related to valued cultural activities and practices. That children look for opportunities to recreate and re-enact their family experiences has important implications for play as pedagogy. A funds-of-knowledge lens enables teachers to be more cognisant of children's lives, and to recognise and support the cultural nuances and complexities of children's play in the centre, thereby bringing deeper meaning to the motivations underpinning their play. Providing rich play environments can also be re-thought in multiple ways. Rather than teachers making decisions about curriculum, children might want opportunities to: engage in conversations about their lives, use real tools and equipment that reflect their experiences, be involved in setting up learning areas, and make decisions regarding the selection and purchase of equipment and resources. Additional relationship-based approaches to pedagogy (Hedges & Cooper, 2018), such as involving families in centre life, can be employed to embed and further develop children's interests, knowledge, and skills from home within ECE contexts.

Conclusion

Play-based pedagogy often focuses on teacher provision of a range of equipment, resources, and experiences that children are able to choose from. However, the ways that children use equipment and resources in ECE settings relate directly to their life experiences. We have argued that because an important function of play is to afford children opportunities to practise participation in real-life activities, teachers need to be aware of, and reflect critically on, their decision-making and pedagogy to facilitate teaching and learning environments that provide children with opportunities to recreate, re-enact, and represent their family and community lives.

Our chapter has invited a rethinking of play as pedagogy in relation to children's family knowledge and valued experiences through the lens of funds of knowledge. The vignettes we have presented highlight the power of home visits to provide insights for curriculum and pedagogy that embed family knowledge and practices centrally within early childhood settings. Our intention was to provoke thought around how teachers build relationships with families in order to provide meaningful play environments that enable children to connect with their family lives and explore their identities as they grow in capability as learners, communicators, and citizens.

References

Brooker, L. (2002). *Starting school: Young children learning cultures*. Buckingham: Open University Press.

Chesworth, L. (2016). A funds of knowledge approach to examining play interests: Listening to children's and parents' perspectives. *International*

Journal of Early Years Education, 24(3), 294–308. doi:10.1080/09669760.2016.1188370.

Cooper, M., Hedges, H., Ashurst, L., Harper, B., Lovatt, D., Murphy, T., & Spanhake, N. (2014). Transforming relationships and curriculum: Visiting family homes. *Early Childhood Folio, 18*(1), 22–27.

González, N., Moll, L. C., & Amanti, C. (Eds). (2005). *Funds of knowledge: Theorizing practices in households, communities and classrooms.* Mahwah, NJ: Lawrence Erlbaum.

Hedges, H., & Cooper, M. (2014). *Inquiring minds, meaningful responses: Children's interests, inquiries, and working theories.* Wellington: Teaching and Learning Research Initiative.

Hedges, H., & Cooper, M. (2016). Inquiring minds: Theorizing children's interests. *Journal of Curriculum Studies, 48*(3), 303–322. doi:10.1080/00220272.2015.1109711.

Hedges, H., & Cooper, M. (2018). Relational play-based pedagogy: Theorising a core practice in early childhood education. *Teachers and Teaching: Theory and Practice, 24*(4), 369–383. doi:10.1080/13540602.2018.1430564.

Hedges, H., Cullen, J., & Jordan, B. (2011). Early years curriculum: Funds of knowledge as a conceptual framework for children's interests. *Journal of Curriculum Studies, 43*(2), 185–205. doi:10.1080/00220272.2010.511275.

Lovatt, D., Cooper, M., & Hedges, H. (2017). Enhancing interactions: Understanding family pedagogy and funds of knowledge "on their turf". In A. C. Gunn & C. A. Hruska (Eds), *Interactions in early childhood education: Recent research and emergent concepts* (pp. 99–112). Singapore: Springer.

Ministry of Education. (2017). *Te whāriki. He whāriki mātauranga mō ngā mokopuna o Aotearoa: Early childhood curriculum.* Wellington: Author.

Wood, E. (2014). Free choice and free play in early childhood education: Troubling the discourse. *International Journal of Early Years Education, 22*(1), 4–18. doi:10.1080/09669760.2013.830562.

8

OPENING THE SCHOOL GATES
Facilitating after-school play in school grounds

Marianne Mannello, Mark Connolly, Sandra Dumitrescu, Cheryl Ellis, Chantelle Haughton, Sian Sarwar and Jacky Tyrie

This chapter reflects practitioner involvement in an action research project from Wales. Wales makes up one of four nations in the UK and has a devolved government. It has its own elected legislative assembly which sets educational policy that is different from the other countries within the UK. This project researched the utilisation of school grounds as a community asset for play. Despite children's right to play being embedded in statute and general consensus that play has positive outcomes for children, evidence suggests that school grounds are under-utilised for this purpose in Wales.

The project which is the focus of this chapter, titled *Open All Hours*, researched the utilisation of school grounds as a community asset for play, through the piloting of a toolkit[1] designed to support democratic use of school grounds.

The project was a partnership between Play Wales, Cardiff School of Education at Cardiff Metropolitan University (Education and Early Childhood Studies team) and Cardiff University's School of Social Sciences. It involved interviews with key stakeholders and was staffed by three student volunteers (one at each school) and university academics. This chapter represents a snapshot of the whole venture. All students attended training, giving them the opportunity to understand and agree to implement the philosophy of the project. The training represented an important element of the research team's wider ethical considerations: it was important that the team remained mindful of its responsibility to *all* participants; students needed to feel confident and equipped to facilitate play during the project; children's safety and welfare were important considerations throughout; and it was vital that head teachers and other school stakeholders were confident that all aspects of the project were conducted in the best interests of the children (BERA, 2018). Monitoring was carried out by the research team and involved using a 'prospective study design' (Mukherji & Albon, 2015, p. 235) adopting action research as its methodological approach. The research team engaged in diagnosis, planning, acting and observing, followed by a period of reflection. The diagnosis identified the under-use of school grounds as places for children to play; the planning involved identifying three schools and recruiting and training undergraduate student volunteers to work as playworkers over a period of six weeks. The project aimed to induce organisational change over a six-week time period and focused on realising the right to play.

Colleagues with local knowledge identified schools. Community profiling in each area demonstrated that there were no obvious municipal play areas nearby. The planning stage involved semi-structured pre-project interviews with stakeholders within each school setting (e.g. caretaker, head teacher, school governor). The research aimed to develop effective partnerships between the schools, universities and a policy advocacy organisation (Solvason, Cliffe & Snowden, 2017) to affect positive social change through action research, drawing on Lewin's (1946) classic model.

Realising the right to play: The policy context in Wales which underpinned the project

The commitment to following a children's rights approach to policy-making in Wales manifested itself in approaches to promoting children's play. The first commitment by the Welsh Government (WG) was the adoption of a play policy (WG, 2002), and more recently the Children and Families (Wales) Measure 2010 (WG, 2012a), which places duties on local authorities to assess and secure play opportunities for children in their area. Wales was the first country in the world to introduce a statutory requirement; some suggest that it 'stands as a beacon to the rest of the world in its approach to supporting children's rights generally, and children's right to play specifically' (Lester & Russell, 2013, p. 11). By establishing a framework through statutory guidance (WG, 2014) and a toolkit (WG, 2012b), local authorities were afforded the opportunity to apply new and experimental responses in assessing and planning for children's play. In the statutory guidance, the government notes the importance of school grounds as community assets:

> Schools provide an important opportunity for play for periods before and after classes. They can provide valuable play space at weekends and during holiday periods. Welsh Government recommends that Local Authorities advise schools to give full consideration to opening this provision during out of teaching hours.
>
> (WG, 2014, p. 30)

Evidence from a national review (Play Wales, 2012) and local authority play sufficiency assessments suggested that school grounds across Wales are substantially under-utilised for play at the end of the school day. The importance of community access to schools, particularly in under-resourced communities, is recognised (Dyson et al., 2016; Welsh Government & Welsh Local Government Association, 2002) with Blank, Melaville and Shah (2003) claiming that the evidence regarding community schools impacts on: student learning; school effectiveness; and community vitality. Qualitative research for Playday (ICM, 2010) found that 81 per cent of adults believe children playing outside helps to improve community spirit and 70 per cent think that it makes an area more desirable to live in; consequently, one of the goals of Open All Hours was to engage with local parents to empower them to sustain the activity when the project finished. Strong neighbourhoods can mitigate parental fears about children playing outside by providing a sense of community and security. Spaces that are good for children are often good for adults too, as Beunderman, Hannon and Bradwell (2007, p. 106) point out: 'the interests of children and the interests of the community at large are not opposed but closely aligned and mutually dependent'. Children playing outside in their local communities have been shown to benefit social relationships for both children and adults (Gleave, 2010). It was within this policy context that the play advocacy organisation Play Wales developed the toolkit for the use of school grounds as a community play resource.

The importance of play in the context of the project

Play involves children doing as they wish in their own time, in their own way, and comes instinctively to children; however, without the support of parents, policy makers and the wider community to make play a priority, children are often denied the freedom, spaces and time to act on their natural instincts. When children have the conditions of enough time to play, access to spaces, permission and resources, then playing and playful behaviour emerge (Lester & Russell, 2010). The importance of play and playing for children's physical, emotional, social and intellectual wellbeing has been well researched and documented (Lester & Russell, 2008, 2010) and there is a range of agreed benefits that children gain from playing.

Researchers have increased our understanding so that there is now

> a higher level of agreement than ever before, that it is authentic, immersed, unconscious play behaviour which is responsible for a whole range of outcomes including good psychic health and neural growth and organisation.
> (Hughes, 2012, p. 317)

A central feature of most descriptions of play is that play is fun and deeply satisfying. Although it is serious on occasions, fun is how most children describe their play, particularly if it involves friends (Ipsos MORI & Nairn, 2011). The fun children experience when playing is a great motivator; 'playing is only really experienced as play when it is absorbing' (Meire, 2007, p. 44). Research suggests that play is not only beneficial to children's physical and emotional wellbeing but also an element of their lives they value most. To children themselves, playing is one of the most important aspects of their lives – they value time, freedom and quality places to play (Children's Commissioner for Wales, 2016, 2018; IPA, 2010; National Assembly for Wales, 2010; Wales Observatory on Human Rights of Children and Young People, 2015).

Although there is a lack of data regarding unstructured play opportunities, it is acknowledged that children's ability to access play in their own neighbourhoods has diminished over time (One Poll, 2013). There is concern that modern trends have negatively impacted on children's ability to access opportunities for playing outside (One Poll, 2013). A range of barriers have been found to limit opportunities to play. These include attitudinal issues reflecting adults' hypersensitivity towards childhood: such as fears for children's safety; concerns over accidents and litigation;

misinterpretations regarding strangers; increased time children spend in structured activities; and changes to the built environment, and a tendency to over-protect and avoid risk can also diminish access to play (Connolly & Haughton, 2015; Furedi, 2002; Gill, 2007; Lester & Russell, 2010). Parents in Wales report dissatisfaction with play facilities in their local area (WG, 2015), citing a lack of suitable outdoor public places for children to play and meet up. While almost all parents (97 per cent) in a Public Health Wales survey (2017) think it is important for their child to play outdoors every day, nearly a third (29 per cent) felt that children under five aren't getting the time outdoors that they need.

Having enough time to play is a recurring issue for children, particularly older ones. They report that school, homework, exams and revision are barriers to play and free time (Children's Commissioner for Wales, 2018). To play, children need time and opportunity; it needn't be complicated, difficult or expensive. Children's time to play has decreased significantly in recent years, becoming organised, structured and highly scheduled, as highlighted in the pre-project engagement with children, school staff and students. While structured activities may offer new opportunities, they do so at the cost of the loss of control children have over their own play (Moss & Petrie, 2002), and the time they have to play on their own terms in their free time. This is a loss as the central point about play is the control it offers children. It is a process of trial and error where children can experiment, try things out and repeat and refine behaviour (Brown, 2014). Central to this behaviour is that children can choose how and why they play. The level of control children have over their own play is part of what makes it play, along with its characteristics of flexibility, unpredictability, spontaneity and imagination (Lester & Russell, 2008; United Nations Committee on the Rights of the Child [CRC], 2013).

While this element of children's lives has been gradually eroded, its importance is reflected in international and national law. Article 31 of the United Nation Convention on the Rights of the Child (1989) recognises the right of every child to rest, leisure, play and recreational activities. In 2013, the CRC adopted General Comment 17 that clarifies for governments worldwide the meaning and importance of Article 31.

In implementing the project, the team referred to the CRC definition of play, which defines children's play as:

> - behaviour, activity or process initiated, controlled and structured by children themselves;
> - taking place whenever and wherever opportunities arise;
> - non-compulsory, driven by intrinsic motivation and undertaken for its own sake, rather than as a means to an end;
> - the exercise of autonomy, physical, mental or emotional activity;
> - having characteristics of fun, uncertainty, challenge, flexibility and non-productivity;
> - a fundamental and vital dimension of the pleasure of childhood;
> - an essential component of physical, social, cognitive, emotional and spiritual development (CRC, 2013, p. 6).

General Comment No. 17 makes a strong assertion in terms of policy and in particular with regard to legislation and planning. The CRC (2013) advised for legislation to ensure the realisation of Article 31 for every child; that all children should be given sufficient time and space to exercise these rights.

The philosophy of the project: The importance of spaces and adults

The philosophy of this project was that play can be supported by improving and protecting existing play spaces, such as school grounds. Characteristics of quality children's spaces include opportunities for wonder, excitement and the unexpected, and opportunities that are not overly ordered and controlled by adults. Children still prefer to play outdoors (Children's Commissioner for Wales, 2016, 2018) and parents are also concerned about lack of space for play opportunities.

Children's development can be supported by tolerant and caring adults who create opportunities and places where children can play freely with confidence (CRC, 2013). Open All Hours aspired to allow children to encounter a rich play environment (see Box 8.1). The project was designed to address the concerns of parents and wishes of children.

> **Box 8.1 A rich play environment**
>
> Quality play opportunities offer all children and young people the opportunity to freely interact with or experience the following:
>
> - **other children and young people** – with a choice to play alone or with others, to negotiate, co-operate, fall out and resolve conflict;
> - **the natural world** – weather, the seasons, bushes, trees, plants, insects, animals and mud;
> - **loose parts** – natural and man-made materials that can be manipulated, moved and adapted, built and demolished;
> - **the natural elements** – earth, air, fire and water;
> - **challenge and risk taking** – both on a physical and emotional level;
> - **playing with identity** – role play and dressing up;
> - **movement** – running, jumping, climbing, balancing and rolling;
> - **rough and tumble** – play fighting;
> - **the senses** – sounds, tastes, textures, smells and sights;
> - **feelings** – pain, pain, joy, confidence, fear, anger, contentment, boredom, fascination, happiness, grief, rejection, acceptance, sadness, pride and frustration (WG, 2014, p. 18).

Establishing principles of working

To demonstrate supportive attitudes towards play, Open All Hours committed to the principle that when implementing the project, we would not:

> - dismiss play as frivolous and a waste of time;
> - unnecessarily restrict it through fear;
> - over-regulate and over-organise it;
> - subvert it for other purposes.

While undertaking training for students, we discussed that being playful, adults can encourage play, but generally it was agreed to be cautious about getting too involved when children were playing. We committed to getting involved when:

- children asked for it. Sometimes children will directly ask us to play. This invitation may be subtle and may consist of a nod, wink, grin or other small signals. These invitations or cues meant we needed to stay vigilant, so we could recognise the cues and respond;
- children needed us to act as a resource, such as providing an extra pair of hands when den-building;
- a child was unhappy or distressed. It was recognised that this is an area where knowledge of the child or children involved is especially important, so students were assigned to the same school for the duration of the project;
- there were serious disputes that the children were unable to resolve themselves. We agreed to be wary of jumping to conclusions as often children are able to resolve disputes themselves;
- there was violence, harm or danger. It was our responsibility to ensure the play environment felt safe and secure even when children were challenging themselves;
- when there was a hazard not detected by the child. While many children are very capable of assessing familiar and obvious dangers, this is not the case for unseen or unknown hazards.

Drawing on the Playwork Principles (Playwork Principles Scrutiny Group, 2005 – see Box 8.2), Open All Hours committed to the philosophy of children leading their play, with no external goal or reward. Key to this was a commitment (as outlined in Playwork Principle 4) to the concept that play is a process that is freely chosen, personally directed and intrinsically motivated. That is, children and young people determine and control the content and intent of their play, by following their own instincts, ideas and interests, in their own way for their own reasons.

Box 8.2 Playwork Principles

These principles establish the professional and ethical framework for playwork and as such must be regarded as a whole. They describe what is unique about play and playwork, and provide the playwork perspective for working with children and young people. They are based on the recognition that children and young people's capacity for positive development will be enhanced if given access to the broadest range of environments and play opportunities.

1. All children and young people need to play. The impulse to play is innate. Play is a biological, psychological and social necessity, and is fundamental to the healthy development and wellbeing of individuals and communities.
2. Play is a process that is freely chosen, personally directed and intrinsically motivated. That is, children and young people determine and control the content and intent of their play, by following their own instincts, ideas and interests, in their own way for their own reasons.
3. The prime focus and essence of playwork is to support and facilitate the play process and this should inform the development of play policy, strategy, training and education.
4. For playworkers, the play process takes precedence and playworkers act as advocates for play when engaging with adult-led agendas.
5. The role of the playworker is to support all children and young people in the creation of a space in which they can play.
6. The playworker's response to children and young people playing is based on a sound up-to-date knowledge of the play process, and reflective practice.
7. Playworkers recognise their own impact on the play space and also the impact of children and young people's play on the playworker.
8. Playworkers choose an intervention style that enables children and young people to extend their play. All playworker intervention must balance risk with the developmental benefit and wellbeing of children.

To facilitate children's discovery of these capabilities and interests, Open All Hours endeavoured to provide minimal resources to facilitate and encourage play. Each team had a small selection of loose parts. The term 'loose parts' was coined by the architect Simon Nicholson (1972); he proposed that the more moveable and adaptable materials an environment contained, the more creative and inventive children would be. Loose parts are anything that can be moved, changed, taken apart and used in different ways, and with no specific instructions. Examples include: sand, water, shells, fabric, buckets, boxes, rope, tyres, wood and scrap materials of all kinds.

The planning phase

In the planning phase, we conducted workshops with children and teachers to assess barriers to playing outside. Children outlined concerns relating to contemporary understandings of childhood, risk and play. The children associated play with structured adult-directed activity: in two of the groups the children enquired about the 'resources' that would be provided. Children reported these barriers:

- unsafe environments, including speed and volume of traffic;
- parents' fears (particularly unknown adults and traffic);
- inadequate facilities;
- too much structured and programmed leisure time.

Open All Hours aimed to demonstrate to adults within the school community the extent to which school play spaces might become absorbed into wider community life. A common theme that emerged across the schools via pre-project interviews was how as adults we affect the conditions which support children's play, by

- regulating time for play opportunities (time);
- impacting on the how and if space is made available (space);
- affecting what children experience (permission);
- providing (or denying) materials (stuff).

Opportunities and challenges: Considering the impact of the project

The acting and observing elements of the research represented the intervention itself during which students facilitated the opportunity for children to engage in free play. A period of reflection during the play sessions and via post-project interviews significantly identified strengths and benefits in relation to increasing access to school grounds. A range of barriers to children's full participation in play were addressed.

Children's control

Playing in a space enhanced with loose parts supported a wide range of observed activity during the project, including flexibility, creativity, imagination, resourcefulness, problem solving, self-esteem and spatial awareness (see Figure 8.1).

Figure 8.1 Preparing the school grounds

The provision of loose parts and people acted as a springboard for play in the schools. Giving parents the opportunity to observe how loose parts were used also impacted upon how parents viewed play:

> Definitely, it's made me think to leave children more to their own devices. It made me think that play can be simple and simple materials. And the children can create play. I thought they'd need more: when I saw what they bought I thought, "Is this all they are going to play with? How long will that entertain them?" Surprisingly we got to 5 o'clock and it was time to go.
>
> (Parent, post project)

The schools had clear expectations of the student volunteers and this in turn led students to have similar expectations. They expected to be leading play and structuring activities for children. What happened once children had the time and space to play was entirely different. Children led their play (see Figure 8.2).

Having enough time and opportunity to play

There was benefit in terms of what parents appeared to get out of the sessions in terms of respite, but also socialisation, talking with advocates for play and sharing concerns about what's happening locally. We observed that parents, particularly those with larger families of young children, valued the time to engage with other parents while children played with their siblings and other children. Having the opportunity to observe their children having space to play after school, and a place to gather and socialise with their friends on their own terms, was powerful for some parents:

> It's been positive. I enjoyed how the children were playing. I was apprehensive whether I wanted to play with them or not, so at times I would have to consciously stop myself getting involved. It was good to see play among the children and them being imaginative and creative.
>
> (Parent, post project)

Figure 8.2 Children taking control of the play

Parents making the most of facilities in their local area

As mentioned above, Welsh parents report dissatisfaction with play facilities in their local area (WG, 2015), citing a lack of suitable outdoor public places for children to play and meet up. The project redressed this concern about space, to some extent, by utilising a community asset which was already seen by parents to be a safe place, where playing was permitted.

> One of the parents said it felt more secure in a school than in a park because it's almost a sanctioned space so she feels that it's safe, that she can relax.
>
> (School teacher, post project)

More outdoor play opportunities for children under five

Because many parents stayed with their school-aged children, many younger children had access to play opportunities they might not normally have. This resulted in different age groups mixing and playing, both together and alongside one another, without conflict.

> Oh, there was quite a big age range – from 18 months to 11 in one family, there was like four children living in a two-bedroom flat, with no access to the outdoors, so six people living in two bedrooms, and I thought, "Well, where do they go, what do they do?" We [the mother and I] spoke quite in-depth. There was an 18-month-old baby. He just wanted to get involved with everyone else. When he arrived, he would happily run around and then he would become tired, a lot quicker than the older children, but his brother, who is known as being quite a difficult child in school, was so protective and he wanted to play with his brother.
>
> (Student volunteer, post project)

A less risk-averse approach to play

School staff themselves, head teachers, teachers and caretakers also benefitted. Within the planning-phase interviews, school staff – especially caretakers – expressed concerns, driven by a perception of and hypersensitivity towards risk. During the project, these attitudes changed as staff found that many of their fears were unrealised, resulting in them relinquishing control of the space, thus fostering community links and a more trusting and democratic use of the space:

> I'm more encouraged, more enthusiastic. I've got to be honest, I don't think my fears were realised at all. It opened our school to the community, it was a start for us because we did have very good community links within school hours, we don't have so much afterwards and that was, for me, I suppose the best thing, seeing the parents sitting there doing their little picnic, their kids playing on the field.
> (School deputy head teacher, post project)

Unexpectedly, there was the outcome of student professional development in terms of family and community engagement. Alongside this was a development in advocacy skills, particularly when engaging with the often adult-led concerns of school staff, who, pre-project, were anxious about vandalism, injuries and accidents. Although the project staff knew there was a potential that students would gain from involvement in Open All Hours and it would add to their repertoire of skills, the speed of the acquisition of skills was noticeable.

Reviewing the project and implementing change

Based on the learning, the toolkit was revised and is used by playwork professionals across Wales to open up school grounds for playing. The schools involved in the Open All Hours project responded positively to considering adopting an 'open all hours' ethos. However, some adults within the school communities still retained views of what children should be doing when playing, and under what conditions, with some imposing rules throughout the project. Throughout, the need to understand the context of the community in which projects might operate was highlighted.

> I recognise the challenges that they might feel that they're under by sending children home who've got wet or paint on their clothes playing after school. A key learning message for anybody that is going to take this forward is know your community, and not just the community but the school community as well.
> (Staff, post-project interview)

Children have always needed effective coping skills, and while our changing world brings many advantages, the need to provide time and space to play is as important as ever. Childhood for many has become full of heightened pressures and busy schedules intended to keep children busy and safe (Children's Commissioner, 2018). When children's time is highly scheduled by others it can hardly be seen as their time. Freely-chosen play, when children themselves choose when, how and what to play, not only offers benefits that protect against stress and other pressures, but also gives children opportunities to discover their own interests and competencies (CRC, 2013).

Children playing outside in their local communities has been shown to benefit social relationships for both children and adults (Gleave, 2010). It was within the children's rights policy context that the play advocacy organisation Play Wales developed the *Use of School Grounds for Playing Out of Teaching Hours* toolkit for the use of school grounds as a community play resource. Play Wales is committed to helping schools make school grounds available to local children out of teaching hours and will continue to widely promote the toolkit for schools. The *Open All Hours* project, which piloted the toolkit, illustrated how schools, as a central resource for the local community, should actively consider the options to make their school grounds available for free play after school and at weekends, thus better supporting children's right to play.

Note

1 Play Wales. (2016). *Use of School Grounds for Playing Out of Teaching Hours*. Cardiff: Play Wales.

References

Beunderman, J., Hannon, C., & Bradwell, P. (2007). *Seen and Heard: Reclaiming the Public Realm with Children and Young People*. London: Play England.

Blank, M., Melaville, A., & Shah, B. (2003). *Making the Difference: Research and Practice in Community Schools*. Washington, DC: Coalition for Community Schools, Institute for Educational Leadership.

British Educational Research Association (BERA). (2018). *Ethical Guidelines for Educational Research*. Available at: www.bera.ac.uk/researchers-resources/publications/ethical-guidelines-for-educational-research-2018.

Brown, F. (2014). *Play & Playwork: 101 Stories of Children Playing*. Buckingham: Open University Press, McGraw-Hill Education.

Children's Commissioner for Wales. (2016). *Beth Nesa? What Next?* Available at: www.childcomwales.org.uk/en/what-next/

Children's Commissioner for Wales. (2018). *Spotlight Report: Article 31*. Swansea: Children's Commissioner for Wales.

Connolly,M., & Haughton C. (2015). The perception, management and performance of risk amongst forest school educators. *British Journal of Sociology of Education*, 38 (2), 105–124. Doi: 10.1080/01425692.2015.1073098.

Dyson, A., Kerr, K., Bottrill, I., & Boyd, P. (2016). *Increasing the Use of School Facilities*. Cardiff: Public Policy Institute for Wales.

Furedi, F. (2002). *Culture of Fear: Risk Taking and the Morality of Low Expectation*, 2nd ed. London: Continuum.

Gill, T. (2007). *No Fear: Growing Up in a Risk Averse Society*. London: Calouste Gulbenkian Foundation.

Gleave, J. (2010). *Community Play: A Literature Review*. London: Play England.

Hughes, B. (2012). *Evolutionary Playwork*, 2nd ed. Abingdon: Routledge.

ICM. (2010). Our Place. Playday 2010 poll commissioned for Playday 2013. Available at: www.playday.org.uk/campaigns-3/previous-campaigns/2010-our-place/2010-opinion-poll/.

International Play Association. (2010). *IPA Global Consultations on Children's Right to Play Report*. Faringdon: IPA.

Lester, S., & Russell, W. (2008). *Play For a Change – Play, Policy and Practice: A Review of Contemporary Perspectives*. London: Play England.

Lester, S., & Russell, W. (2010). *Children's Right to Play: An Examination of the Importance of Play in the Lives of Children Worldwide*. Working Paper No. 57. The Hague: Bernard van Leer Foundation.

Lester, S., & Russell, W. (2013). *Leopard Skin Wellies, a Top Hat and a Vacuum Cleaner Hose: An Analysis of Wales' Play Sufficiency Assessment Duty*. Cardiff: University of Gloucestershire & Play Wales.

Lewin, K. (1946). Action research and minority problems. In: G. W. Lewin (Ed.), *Resolving Social Conflicts* (pp. 56–70). New York, NY: Harper.

Meire, J. (2007). Qualitative research on children's play: A review of recent literature. In: T. Jambor & J. Van Gils (Eds.), *Several Perspectives on Children's Play* (pp. 27–78). Antwerp: Garant.

Moss, P., & Petrie, P. (2002). *From Children's Services to Children's Spaces: Public Policy, Children and Childhood*. New York, NY: RoutledgeFalmer.

Mukherji, P., & Albon, D. (2015). *Research Methods in Early Childhood*, 2nd ed. London: Sage.

Ipsos MORI & Nairn, A. (2011). *Children's Wellbeing in UK, Sweden and Spain: The Role of Inequality and Materialism*. Available at: http://bit.ly/lAEk9p.

National Assembly for Wales, Children and Young People's Committee. (2010). *Provision of Safe Places to Play and Hang Out*. Cardiff: National Assembly for Wales Commission Copyright.

Nicholson, S. (1972). The theory of loose parts: An important principle for design methodology. *Studies in Design Education Craft & Technology*, 4 (2), 5–14.

One Poll. (2013). Playday 2013 opinion poll commissioned for Playday 2013. [Online]. Available at: www.playday.org.uk/2013-opinion-poll/.

Play Wales. (2012). *State of Play*. Online. Reports available on request. Cardiff: Play Wales.

Play Wales. (2016). *Use of School Grounds for Playing Out of Teaching Hours*. Cardiff: Play Wales.

Playwork Principles Scrutiny Group. (2005). *Playwork Principles*. Cardiff: Playwork Principles Scrutiny Group.

Public Health Wales. (2017). Nearly a third of under-fives aren't getting enough outdoor play. Available at: www.wales.nhs.uk/sitesplus/888/news/45907/

Solvason, C., Cliffe, J., & Snowden, M. (2017). Researching in school – Creating a meaningful school/university alliance: A reflection. *Educational Action Research*, 26 (4), 589–602. Doi: 10.1080/09650792.2017.1388828.

United Nations Committee on the Rights of the Child. (2013). *General Comment No. 17 (2013) on the Right of the Child to Rest, Leisure, Play, Recreational Activities, Cultural Life and the Arts (Art. 31)*. Geneva: Committee on the Rights of the Child.

Wales Observatory on Human Rights of Children and Young People. (2015). *Little Voices Shouting Out: Children's Report from Wales to the Committee on the Rights of the Child*. Swansea: Wales Observatory on Human Rights of Children and Young People.

Welsh Government. (2002). *Play Policy*. Cardiff: Crown Copyright.

Welsh Government. (2012a). *The Children and Families (Wales) Measure 2010 (Commencement No.5) Order 2012*. Cardiff: Welsh Government Crown Copyright.

Welsh Government. (2012b). *Play Sufficiency Assessment Toolkit*. Cardiff: Welsh Government Crown Copyright.

Welsh Government. (2014). *Wales – A Play Friendly Country*. Cardiff: Welsh Government Crown Copyright.

Welsh Government. (2015). *National Survey for Wales, 2014–2015*. Data collection. UK Data Service. SN: 7767. Available at: http://doi.org/10.5255/UKDA-SN-7767-2.

Welsh Government & Welsh Local Government Association. (2002). *Report of the Wales Assembly Government/Welsh Local Government Association Task and Finish Group – 'Narrowing the Gap in the Performance of Schools'*. Cardiff: Welsh Government & Welsh Local Government Association.

9

PEDAGOGICAL DOCUMENTATION AS 'AGORA'

Why it may be viewed as a form of citizenship for children, parents and communities

Elisabetta Biffi

Play is the core activity in early years education and for good reason: it remains the principal experience through which the child learns to know itself, others and the world, all throughout development and beyond. It is educational experience (self-formation, understanding one's relations with others, acquiring knowledge and competences) with multiple meanings that is embodied in multiple practices, which may be directed and structured to varying degrees. To understand this complexity, pedagogical documentation can make a key contribution if it is understood as a practice that allows us to bring to light, to reveal, not only what goes on in the educational setting – recording action – but also the theoretical ideas about children and education that inform the experience (Fleet, 2017, p. 14). This chapter – from an Italian perspective – focuses on the role of pedagogical documentation as an 'agora'[1] in which the different voices composing the life of an early childhood education facility – those of children, teachers, families and the broader community – are included so as to guarantee a form of citizenship education for all the actors around the meanings of 'play'.

Introduction to play in pedagogical documentation

As reported in the literature, pedagogical documentation is a key element in early childhood pedagogy (Dahlberg, Moss & Pence, 2013;

Fleet, Patterson & Robertson, 2017). Within early childhood education and care (ECEC) settings, documentation primarily contains the teachers' perspective, given that it is mostly assembled by teachers, yet its 'pedagogical' nature demands that the children's voices should also be present, given that children are the protagonists of life at ECE facilities and the main actors in the educational process (Dahlberg, Moss & Pence, 2013).

It is not a matter of recording play but, in a certain sense, of exploring – we might say *studying* – via the documentation data the *what* and *how* of play in ECE settings. Indeed, when it is understood as a process of discovery rather than the description of a product, pedagogical documentation facilitates the sharing, both internally and externally to the ECE setting, of the meaning and role of play in the early years, thus contributing to the construction of a culture of child's play that communicates to children the value and rigour of play as a practice. To fulfil this aim, however, pedagogical documentation must be multivocal, taking 'centre stage' in the public square of the ECE community, and offering opportunities for dialogue among the various actors in educational events – children, teachers, families and the local community. Exploring this possibility is the underlying aim of this chapter.

The culture of play and the culture of childhood

Our understanding of *a child* is a cultural issue: historical perspectives in childhood studies have brought to light the constructed nature of childhood.

The twentieth century saw a series of shifts between viewing children as needing protection or as needing to be civilized through education (Daniel & Ivatts, 1998), between a concept of children as weak by virtue of their inferior abilities or as oppressed by adults and in search of emancipation (Hart, 1992). These visions alternately shaped social welfare and educational policy (and vice-versa) in the period spanning the 1800s and 1900s (Jenks, 2014) and indeed right up to the recent debate on the rights of children: a debate in which the definition of what we understand by *childhood* and *child* is still in question, in the last – unfinished – act of a process that began long ago. The latest act in this long process has been, indeed, the cultural revolution of the 1900s, known as the 'century of the child', which laid the ground for the Convention on the Rights of the Child (1989).

This international agreement is the most recent expression of the contemporary – albeit predominantly Western – vision of childhood. Within the Convention itself, a specific space is dedicated to 'playing activities' (Article 31): 'Children have the right to rest and leisure, to engage in sport and play and recreational activities appropriate to the age of the child and to participate freely in cultural life and the arts.'

But this image of play as specific to children, and a specific entitlement, is informed by a particular cultural perspective on childhood. In parallel with the construction of an awareness of childhood as a peculiar life stage, the modern age has also seen an increasing focus on the spaces (ECEC centres and schools), practices (routines and teaching-learning methods) and objects dedicated to children. At the same time, play has become an 'educational category' associated with the child, facilitating – as outlined by Piera Braga in her work on play (Braga, 2005) – the advancement of educational and psychological theories on the role of play in child development. This advancement began with the definition of Susanna Millar (1968), who argued that play should be conceptualized not in terms of a *what*, or a specific activity, but as a *how* or a *playful attitude* endowing the act of play with one defining characteristic: it comprises free, voluntarily performed actions that engage the performer in a way that is pleasant or gratifying. Thus, the key difference between play and non-play is not so much the activity per se as the stance of the person implementing it. For Jean Piaget (1952), it is the *symbolic* dimension of play that sets it apart from non-play and confirms its cultural nature.

Johan Huizinga (1938) was the first to posit play as the foundation of culture, given its capacity to draw together social coexistence and civilization by defining rules that produce particular social relations: each game has its own rules, which if transgressed bring about the collapse of the play world. These rules establish the boundaries of play as a world that is both part of, and outside of, reality, almost as though play were a border zone: a transitional space, according to Donald Winnicott (1971), or an area that lies between experiencing the *self* and that which is *other than self*. It is the playful attitude that enables this area of transition to be generated, this bridge between the inner and outside worlds, contributing to create even relational spaces between the child and the others (Alcock, 2013).

The cultural valence of play may be deduced from the fact that it is simultaneously both 'pretend' and real in nature. In this regard, an interesting line of reflection has been developed by anthropologists of education and social psychologists, who have interpreted play as a means of adaptation (Bruner, Jolly & Sylva, 1976). Barbara Rogoff, in her work on the cultural nature of development (2003), points out that different modes of play are related to the extent to which children have access to involvement in their community's activities and that these modes are clearly linked to different visions of the participation and role of children in community life.

From this perspective, childhood and play are two sides of same coin, dimensions that mirror and narrate one another and that are both historically and culturally situated. A fine example of how this works is offered by Joseph Tobin's analysis of educational models and adults' ideas about educating children, based on video observations of a typical day in ECEC centres in China, Japan and the United States in the late 1980s: Tobin invokes play when discussing the cultural meanings implicit in educational practice (see Tobin, Wu & Davidson, 1989). Specifically, the staff of early childhood educational services – teachers, educators and coordinators – need to be committed to sharing with the children's parents, but also with the adults in the local community more generally, the various levels of meaning of children's play practices: individual and social, real and symbolic. This sharing primarily, though not exclusively, takes the form of documenting children's play experiences.

Documentation informs educators' decision-making processes and lays the bases for engaging all the actors in the community. This is well illustrated by Alma Fleet, who advocates approaching pedagogical documentation as a means of exploring the Local Interpretation of Larger Ideas (Fleet, 2017). She suggests that pedagogical documentation may be viewed by educators as both a method for exploring and reflecting on their own professional decision-making processes and a vehicle for engaging other actors, including families and local communities, in growing with and alongside the children (Fleet, 2017). Within this framework, pedagogical documentation will be presented in this chapter as a *magnifying glass* that gives observers access to the experience of play in ECE settings, allowing them to develop in-depth understandings of what a child authentically can be.

The role of pedagogical documentation from the cultural construction of childhood to developing a shared understanding of children

As childhood studies have established, from different disciplinary perspectives, documentation has always contributed both to advancing our understanding of the child development process and to constructing our cultural image of childhood. Documentation based on child observations was first introduced in the 1890s by the American Child Study movement (Singer, 1992), and was initially informed by an open-ended exploratory perspective that sought to develop an understanding of the whole child. In the early decades of the twentieth century, however, under the influence of the behaviourist paradigm, observation began to be used as a tool for studying child behaviour. The new positivist outlook shifted the emphasis within documentation from flexible note-taking to tests and measurement: children were being observed in order to be categorized rather than to be understood.

Subsequently, anthropologists began to draw on multiple forms of documentation to explore childhood: in addition to written records of observations, children's artefacts and documents produced by healthcare organizations, welfare services and institutions began to be viewed as valuable sources of information. The interpretation of these kinds of documentation gained popularity as a research strategy for investigating children's cultural and social experience within the ethnographic stream of educational research that began to flourish in the 1970s (e.g., Best, 1983; Erickson, 1986). This tradition introduced qualitative research methods from sociology and anthropology (e.g. Lewis, 2011; Spradley, 2016a, 2016b), seeking above all to interpret experience and to provide 'thick description' (Geertz, 2017) through observational data collected from field notes, interviews and visual material such as artefacts and images (Wien, Guyevskey & Berdoussis, 2011). In addition, following the work of Gregory Bateson and Margaret Mead, who began to use photographs and film in the 1930s to capture the essence of the peoples they were observing, photographic images of children began to be circulated in society at large, wielding a major impact on audiences. It is important to note here that although the use of photography as a form of documentation for studying people came to be rejected as 'unscientific' by the research community (Wiedel, 1995), images have always played a strong role in the cultural construction of childhood, and so too in our contemporary era, which is dominated by an image-based media culture.

Crucially for our line of reflection here, while the aim of the studies just reviewed was to *understand children*, they also *produced childhood*, defining this cultural object by offering images, narratives and descriptions of what a child was supposed to be. Thus, in addition to offering a tool for developing our knowledge and understanding of children and childhood, documentation also became a tool for gradually constructing a sort of collective awareness of what was meant by childhood. A key part in this process was played by childhood services offering healthcare, welfare and education, given that by virtue of their role they have always been in direct contact with children. As many scholars of the history of education have observed, institutions not only document their work, or *object* so to speak, but through these same documentation practices also produce their *subject*. Hence, we may reasonably argue that documentation practices in early childhood services contribute to – or are key instruments of – the *production* of childhood.

Maurizio Ferraris, a philosopher who has studied the concept of *documentality* (Ferraris, 2009), draws attention to the fact that a document is a 'social act', which not only serves as a record of events but is a form of social action in its own right. Thus documentation, in the context examined here, produces the very education and the childhood that it documents: it both defines and regulates them.

'Pedagogical documentation can never be an innocent activity; it always has social and political implications and consequences': following Michael Foucault, Gunilla Dahlberg argues that 'if we are not alert and observant, pedagogical documentation may get swept up into strategies to "predict and control" children more effectively through processes of normalization and surveillance' (Dahlberg, 2012, p. 229). This citation makes explicit the 'fine line' in the practice of documentation between giving voice to bearers of difference and excluding them. This ethical dimension is simultaneously the most powerful and the most fragile aspect of the documentation approach that is going to be discussed here. Powerful, because it offers the potential for local education services, as the Reggio Emilia model proves, to attain international levels of excellence and maintain them over time. Fragile, because when it is not applied in a mindful way, it can end up reproducing externally imposed stereotypes of education and childhood. For instance, given the contemporary tendency to represent childhood as the 'golden years', often by using stereotypical images of clean, happy children, even pedagogical documentation is at risk of reinforcing an objectifying notion of childhood, and thereby failing to capture the complexity of this life stage, which is also made up of failures. Similarly, when educators are too anxious to meet the expectations of parents, only showing pictures of quiet, smiling, happy children, they reinforce a reassuring image of childhood that is far removed from the real-life experience of anyone who works with children on a daily basis.

Homing in now on the theme of this book, play, we crucially need to examine how children's play may best be documented; for example, the toy industry offers evocative images of children at play that stereotypically associate the concept of play with the use of the 'toy' object. Yet empirical research in ECE settings suggests that play often does without objects, or applies divergent thinking to them; for example, by turning everyday objects into toys (a branch that becomes a sword, a blanket that becomes a cloak, etc.). Furthermore, while stereotypical images often portray children as smiling during play, the gaze of early childhood educators can remind other adults of the considerable effort and commitment demanded by serious play. In this sense, documentation has the power to reinforce or challenge adult prejudices and representations concerning the educational value of play.

This has key implications for the use of documentation in the context of the relationship between the ECE facility and the family: documentation should be carefully revisited when there is a tendency for it to only display what its external audience (i.e. families) expects to see, and, above all, when it is exclusively at the service of a requirement for control: for example, the use of instant messaging conversations between parents and teachers, often merely serving to reassure parents about their children's safety and wellbeing while attending day care.

Playing with pedagogical documentation for building an agora, among children, teachers, families and the local community

By narrating the ways in which adults – in their capacity as educators – relate to children, documentation essentially provides an account of the educational process itself (Formosinho & Formosinho, in Formosinho & Pascal, 2016, p. 48). It showcases both effective styles of interaction that are respectful of the peculiar characteristics of very young children and the community dimension and collective participation that characterize the ECE setting, understood as a living space that is shared between adults and children and among the children themselves.

In this final section, we shall reflect on ways in which documentation can provide a space for shared dialogue among the actors in the educational process, based on a series of examples of the use of pedagogical documentation at ECEC facilities.

Sharing with the children

Anna,[2] a teacher, observes a group of three-year-olds who are intent on making constructions with recycled objects (bottle caps, small pieces of wood, stones). She stops to photograph the children at work. Later, she shows the children the photos of their work and begins a conversation with them: What did we do this morning? How can we tell our families about it? This leads to a conversation about selecting photos to display on the wall of the classroom.

Pedagogical documentation clearly offers a key space for giving voice to children. But, as mentioned earlier, this must not merely involve adults reporting excerpts from their utterances or presenting parts of their artworks: rather, the children themselves must be involved in the process of selecting what is to be shared. Documenting is in itself an activity that contains an element of play and fun for children, as described in an enthralling manner by Franca Zuccoli in her book *Dalle tasche dei bambini* [From children's pockets]. Children can be excellent collectors; they often keep objects and fragments of objects that can seem insignificant to our adult gaze but that, on the contrary, provide a valuable record of their process of discovering the world and their incessant thinking about and attributing meaning to their experience. In these terms, children may be directly involved in the documentation process, understood as a complex process of observation–selection–collection–presentation in relation to their experience in the educational setting.

This demands a paradigm shift from the adults, who must learn to view the children as 'competent interlocutors' rather than 'end users'. Hence, participation is closer to a 'state of mind' in the adult than to a 'behaviour' of the child. Thus, in the context of ECEC services, early work on developing shared memory is key to fostering that sense of community that will help children to identify themselves as part of the whole community.

Sharing with parents

The educators have set up a meeting with the parents of 20-month-old Sofia. They would like to explore the theme of 'risk' with them: this is because the parents themselves have frequently expressed their concern that the little girl might be in danger of hurting herself while playing outdoors – for example, while climbing onto the slide, or jumping off the low walls in the playground – because they feel that she is still insecure in her movements. In preparation for the parent–teacher meeting, the teachers collect photographs and videos of Sofia while climbing up the slide and playing outdoors. They next select one excerpt in which she confidently climbed to the top of the slide and slid down without incident, and another in which she stumbled as she was climbing up, picked herself up and resumed climbing. At the meeting with parents, the educators explain why they asked to meet them, and then show them the assembled documentation. The opportunity to see their child in action while encountering and dealing with risk makes the parents feel that their concerns were legitimate and allows the teachers to share Sofia's ability to independently cope with difficulty.[3]

The theme of parent engagement is vast and raises multiple questions about the concept of education underpinning the work of the ECEC centre. Within our reflection, documentation can be considered as a concrete object on which teachers and parents can converge their perspectives. In a certain sense, teachers may view educating parents as part of their brief, and this will lead them to use documentation not only to display the children's achievements and activities but also to inform and educate parents. More specifically, actively using documentation to inform the dialogue between teachers and parents offers a tool for educating parents in terms of developing an in-depth understanding of their child and his/her learning processes. Different forms of documentation should be deployed to engage parents in conversation and dialogue about what has been documented, e.g. by displaying documentation on the classroom walls, through regular meetings and conversations or via e-mail/chat.

An interesting example of the use of documentation in terms of parents' engagement is given in the work of Jeanette Clarkin-Philips and Margaret Carr (2006), describing efforts by teachers to engage parents by personally inviting them to contribute comments on their children's learning at home (through the strategy of using learning stories as a documented assessment record), referring to the concept of 'relational agency' (Edwards & D'Arcy, 2004). These authors pointed out that teachers hold a position of authority in an educational institution: it is therefore crucial that they adopt a non-judgemental attitude to allow families to share their ideas without any fear of being considered 'bad' or 'inadequate' parents.

Parent engagement and participation is, indeed, a cultural issue in its own right: belief in the importance of parents' participation in school life cannot be taken for granted. For example, parents may be culturally predisposed to view not discussing with teachers what is done at school as a form of respect; or they may lack a clear understanding of their own role in children's learning in the educational setting. Therefore, teachers must bear in mind that active participation by parents needs to be preceded by the construction of a 'shared culture of belonging' with children, parents and the community.

Sharing among teachers/educators

The project presented here was implemented in a large Northern Italian town near Milan, with 18 educators working at five different ECECs, who were guided through a process of reflecting about how to share the meanings of the children's play with the parents.[4] While focusing on this theme, they began to collect photos of the ways in which education took the form of play during daily life in the classroom. The images were chosen to illustrate the educational value of play in terms of both art and science, and thus with a great degree of openness. As a result, the photos selected were not necessarily the best pictures of the children or those in which they were centre-screen, but those which bore best witness to the children's exploratory processes.

Once the 'catalogue' had been assembled, the team of educators and representatives of the town council decided to exhibit it to the public during the annual open day of presentation of the town's ECEC facilities at the start of the enrolment period. The introduction to the catalogue was an essay by the municipal pedagogista, entitled 'What Is a Child': 'Children play and through their play construct meaning, organize knowledge, have experiences on their own and with others, and express themselves. [...] This is why children's play invariably bears intrinsic scientific, artistic and relational value' (p. 9).

Within this process, the educators were invited to think of themselves as researchers: the main competence required for this role is the ability to engage in reflective thinking, understood not as a strategy but as a *mental habit* (Dewey, 1933; Schön, 1987). Teachers are called to the frontline of an open-ended inquiry into childhood and childhood educational experience through play. By narrating the ways in which adults relate to children, documentation essentially provides an account of the educational process itself. It showcases both effective styles of interaction that are respectful of the peculiar characteristics of very young children, and the community dimension and collective participation that characterize the ECE setting, understood as a living space that is shared between adults and children and among the children themselves. The opportunity for the team of educators to share images of what they meant by 'play' allowed them to establish a shared culture of the play that was broader than the specific ideas of individual teachers.

Sharing with the local community

Coming back to the project outlined above, the next step after the construction of the catalogue was the production of a joint exhibition. The exhibition was held at the public library and was supplemented by open workshops run both outside and inside the library, at which children could freely take part in the types of play experience on display in the exhibition.

The decision to organize the exhibition at the public library – instead of at the ECEC centres themselves – had a specific cultural aim: to build awareness of educational culture by bringing the education services into the town centre and making them more visible to a public that might not be familiar with their role. At the same time, by holding outdoor workshops (as integral part of the exhibition), children were directly engaged in the type of play presented inside the library. This was reflected in the fact that the exhibition could only be accessed through the areas in which the workshops were being conducted and all those walking by were invited to take part in the workshops: children and parents attending the exhibition, but also other users of the library and even casual passers-by.

Pedagogical documentation has, indeed, a key role to play in this regard by offering continuous feedback to the local area with respect to the value of its investment in early childhood services, and a method of sharing responsibility for and attributing meaning to local investment in ECE. The role of the local community in the life of an ECEC service introduces another critical issue for reflection, which is how the macro curriculum and national assessment requirements may be reconciled with local situations. ECEC services must be aligned with the needs and resources of the local community if they are to 'service' it. On the other hand, they are obliged to implement a curriculum that has been designed by centralized institutions at the national level (and beyond, if we consider the efforts currently underway to develop a common European Union curriculum).

Conclusion

Pedagogical documentation allows us to give body to this experience, making it visible, observable and available for sharing, and offering a point of encounter among different adult perspectives on it. It helps to bring to light adult stereotypes about play, which in reality are underpinned by adult stereotypes of the child. The mediation of the teacher/educator remains crucial to this process, not because teachers are child experts in the broader sense, but because they hold professional competence in how to observe and listen to children. Thus, while documentation can fulfil the desire to give voice to children, it also reminds adults of the responsibility that they bear in 'narrating children'. Pedagogical documentation therefore acts as a litmus test of the authenticity of alleged processes of 'giving voice': when it consists of the rigorous narration of a process of co-construction, it comprises space for both adult and child.

Given this background, the hypothesis explored in the chapter is that pedagogical documentation may be considered as the space-time for the dialogue within the agora of the ECEC centre: for children, to whom it affords a means of genuine participation in their own educational processes; for teachers, to whom it offers the space for self-professional reflection; for parents, to whom it offers the opportunity to share their perspectives on their children with the teachers; and finally, for all the adults in the community.

Notes

1 In ancient Greece, the 'agora' was a public gathering space for markets and assemblies, including artistic and political events.
2 This account is based on material collected during professional development sessions and research meetings with the staff of ECE centres over

the last few years. My special thanks go to Daniela Corradi, Marta Poletti and Alessandra Dedè for their help with writing up these experiences.
3 See previous note.
4 We are referring to the exhibition *Play at Nursery School between Art and Science* (Cinisello Balsamo, 2017) organized by the educational services of Cinisello Balsamo. My special thanks to the municipality, the pedagogista of the services, Enza Stragapede, and the organizers of the exhibition, Alessandra Dedè and Daniela Corradi, for the contribution offered to this description.

References

Alcock, S. (2013). Toddlers complex communication: Playfulness from a secure base. *Contemporary Issues in Early Childhood*, 14(2), 179–190.

Best, R. (1983). *We've all got scars*. Bloomington, IN: Indiana University Press.

Braga, P. (2005). *Gioco, cultura e formazione. Temi e problemi di pedagogia dell'infanzia*. Parma: Junior.

Bruner, J., Jolly, A., & Sylva K. (Eds) (1976). *Play: Its role in development and evolution*. New York, NY: Basic Books.

Clarkin-Phillips, J., & Carr, M. (2006). *Strengthening responsive and reciprocal relationships in a whānau tangata centre: An action research project*. Wellington: Teaching & Learning Research Initiative.

Dahlberg, G. (2012). Pedagogical documentation: A practice for negotiation and democracy. In C. Edwards, L. Gandini & G. Forman (Eds), *The hundred languages of children: The Reggio Emilia experience in transformation* (pp. 225–232). Santa Barbara, CA: Praeger.

Dahlberg, G., Moss, P., & Pence, A.R. (2013). *Beyond quality in early childhood education and care: Languages of evaluation*. Abingdon: Routledge.

Daniel, P., & Ivatts, J. (1998). *Children and social policy*. Basingstoke: Macmillan.

Dewey, J. (1933). *How we think: A restatement of the relation of reflective thinking to the educative process*. New York, NY: D.C. Heath and Company.

Edwards, A., & D'Arcy, C. (2004). Relational agency and disposition in sociocultural accounts of learning to teach. *Educational Review*, 56(2), 147–155.

Erickson, F. (1986). Qualitative methods in research on teaching. In M. Wittrock (Ed.), *Handbook of research on teaching* (3rd ed., pp. 119–161). New York, NY: Macmillan.

Ferraris, M. (2009). Documentality, or Europe. *The Monist*, 92(2), 286–314.

Fleet, A. (2017). The landscape of pedagogical documentation. In A. Fleet, C. Patterson & J. Robertson (Eds), *Pedagogical documentation in early years practice: Seeing through multiple perspectives* (pp. 11–26). London: SAGE.

Fleet, A., Patterson, C., & Robertson, J. (2017). *Pedagogical documentation in early years practice: Seeing through multiple perspectives*. London: SAGE.

Formosinho, J., & Formosinho, J. (2016). Pedagogy-in-participation: The search for a holistic praxis. In J. Formosinho & C. Pascal (Eds), *Assessment and evaluation for transformation in early childhood* (pp. 26–55). London: Routledge with EECERA.

Geertz, C. (2017). *The interpretation of cultures*. New York, NY: Basic Books.

Hart, R. (1992). *Children's participation: From Tokenism to citizenship*. Firenze: UNICEF International Child Development Centre.

Huizinga, J. (1938). *Homo ludens: Proeve eener bepaling van het spel-element der cultuu r* [*Homo ludens*: A study of the play-element in culture]. Haarlem: Tjeenk Willink.

Jenks, C. (2014). *Childhood*. London: Routledge.

Lewis, O. (2011). *The children of Sánchez: Autobiography of a Mexican family*. New York, NY: Vintage.

Millar, S. (1968). *The psychology of play*. Harmondsworth: Penguin.

Piaget, J. (1952). *The origins of intelligence in children* (M. Cook, Trans.). New York, NY: International Universities Press.

Rogoff, B. (2003). *The cultural nature of human development*. New York, NY: Oxford University Press.

Schön, D.A. (1987). *Educating the reflective practitioner: Toward a new design for teaching and learning in the professions*. San Francisco, CA: Jossey-Bass.

Singer, E. (1992). *Childcare and the psychology of development*. New York, NY: Routledge.

Spradley, J.P. (2016a). *The ethnographic interview*. Long Grove, IL: Waveland Press.

Spradley, J.P. (2016b). *Participant observation*. Long Grove, IL: Waveland Press.

Tobin, J., Wu, D., & Davidson, D. (1989). *Preschool in three cultures: Japan, China, and the United States*. New Haven, CT: Yale University Press.

United Nations. (1989). *UN Convention on the Rights of the Child. UN General Assembly*. Vol. 1577. New York: Treaty Series.

Wiedel, J. (1995). Being there: Using pictures to see the invisible. In M. Schratz & R. Walker (Eds), *Research as social change: New opportunities for qualitative research* (pp. 65–89). London: Routledge.

Wien, C.A., Guyevskey, V., & Berdoussis, N. (2011). Learning to document in Reggio inspired education. *Early Childhood Research and Practice*, 13(2), 1–12.

Winnicott, D.W. (1971). *Playing and reality*. London: Psychology Press.

Zuccoli, F. (2011). *Dalle tasche dei bambini ... Gli oggetti, le storie e la didattica*. Bergamo: Edizioni Junior.

EDITORIAL PROVOCATIONS
Engaging readers and extending thinking

Sophie Alcock

Adapting the well-known African proverb, it takes a community to raise a child. Themes underpinning Section 3 include communication, politics and pedagogical documentation in exploring how communities can make provision for children's desire to play. Communities may be viewed as central to citizenship and belonging, containing families and places such as early childhood centres, schools and more. The chapters in this section present three different angles on community and play, adding to perceptions of how children can play in and with their communities.

The context for Chapter 7 is a community-based early childhood care and education setting in New Zealand-Aotearoa. Hedges, Cooper and Weisz-Koves locate children's play within a focus on family funds of knowledge and children's interests, as played out in the early childhood setting. Vignettes illuminate the ways in which common family values and practices influence children's interests and play. Children can create meaning and sense in early childhood settings through playing with and through family and community-based funds of knowledge. As the authors write:

> because an important function of play is to afford children opportunities to practise participation in real-life activities, teachers need to be aware of, and reflect critically on, their decision-making and pedagogy to facilitate teaching and learning environments that provide children with opportunities to recreate, re-enact, and represent their family and community lives.
>
> (Chapter 7)

Community spaces and places to support children's play is the focus of Mannello et al. in Chapter 8. They describe the Open All Hours action research project that involved schools in Welsh communities opening the gates to their playgrounds and supporting playworkers to facilitate children playing in school grounds outside school hours. The tool kit developed out of this community-based project has continued to influence other communities in Wales to also open their school gates. The authors describe how perceived risk around children's outdoor play – an everyday issue in these hypersensitive risk-averse times – was managed through dialogue and clear communication early on in project planning processes.

Wales is unique in being the only government to exceed the UN Convention on the Rights of the Child by legislating a more detailed national play policy: Local authorities must explain how their communities make provision for children's play. Children's 'right to play' is kept up front and endorsed by the Welsh government.

- Might government interest reduce public risk-averseness around children's outdoor play in local communities?
- How might we interpret increasing community interest and the spread of forest, bush and other outdoor play-based early childhood programs in many countries, alongside climates of risk-averseness?

From Italy, Biffi rounds out this section with her focus in Chapter 9 on the documentation of pedagogy in communities, historically contextualising trends in child observation and pedagogical documentation processes. Pedagogical documentation is positioned like the agora as a central community meeting place – public market – that combines artistic, political, spiritual and other dimensions of citizenship. From this multi-perspectival context, pedagogical documentation can enliven and challenge community members' – citizens' – perceptions and understandings of children, play and pedagogy. Documentation thus becomes democracy in practice.

Together, these three chapters provide appropriately broad and challenging overviews of different ways of viewing and embedding families and communities in rethinking play as pedagogy. As these voices are often undervalued, these may serve as timely reminders for readers who are considering the important voices in these debates.

Section 4

WORKING WITH SYSTEMS

10

SPINNING THE KALEIDOSCOPE

A conversation around play, learning, policies and systems

Alma Fleet and Michael Reed

This chapter provides opportunities to reflect on complications in the constantly moving realm of policy development relating to the early childhood landscape. In particular, the impact of systems on 'the child's right to play' is considered in the context of issues associated with early childhood pedagogy. The chapter evolved via many conversations; it walks an interesting academic line between informed opinion and poetic licence, asking the reader to imagine multiple conversations over time. Chapter content reflects some of the dilemmas (rather than solutions) that were exposed in the course of those conversations. We ask you to read them and, as you do, to make some mental and/or written notes to help continue the conversations as a companion to study or to fuel practitioner-led reflections on play and learning.

Let's imagine we're sitting around a table in a comfortable, encouraging environment. The computer sits alongside tea and coffee, and we think together.

We started with some agreement

Children love to play; 'play' is one of the few opportunities children have to experiment, sometimes face disappointment, and interact with others – especially if they do so in a safe, welcoming environment. Further, the United Nations (1991) position is that children have a *right* to play.

We pressed 'Pause' here and asked, 'how do we know'?

In Chapter 5, Fleet and Kemenyvary included the views of children as part of their investigation; value is given to their voices. This approach really made us think about ways to engage in further research with children, both to harness the collective energy emanating from any group of children and to explore individual perceptions; it also recognises that learning is shaped by the ways educators interact with children and children interact with each other. The children's views about play tell us much about shared social expectations. It also respects what each child brings into a learning space, seeking what each has contributed as well as what has been attained. Educators and researchers in this sector care about children, their wellbeing and learning, as well as the views of families and communities. So, we agreed, listening to children is important to understand play, systems, and pedagogy. A competent system would do this.

At this point we spent time thinking about what was meant by a 'learning space'.

Mike writes

An educator is the guardian of a learning space which may be a formal space with a defined purpose. Space can also be given over to the guardianship of the children themselves, their parents, carers, or community. It can also be space which encourages learning opportunities that can be short and spontaneous. Educators and children do not operate in isolation; children's learning is also shaped by environments – they learn to trust the environment, trust each other, and develop shared social expectations.

Learning spaces are not static; they change as adults and children enter and exit those spaces. Children inhabit the spaces in pairs, groups, or as interested bystanders who find something they have in common or want to learn about or explore. These coming-togethers are sometimes fleeting, sometimes last a while, and then disband. OK, so any space means establishing social frontiers, because play-spaces change as adults and children revise their opinions and respond to what they contain and, importantly, who inhabits them. I say 'frontiers' because children are on a learning mission which is often exciting, challenging, and, for them, very new. Children are just like the researchers in this book: they see frontiers that are there to be explored, often in the company of other explorers.

- But what about challenges. Is the description realistic?

There are external pressures on those spaces due to time, educational policies, systems, statutory learning goals, and the availability of resources. Everybody, including the children, has to be able to adapt to these external pressures. It's a delicate balancing act performed by educators every day. I can certainly see why educators feel pressure from systems which ask them to produce learning outcomes and they must feel pressure to provide activities that can demonstrate how 'teaching and learning' is meeting those goals. There is also pressure from those who look on in dismay because some educators fail to continually expose children to self-directed play opportunities. The middle ground is disappearing.

Now, after pausing again we think of our reading from this book and elsewhere, and share some thinking.

We wish to distance ourselves from any claims of 'expert' knowledge; we say this because there is a danger that author-views may give that impression. As the authors of this chapter, we are from different countries, with different experiences. Inevitably, we have drawn on many sources and conversations with colleagues to raise issues for consideration; this is a position of curiosity rather than certainty, of puzzlement rather than instruction.

Surely, the terrain of play and pedagogy is about being open to multiple interpretations that acknowledge complexity of contexts and the importance of pursuing the investigation. For example, and here we shall use some research evidence: Wood & Chesworth (2017, para 1) note that the 'field of play scholarship is extensive, international, multidisciplinary and progressive in providing different ways of understanding play from a range of perspectives', and in commenting on a recent UK review note that it:

> highlights a persistent tension – a progressive focus in research, but a potentially regressive framing of play in policy contexts. This is captured by the juxtaposition between what play is, and what play means for children, and what play does, and what play produces, from the perspectives of policy … a consistent concern across all five themes of the Review is that practitioners are pulled in different directions as they navigate policy, practice, and their own beliefs and aspirations.
>
> (para 2)

For an example, more than 25 years ago an investigation into children's participation in matters concerning them, in the context of the UN Convention on the Rights of the Child (1991), resulted in an issues paper including the following reflection on children's play:

> in many developing countries a lot of the work in the family is carried out by five-year-olds, and older children are often exploited in grinding industrial or agricultural labour. There is little time for play ... if one observes children playing with one another in an environment rich with materials, what they are doing looks a lot like work. It is for this reason that the static traditional playgrounds with fixed equipment are most interesting to children when they are being built or dismantled. Consequently, the countries of Northern Europe have developed "adventure playgrounds", places with many materials and much participation by children building in them. Squint a little and children in an adventure playground look like adult workers at a building site.
>
> (Hart, 1992, p. 20)

This positioning highlighted aspects of 'play' that continue to confound educators and policy-makers, though children and families tend to move with whatever cultural milieu surrounds them. Note the Australian Aboriginal voices on play reported by Fasoli et al. (2010). As Alison commented there (p. 216), 'when children are playing they are also learning about their environment and their culture. Every time something new comes along, it gives them strong emotions.' Reflecting on her work with Alison Wunungmurra and more recent research with Galiwin'ku Yolŋu colleagues in the Growing Up Children in Two Worlds project (www.cdu.edu.au/health-wellbeing/growing-up-children-in-two-worlds), Lyn Fasoli shared some of the team's understanding that, 'Children's play is a highly valuable activity in Yolŋu culture. Adults enjoy watching their children re-playing or play-practising cultural skills and activities they have observed in adults, such as ceremonial dancing, hunting or building shelters' (personal communication, 1 October 2018). Systems and policies that are distanced from such cultural ways of being risk alienating communities and distancing children from heritage.

There are, however, strategies that educators and researchers can use to support calls for grounded policies. Note, for example, the Talking Pictures project jointly supported by Batchelor Institute (it includes targeted teacher education for students of Aboriginal and/or Torres Strait Islander background) and the Telstra Foundation (sponsorship for children's cameras). This project investigated 'what young Indigenous children and their families think about play. Children were the data collectors. They took over 200 photos of their own play activities and selected the 15 that best showed their ideas about play' (Fasoli, 2008, n.p.). The children (four- to eight-year-olds) were from two remote communities. Tellingly, the project was subtitled 'Kids play what they see', and included parent comments like, 'I hope they're learning culture while they play' (Gapuwiyak community) and, 'Whatever they're feeding their minds on, that's what they're going to become' (Jilkminggan community).

Now we 'fast forward', because systems, policies, and policy reviews are rarely static. For example: Canada has recently taken major steps in the policy landscape in a consultative collaboration between government and groups of First Nations peoples, releasing the following press statement:

> Children hold a sacred place in the cultures of Indigenous peoples and with that comes a sacred responsibility to care for them. The Assembly of First Nations, Inuit Tapiriit Kanatami, the Métis National Council and the Government of Canada are working together to improve early learning and child care for Indigenous children by jointly releasing a co-developed Indigenous Early Learning and Child Care Framework. www.childcare canada.org/documents/research-policy-practice/18/09/govern ment-canada-assembly-first-nations-inuit-tapiriit-kan.
> (Government of Canada et al., 2018)

The Preamble to this ground-breaking document states that:

> Alongside a distinctions-based approach that respects the specific priorities of First Nations, Inuit and the Métis Nation, the Framework describes an overarching vision for a comprehensive and coordinated early learning and child care system led by Indigenous peoples, establishes shared principles, and includes specific gender and geographic considerations that represent the views of all Indigenous children and families.
> (Government of Canada et al., 2018)

We are pleased there is grounded consultation and that educators are involved; it will be interesting to see how 'play' emerges from this consultation.

Now we find ourselves asking how we can include other voices in this conversation? (We are very taken by non-standard academic viewpoints such as online blogs.)

In considering bird's-eye views of this landscape, Colliver (2011) suggested that, 'Comprehensive review and examination of the early childhood play-based learning literature suggests that this contention [re the value of play] may be understood in terms of five critical debates', and that consideration of these 'offers a useful framework for play-based research activity, the continued development of play-based pedagogies and policy formation' (para 3). The framework he proposed captures many of the conversations unfolding in this chapter. The debates related to:

1. The educative value of play time;
2. Play as a site for power differentials (both student–student and teacher–student);
3. The ethnocentricity of pro-play rhetoric;
4. The universalist treatment of individuals through play advocacy; and
5. The privileging of 'expert' stakeholder perspectives in play research.

(para 1)

While continuing to unpack these ideas the following year (Colliver, 2012), he notes (personal communication, 2018) that the five debates continue to rage but have not been extensively extended to digital play, which he is exploring currently. We remind readers that an aspect of that play is explored in this volume (see Robertson) and is being pursued elsewhere, as reflected in a BERA Blog post (Arnott, Palaiologou & Gray, 2018).

At this point we press the 'Pause' button and say: Volume 6 in this series spends time on policy intersections with pedagogy, so we'll just mention two systemic efforts specific to the play and policy landscape.

In England, the Office for Standards in Education, Children's Services and Skills is the body charged with inspecting early education services, using a framework that determines the quality of provision (Ofsted, 2015a). The service produced a document exploring perceptions of teaching and play in the early years (2015b). Alma notes that the report suggests there is 'no one way of approaching play' and that 'leaders did not think of teaching and play as separate endeavours' (pp. 5–6). She comments that this seems to show slippage in the lack of an attempt to define what is meant by 'play' in this context, and wonders whether consideration was given to the pedagogy of play.

Mike suggests that it is valuable to read the document, but to look at it in terms of how/where it positions the status of play in the curriculum – what professional expectations are embedded into what it says – and question whether it values the ability of educators to engage in pedagogical reflection about play. Should play and learning opportunities encompass children's dispositions to learn, or be focused on meeting goals and outcomes expected of a child entering school? Of course, this is not to suggest a binary choice between one or the other; the point is that systems drive approaches to learning. There must always be caution if definitions of 'play' and 'learning' are universally applied to widely varying educational settings, as part of a regulatory pattern impacting on pedagogy.

Alma cites the efforts of the Australian government in releasing the first national framework for the early childhood sector in that country, the *Early Years Learning Framework* (EYLF) (DEEWR, 2009). Jennifer Sumsion had a lead role with Linda Harrison on the consultation team that shepherded this formative document into existence. The process was not straightforward (see Sumsion et al., 2009) due to state, territory and national differences in policies and philosophies about ways to support/extend the education and wellbeing of young children. In fact, original processes for developing the document spanned the birth-through-eight age range, in hopes of creating a frame encompassing transition into the first years of formal schooling. With realities of pragmatics and political ideologies, this ambitious goal was 'one bridge too far'. Nevertheless, the EYLF (DEEWR, 2009) included in its introduction a clear focus on 'play-based learning', citing the UN's Convention on the Rights of the Child (1991) as recognising 'children's right to play and be active participants in all matters affecting their lives' (p. 5). In this context, play-based learning was defined as: 'a context for learning through which children organise and make sense of their social worlds, as they engage actively with people, objects and representations' (p. 6). The document expands the definition of play for readers. No claim was made as to how governments might support the implementation of this non-regulatory pedagogical frame. States and territories were enabled to continue referring to/framing their policies and practices around local documents/guidelines, while being expected, under the umbrella of the National Quality Framework (Australian Children's Education and Care Quality Authority, 2018), to reflect the directions encapsulated in the EYLF. It remains to be seen how these ideas are being interpreted, envisioned, and enacted across the diverse contexts that constitute Australia.

'Fast forward' again, to an evolving discussion related to 'pure play' which evolves in Sophie Alcock's chapter in this book, where she says: 'Being alongside children while observing them playing wildly can be emotionally challenging, particularly when teachers interact affectively with the children.'

Alma muses: I'm thinking that we're talking about/conceptualising a multi-layered/non-linear continuum of interpretations of what people think we're talking about – from something that could be considered 'pure play' in the safe childhood investigative, exploratory, child-owned sense, through a range of understandings including adult–child joint explorations and children playing while they work (skipping rocks over water while catching creatures for food) to the playful possibilities emerging as part of a teacher's agenda, but interpreted through children's ways of being/hands-on decision-making in a group setting. Newer interpretations broaden the focus to include invitations from the non-human/materials and environment (see, for example, Jobb, MacAlpine & Pacini-Ketchabaw, in press; Merewether, 2018). The boundaries are not as formal as might be presumed by dichotomous views such as adult vs child initiation/ownership, or time-tabled vs open-ended play. Interpretations need to be heavily contextualised. Whereas the extremes are perfectly clear (children's joyful or mesmerising engagement in a child's world vs enforced unsafe child labour sites), the layers of complexity are not so clear; judgments about the worthwhileness of events/activities at different points on the continuum are not helpful. Is an infant crawling towards an enticing object with rapt fascination 'playing' or simply exploring the world? Does it matter? Perhaps only if the child is not ever allowed to explore and gain confidence in her capacity to do so. In which case, a 'system' that constrains the child to restricted movement for long periods of time can be seen as not only pedagogically unsound, but in conflict with the child's rights. Definitions and perceptions are key in this conversation.

At this point, we again press 'Pause' because while there is agreement that we are identifying and exploring dilemmas, we seek some further reading.

For example: the following are contextually embedded, but rigorous and applicable to many contexts. While arguing the centrality of play/playfulness in early education, Singer (2013) claims that curriculum founded on play can be problematic, as it can undervalue essential characteristics of play. Issues are raised re adult–child power differentials as well as the primacy of pleasure when play itself is seen as a resource. Similarly, Wood (2014) takes a post-structural position to the debate. Studying the play-decisions of 10 young English children, the use of a sociocultural frame foregrounds context, relationships, and agency in ways that suggest implications for policy and its implementations. We note also the importance of major reviews such as that in England by Santer and Griffiths with Goodall (2007).

'Fast forward' again. This time we have assimilated so much information (a position a conscientious student is in when preparing for an assignment) that we can only draw some of what we call 'dilemma points' together.

Alma writes

We seem to be saying the same thing over and over without being heard; it's like talking to a river running by, with the context, information, and potential insights disappearing in rushing water around the river's bend. Of course, one of our challenges – while we wonder what we are actually talking about when we challenge deeper investigations into the play landscape – is what we mean by 'systems'? When we say that systems can enhance or constrain the possibilities for interpreting and offering play-spaces, loose parts or playful pedagogies, are we imagining guidelines? Frameworks? Informal structures? Formal employment?

Mike writes

For a start, Pascal et al. (in press) argue that systems are rarely static; change systems constitute ever-changing responses to a variety of influences. They are shaped by structural factors related to the nature, scope, and capacity of early years programs and process factors which determine how these operate in the community. They identify the dilemma facing early educators as they apply curriculum guidelines encompassing care, welfare, education, and development. This dilemma includes how best to develop an approach which promotes a balance between adult- and child-led activities and recognises the value of free play. Reed and Walker (2017) argue the result is that the professional role is embedded into complex structural system requirements: for example, promoting inter-professional working, safeguarding children's welfare, supporting children to meet national early learning goals and promoting inclusive education. These are all measured/rated by regulation and inspection requiring an educator to demonstrate sound pedagogical practice including warmth, security, care, and consideration, as well as forging positive relationships with families and communities.

The key question is whether these regulatory systems are the driving forces shaping professional practice and determining professionalism, or is there more to being a competent, adaptive, reflective early educator? The answer might be to see (modern) professionalism as not only the educator's ability to understand relationships between day-to-day practice and systems, but to recognise wider overlapping dimensions. Wenger-Trayner et al. (2014) question what we mean by effective professional practice: are there different institutional demands within the early education sector; are there differences in scale; are there power dimensions and change over time? Building on Wenger-Trayner et al. (2014), it is important to recognise:

- The way different professional communities within a sector exhibit and share competing and overlapping structural and process practices; not everyone will interpret systems and regulation in the same way.
- That home-based community-provision or voluntary sector provision will have different demands; is a one-size-fits-all regulatory requirement appropriate?
- The importance of status and power, including differences between professional groups and institutions, noting a bedrock for integrated working where there is need to work alongside other professional groups.
- Patterns of change: recognising how things change over time, and the time it takes to change professional expectations and perspectives.

'Fast forward' to an attempt to reconcile some of the dilemmas (what we said we would not do, but a lifetime in academia means we have to try).

Alma writes

But if that's our definition (for this purpose), how does 'the system' cope with accountability requirements in a play-based environment? This brings us to the 'assessment' question, in a sector which tends to only acknowledge the term for systemic purposes – i.e. it's the term used by employers and governments to frame reporting responsibilities, that is, to demonstrate on the record that we are, in fact, making a difference in the lives of children in our care – or that we are at least aware that they are growing over time! This is satisfying for some, but a headache for many more, as there are often philosophical and pragmatic issues involved in reconciling ways to share learning with children, and then to represent learning in an authentic way (as has been noted in several chapters in this volume).

Introducing a focus issue devoted to the topic, Hayward et al. (2016, p. 169) noted that 'The idea that curriculum, pedagogy and assessment are inter-related and enacted in harmony seems common sense. Sensible it may seem, but common it is not.' While dealing largely with formal schooling and older children, their thesis remains the same for this conversation; it echoes the thoughts put forward earlier, as reflected in the following example, closely linking play and assessment in holistic, authentic ways, while acknowledging systemic expectations.

Let's imagine a scenario that values young children's playful engagement with each other, materials and the environment in a group setting with educators (teachers, early childhood workers, or other professionals, depending on the nomenclature of the location). The adult has been sharing Pamela Allen's *Is Your Grandmother a Goanna* (2009) with a group of children who have joined her when she settled for a quiet moment in a cushioned area, with curriculum intentions ranging from the valuing of children's literature, to the pleasures of shared reading, to discovery of connected text, to invitational literacy (including opportunities to chorus and then memorise and then recognise text). Well, that's not 'play', but it's lovely pedagogy as children are enjoying the opportunity to enthusiastically join into the teacher's rendition of the dialogue, being enveloped in fundamental literacy understandings, and also navigating mathematical language related to time and place. Later in the day, several of the children – of their own volition – in their own space and time are seen to be pushing boxes and chairs into position to create a train; donning hats to be the conductor; grabbing puppets and other paraphernalia to turn into animals; and generally shrieking on and off the train, tooting, laughing, and commenting on their play. This unfolding scenario can be recorded in various ways including anecdotal narratives, photo essays to be revisited with children at a later time, short video clips for sharing with families in the site's lobby, and so on. From the point of view of systemic privileging, the children have been given provocation, opportunity, time, space, and the availability of resources to relive the experience, adapting it as the moment and the invitations of the environment suggest, engaging in problem-solving, decision-making, and the group dynamic during their play. In terms of assessment, the keen-eyed educator can record/tick-off multiple literacy or mathematical achievements related to textual features like rhythm and rhyme or conceptual features related to time passing and so on and so on. The fact that the play has emerged spontaneously does not lessen the potential for learning to be visible!

This style of educational encounter has been chosen for illustrative purposes as it is likely to be familiar to many readers. The shape of play and children's engagement with it will, of course, vary widely depending on the age of the children, their situation, and the geographical provision. In other instances of children's play, the provocation may not be identifiable, but characteristics of the play or some events or patterns or relationships within it can contribute to pedagogical documentation, which when dated and analysed becomes part of the record-keeping available to children, educators, families, and assessors, as well as contributing to ongoing professional reflection, planning, and evaluation (Fleet, Patterson & Robertson, 2012, 2015, 2017).

We now press 'Rewind' and return to a previous part of the recording, where we agreed that play isn't always peaceful!

Agreed, but systems can't legislate for literature-inspired playfulness, so the conversation needs to include other options. In this volume, Alcock has challenged us to think about play related to the acting-out of power dynamics. Extending that flight of thought to the physical domain, there are warnings about over-enthusiastic managing of 'risky play' (see Brussoni et al., 2012). Similarly, Wyver et al. (2010) caution against 'surplus safety' in policy development around what might be called exploratory rough-and-tumble play, while Little (2017) explores possibilities for managing risky play in regulated environments.

'Fast forward' to a point where we need to finish the chapter (the conversation itself is ongoing) and therefore reflect again on play and systems.

Our conversations over time have allowed us the privilege of listening to a wide variety of professional, community, and children's voices about play, learning, and systems. So here is the final dilemma.

Play and learning sit on a huge expanse of early education water that extends worldwide. Introducing systems and new policies is like throwing a rock into that water, creating ripples which eventually reach all shores. If these ripples are strong, they change the landscape. Are those ripples responsive to the communities and settings they touch, and are their responses heard?

Without considering which systems work, and with professional voices articulating how best to find a balance between systems and pedagogy, there is a danger that systems can become immune to failure. They are therefore not fully accountable to those who actually enact policy in the workplace.

So, sitting around this table, the tea and coffee have gone cold while the ideas have been spinning around. We have not highlighted 'everything' of potential relevance here, though we have proposed issues which we suggest need further consideration – and, Our Reader, these challenges we leave with you.

References

Allen, P. (2009). *Is Your Grandmother a Goanna?* London: Penguin.

Arnott, L., Palaiologou, I., & Gray, C. (2018). The changing nature of young children's learning ecologies, experiences and implications for pedagogy in the digital era. BERA Blog. Retrieved from www.bera.ac.uk/blog/the-changing-nature-of-young-childrens-learning-ecologies-experiences-and-implications-for-pedagogy-in-the-digital-era.

Australian Children's Education and Care Quality Authority. (2018). *Guide to the National Quality Framework*. Retrieved from www.acecqa.gov.au/sites/default/files/2018-03/Guide-to-the-NQF_0.pdf.

Australian Government. Department of Education, Employment and Workplace Relations (DEEWR). (2009). *Belonging, Being and Becoming: The Early Years Learning Framework for Australia*. Canberra, ACT: Commonwealth of Australia.

Brussoni, M., Olsen, L.L., Pike, I., & Sleet, D.A. (2012). Risky play and children's safety: Balancing priorities for optimal child development. *International Journal of Environmental Research and Public Health, 9*, pp. 3134–3148. doi:10.3390/ijerph9093134. Retrieved from www.mdpi.com/journal/ijerph.

Colliver, Y.J. (2011). State of play: Five debates that characterise play literature. Paper presented at the annual Australian Association of Research in Education conference. Hobart.

Colliver, Y.J. (2012). The five debates: Simplifying the contemporary play literature. *Early Childhood Folio, 16* (1), pp. 15–21.

Fasoli, L. (2008). Thinking about play: Perspectives on play from two remote Indigenous communities in the NT. Presentation at the 10th Annual Unpacking Conference: Possibilities of Representation. March 14/15. Macquarie University, Sydney.

Fasoli, L., Wunungmurra, A., Ecenarro, V., & Fleet, A. (2010). Playing as becoming: Sharing Australian Aboriginal voices on play. In M. Ebbeck & M. Waniganayake (Eds). *Play in Early Childhood Education: Learning in Diverse Contexts*. Melbourne: Oxford University Press (pp. 215–232).

Fleet, A., Patterson, C., & Robertson, J. (2012). *Conversations: Behind Early Childhood Pedagogical Documentation*. Mt Victoria: Pademelon Press.

Fleet, A., Patterson, C., & Robertson, J. (2015). Assessment: A critical companion to early childhood pedagogy. In M. Reed & R. Walker (Eds). *A Critical Companion to Early Childhood*. Los Angeles, CA: SAGE (pp. 296–306).

Fleet, A., Patterson, C., & Robertson, J. (2017). *Pedagogical Documentation in Early Years Practice: Seeing through Multiple Perspectives*. London: SAGE.

Government of Canada, Assembly of First Nations, Inuit Tapiriit Kanatami and Métis National Council. (2018). *The Indigenous Early Learning and Child Care Framework*. Retrieved from www.childcarecanada.org/documents/research-policy-practice/18/09/indigenous-early-learning-and-child-care-framework.

Hart, R.A. (1992). *Children's Participation: From Tokenism to Citizenship*. Innocenti Essays No. 4. Florence: UNICEF. International Child Development Centre – United Nations Children's Fund.

Hayward, L., Higgins, S., Livingston, K., & Wyse, D. (2016). Editorial. *Curriculum Journal, 27* (2), pp. 169–171. doi:10.1080/09585176.2016.1179526.

Jobb, C., MacAlpine, K., & Pacini-Ketchabaw, V. (in press). Educators experimenting with common worlds pedagogies. In L. Gibbs & M. Gasper (Eds). *Challenging the Intersection of Policy with Pedagogy*. Series Editors, A. Fleet & M. Reed. Abingdon and New York, NY: Routledge.

Little, H. (2017). Promoting risk-taking and physically challenging play in Australian early childhood settings in a changing regulatory environment. *Journal of Early Childhood Research, 15* (1), pp. 83–98.

Merewether, J. (2018). New materialisms and children's outdoor environments: Murmurative diffractions. *Children's Geographies*. Online first. doi:10.1080/14733285.2018.1471449.

Office for Standards in Education, Children's Services and Skills (Ofsted). (2015a). *Early Years Inspection Handbook*. Retrieved from www.foundationyears.org.uk/files/2015/05/Early_years_inspection_handbook.pdf.

Ofsted. (2015b). Teaching and play in the early years – a balancing act? A good practice survey to explore perceptions of teaching and play in the early years. Reference no: 150085. Retrieved from https://assets.publishing.service.gov.uk/government/uploads/system/uploads/attachment_data/file/444147/Teaching-and-play-in-the-early-years-a-balancing-act.pdf.

Pascal, C., & Bertram, T., with Goodman, D., Irvine, A., & Parr, J. (in press). Pedagogic system leadership within complex and changing ECEC. In S. Cheeseman & R. Walker (Eds). *Pedagogy in Early Education: Pedagogies for Leading Practice*. Series Editors, A. Fleet & M. Reed. Abingdon and New York, NY: Routledge.

Reed, M. & Walker, R (2017). Reflections on professionalism: Driving forces that refine and shape professional practice. Varhaiskasvatuksen Tiedelehti. *Journal of Early Childhood Education Research* 6 (2), pp. 177–187.

Santer, J., & Griffiths, C., with Goodall, D. (2007). *Free Play in Early Childhood: A Literature Review*. London: Play England and National Children's Bureau. Retrieved from www.playengland.org.uk/media/120426/free-play-in-early-childhood.pdf.

Singer, E. (2013). Play and playfulness, basic features of early childhood education. *European Early Childhood Education Research Journal*, 21 (2), pp. 172–184. doi:10.1080/1350293X.2013.789198.

Sumsion, J., Barnes, S., Cheeseman, S., Harrison, L., Kennedy, A., & Stonehouse, A. (2009). Insider perspectives on developing *Belonging, Being & Becoming: The Early Years Learning Framework for Australia*. *Australasian Journal of Early Childhood*, 34 (4), pp. 4–13.

United Nations. (1991). *UN Convention on the Rights of the Child. Article 31*. Retrieved from http://ipaworld.org/childs-right-to-play/uncrc-article-31/un-convention-on-the-rights-of-the-child-1/.

Wenger-Trayner, E., Fenton-O'Creevy, M., Hutchinson, S., Kubiak, C., & Wenger-Trayner, B. (Eds). (2014). *Learning in Landscapes of Practice: Boundaries, Identity, and Knowledgeability in Practice-Based Learning*. Abingdon and New York, NY: Routledge.

Wood, E., & Chesworth, L. (2017). Play and pedagogy. BERA Blog. Retrieved from www.bera.ac.uk/blog/play-and-pedagogy.

Wood, E.A. (2014). Free choice and free play in early childhood education: Troubling the discourse. *International Journal of Early Years Education*, 22 (1), pp. 4–18. doi:10.1080/09669760.2013.830562.

Wyver, S., Tranter, P. Naughton, G., Little, H., Sandseter, E.B.H., & Bundy, A. (2010). Ten ways to restrict children's freedom to play: The problem of surplus safety. *Contemporary Issues in Early Childhood*, 11 (3), pp. 263–277. doi:10.2304/ciec.2010.11.3.263.

Further reading

Multiple online and library-shelf references exist to assist you in continuing the conversation. We offer a few:

Edwards, S. (2017). Play-based learning and intentional teaching: Forever different? *Australasian Journal of Early Childhood*, 42 (2), pp. 4–11. doi:10.23965/AJEC.42.2.01.

Gibson, J.L., Cornell, M., & Gill, T. (2017). A systematic review of research into the impact of loose parts play on children's cognitive, social and emotional development. *School Mental Health*, 9 (4), p. 295.

Lowell, A., Maypilama, E.L., Fasoli, L., Gundjarranbuy, R., Godwin-Thompson, J., Guyula, A., Yunupiŋu, M., Armstrong, E., Garrutju, J., & McEldowney, R. (2018). Building *Yolŋu* skills, knowledge, and priorities into early childhood assessment and support: Protocol for a qualitative study. *JMIR Research Protocol*, 7 (3), p. e50. doi:10.2196/resprot.8722. Retrieved from www.ncbi.nlm.nih.gov/pubmed/29514777.

Pyle, A., & Danniels, E. (2017). A continuum of play-based learning: The role of the teacher in play-based pedagogy and the fear of hijacking play. *Journal of Early Education and Development*, 28 (3), pp. 274–289.

Pyle, A., DeLuca, C., & Danniels, E. (2017). Context and implications document for: A scoping review of research on play-based pedagogies in kindergarten education. *Review of Education*, 5 (3), pp. 352–353. doi:10.1002/rev3.3098.

11
INFLUENCES OF MACROSYSTEMS ON CHILDREN'S SPACES
Regaining the paradigm

Mandy Andrews

This chapter refers to the 1989 paper 'The developing ecology of human development: Paradigm lost or paradigm regained' (Bronfenbrenner, Ed.) in which he decries how studies purportedly subscribing to his ecological orientation have focused far more on the systems and 'the nature of developmentally relevant environments, near and far, than about the characteristics of developing individuals' which characteristics, and adventures in turn influence, the environments in which the individuals develop (p. 95). If we recognise that Bronfenbrenner's model was influenced by Kurt Lewin's psychological field of forces (Lewin, 1931, 1935) with its powerful pressures and reductive challenges in interaction, life and 'becoming' can be perceived as two-way interactions between the child and community and the policy/ideology intent on shaping the child. Just as policy/ideology impacts on children's spaces, so children too can have an impact on the conceived grounds they are given. Lewin also emphasised that spaces are not just physical but also psychological. Within such a concept of interaction, where the child has agency, space can be understood as physical, perceived *and* conceived, *but also regained and lived (Lefebvre, 1974/1991). This opens the door to postmodern and post-humanist understandings, in which children can select and acquire spaces for play (or do the spaces select them?). Such an intra-active perception is contrary to the systemic macrosystemic striations often perceived in Bronfenbrenner's model when seen as nested controlling influences on children and their spaces operating in a top-down or* '*outward-in*' *model. In taking this interactive/intra-active perspective, we can consider where children are expected to play, where they really choose to play, what the landscapes and materials offer to children, and perhaps ultimately, to policy decisions and ideological understandings.*

Childhood is a social construct. Play is also a social construct with many interpretations; the places for children to play may be politically and socially conceived. However, although we may generally understand the notions of 'child', 'childhood' and 'play' or even 'playground' these terms may mean different things to different people. This difference arises from the individual experiences, philosophical and political ideologies that dominate any society at any time. Such ideologies will also shape our pedagogies and ways of being or becoming with children.

Since 1989, for example, the United Nations Convention on the Rights of the Child (UNCRC) has influenced understandings about children and childhood. Article 31 highlighted the child's right to play. In the UK, there was a brief period of focus on this right to play with the funding of Play England and encouragement for each local authority to develop a play strategy to draw down play area funding. Tired community playgrounds were subsequently reclaimed and renewed or newly built. Funding, however, has since been reduced; in 2013 the UN Commission issued a statement of concern at the poor recognition given to the rights to play contained in Article 31, citing findings of

> poor recognition of their significance in the lives of children ... lack of investment in appropriate provisions, weak or non-existent protective legislation and the invisibility of children in national and local level planning. In general, where investment is made, it is in the provision of structured and organized activities, but equally important is the need to create time and space for children to engage in spontaneous play, recreation and creativity.
> (2013, UNCRC General Comment No. 17: point 2.)

There are several conceptual understandings here that could be unpacked, such as 'space' for play, 'time' and the conceptualisation of 'spontaneous play', 'recreation' and 'creativity'. There are also questions of power and responsibility, with mention of the 'invisibility of children' in national and local level planning. It is sufficient, however, to note that policy was in place for the benefit of the child but was not meeting the need UNCRC was advocating for.

In Sheffield, a study identified that four generations of children of the same age had increasingly reducing access to the environment, to roam and play with geographical freedom (Woolley & Griffin, 2015). An 8-year-old child in 1926 was able to roam freely for distances of up to 6 miles, whilst in 2007 an 8-year-old child in the same location had a roaming distance of only 300 yards. What had happened to so restrict children's 'spontaneous play'? Perceptions of child capability were perhaps reducing, maybe social context and demographics had impacted upon children's lives with perceived dangers of heavier traffic, or people were possibly more aware of the dangers highlighted by media coverage of serious accidents and child abduction. Whatever the reason, it is claimed that there are fewer children 'playing out' than a decade earlier, and because of the rarity of children on the street, they are in danger of becoming perceived to be 'out of context' when they are playing out, and in turn this could create a spiral of increasing restriction on spontaneous (outdoor) play.

The context, and social and ideological understanding, are important in shaping the social and political responses of the time and, consequently, the impact on the developing child. This understanding of pedagogy, play and politics takes us into an arena of acknowledged complexity – in policy, ideology, context and interaction: an arena that moves beyond cosy nested systems to generate new play areas and binary pressures for and against, to one that recognises equalising benefits in postmodernity, decentralisation, 'entanglements' and intra-actions, chance encounters and creative innovation. One that allows children to claim and reclaim play spaces.

Since the 1980s, much use has been made of Bronfenbrenner's 'Ecology of Human Development' (Bronfenbrenner, 1979) as a model to consider policy and environments affecting or effecting children's development. His model placed responsibility, just as the UNCRC does, on the states and governments to put into place policies to support the developing child based on a linear concept of time and progression as development, a 'person–process–context' model. Bronfenbrenner (1979) argued in some of his works that the child was the site of the future, and that it was the responsibility of communities to ensure the right environmental conditions for child development. Bronfenbrenner's ecological model is often drawn as a series of concentric circles with the child at the centre, nested in the family surrounded by influences of community, school and then of parental culture and work, policy, governance and social norms, and finally the overarching patterns and ideological influences of a given cultural/social context. It was written initially as an argument for moving away from experimental understandings of child development where the developing child had been considered in isolation from their context. Bronfenbrenner's (1979) ecological model prompted priority consideration of children's environments as influencing factors on their development:

> The ecology of human development is the scientific study of the progressive, mutual accommodation between an active, growing human being and the changing properties of the immediate settings in which the developing person lives as this process is affected by the relations between these settings and by the larger contexts in which the settings are embedded.
> (Bronfenbrenner, 2005, p. 107)

Ideological and conceptual understandings shift as cultural understandings change. Some theoretical models slip from being avant-garde into common usage. Such usage may result in the model being re-interpreted, simplified and given a contemporary 'spin'. Bronfenbrenner's model has become so commonly used that it is no longer a challenging philosophical model, but a secure and familiar 'map' for analysis of each concentric circle, often to affirm what is expected in layers of social policy. Bronfenbrenner had even promoted this idea in his paper of 1985, in which he argued that the process or system of making human beings human was breaking down in modern society and there was a need for conceived government intervention to make it work again. Later – in 1989 – he complained about the success of his own model which had become over-used to explore contexts and contextual influences without reflecting on the developing child as an influence on these contexts; he wished to regain the paradigm.

Revisiting Bronfenbrenner's early texts and seeking again the context and understandings below the surface brings it to life with renewed interpretation that becomes relevant to the philosophical and theoretical shifts towards postmodernism, the material turn and even emerging posthuman positionality as these begin to influence pedagogy today. Bronfenbrenner's early models said that rather than the child being passively nested within its family's arms, the child was agentic in prompting change in the family, community, policy and even ideological arenas.

Adulteration of children's lives

Children's lives are largely controlled by adults, their play experiences adulterated by adults (Sturrock & Else, 2001). Policy shapes lives. Children must attend school, roads are laid in certain places, playgrounds and open spaces are conceptualised for certain purposes. Children may be 'taken' to play at certain times of the day and then after half an hour 'taken home' again in a very time-bound way of life. Communities acting in dialogue also shape children's lives – think of the expectation of children playing, or not playing, on a certain street. A green with many houses overlooking it inhabited by families with young children may have a culture of 'playing out'. A green overlooked by many elderly people who are fearful of noise and ball-playing on the green may end up with a 'No ball games' sign and an expectation that it is irresponsible to let your children 'play out'. Parents and older family members reinforce the cultural norms in shaping children's behaviours and affective responses. Children rarely have a say in these decisions.

Whilst Bronfenbrenner's model was developed in part as an 'organised' system of nested influences at the centre of which was the child, postmodern philosophers such as Deleuze and Guattari (2005) promote a way of being that is not a hierarchical striated structure, instead recognising a flattened structure with random interactions of people, materials, things and entanglements leading creatively to different actions and ways of being. In this conceptual world, things are 'self-organising', not obeying determined laws and rules, but emerging from chance encounters and nomadic behaviours. In these conceptualisations, play can be stimulated by others, landscapes, things, animals and creatures and so on, indeed as a process of intra-active engagement. In the developing theoretical constructs, it is possible to see a shift from focus on the developing and adapting individual, who may be supported by an informed adult looking on benevolently, through engagement with the environment to an understanding of complexity and relational activity that is almost random.

Bronfenbrenner developed his ecological theory during a period of friendship with Kurt Lewin, who was interested in field theory and most famous for his consideration of force field analysis: that all things have 'tensions' with driving forces on one side and alleviating forces on the other. When facing change, you can either drive further or consider how the alleviating forces may be adjusted and adapted to ensure that the forward movement required occurs. A deeper reading of these two works revealed that Bronfenbrenner drew on the work of Lewin. An understanding of this link and also of the influence of quantum physics on Lewin's work, and consequently on Bronfenbrenner's ecological model, can adjust our understanding of both their meanings. This reveals the relevance of his model to the conceptual journey to the current emergence of postmodern and posthuman thinking about children and their play, also informed by quantum physics. If we add to the mix Lefebvre's (1974/1991) understandings of power and resistance (play at the edge of the force field), we can also think about adult positionality in relation to children's play and access to play spaces. This opens the door to postmodern, and posthuman, conceptualising of intra-action.

Bronfenbrenner's ecological approach

Bronfenbrenner's model is very well known in early childhood research and developmental assessment. Often illustrated as a series of nested arenas, it offers opportunities for analysis of the contextual influences on a child's changing development, with the later addition of the chronosystem as development over time. The child is very firmly situated in the centre of this ecological model, the intention of which was to broaden conceptualisation of development beyond the singularity of the child to a recognition of external influences. Bronfenbrenner felt that development should not be studied in false laboratory-type conditions but in 'the actual environments in which human beings live and grow' (Bronfenbrenner, 1979). These ideas of the importance of context are ideas we now take for granted with naturalistic child observations *in situ* but were innovative at the time.

Bronfenbrenner initially described his new ecological model of human development as

> the scientific study of development as a function of the progressive, reciprocal interplay, through the life course, between an active, growing human organism and the changing properties of its environment, both immediate and more remote.
> (Bronfenbrenner, 1989, p. 95)

The model focused on the many contextual systems that impact upon a child's development. The innermost of these circles, in which the child is usually centrally positioned, is the microsystem – the arena in which interconnections between people closest to the child are formulated towards each other as a group engaged in common, complementary or independent tasks. This is frequently considered as the relationship between child and parents, but could be child and siblings, extended family, perhaps pets. The second arena of the ecological environment is the mesosystem – which comprises relationships between two or more settings in which the child is an active participant. This can include interconnections for the child between home, school, peer groups, different family contexts. The mesosystem recognises the many systems of localised influence jostling for priority as a system of microsystems. This area draws on Lewinian ideas of force fields of inner and outer pressures working with or against each other.

Beyond the mesosystem is the exosystem – an arena which does not in itself contain a developing person, but which envelops the mesosystem. Events occur in the exosystem that affect the arenas or systems containing the person. Therefore, in the exosystem we have things such as parents' workplace, processes of schooling, local government policies and so on. Social institutions that make decisions ultimately affecting conditions of family life function as exosystems. The final outer ring of the environment in the labelled versions of this model was the macrosystem, which encompasses the overarching patterns of stability for the society in which the micro and mesosystems operate. These reflect the cultural norms, social organisation, belief systems and lifestyles in which the child or person is developing.

Bronfenbrenner's work clearly placed developmental influence not only in the genetic unfolding nature of the child, but also in the phenomenon of the transformative interaction and influence of environment upon the child and later of the child upon environment:

> from its beginnings, development involves interaction between organism and environment. Moreover, interaction implies a two-way activity. The external becomes internal and becomes transformed in the process. But because, from its beginnings the organism begins to change its environment the internal becomes external and becomes transformed in the process.
> (Bronfenbrenner, 1993, p. 177)

This understanding opens the door to a wider environmental consideration of children's activities as intra-active and embodied in which encounters become internalised.

An aspect of Lewin's work also focused on perception and response, acknowledging 'features of the environment that threaten, beckon, reassure, and steer one's course across a terrain' (Bronfenbrenner, 1977, p. 45), perhaps offering a nod towards the agency of things to change the course of a person's action. Lewin conceived of groups as interconnections, not with so much focus towards interpersonal feelings as a recognition of the relationships of various parties towards each other as they moved towards common purposes; or were engaged in complementary but independent tasks.

Lewin analysed how rigid epistemological frameworks and labels (such as taxonomies of play and lists of play types) restrict understandings of children and their capabilities as they pre-empt and combine crudely a range of ideas generating 'illusions'. Such an approach sets adult apart from child and leads to a conceptualisation of erroneous children who do not behave like adults. In this way, Lewin argued, we had developed 'utilitarian concepts of pedagogy' (Lewin, 2013, p. 15) in which standardised adulthood was the product. Just as we now understand 'play', 'playful' and 'not play' as a spectrum, so too, drawing on modern quantum physics, Lewin presented that binary configurations such as 'man: woman'; 'dry: wet'; 'adult: child'; 'work: play' have been almost entirely replaced by continuous graduations. He acknowledged there is something in the middle that is neither child- nor adult-led, but people of different ages 'becoming' together as they move towards a new level of knowledge, ability and understanding that is not predefined. Each encounter is thus unique within the process of a particular dynamic moment. For Lewin, any behaviour is a function of the individual in relation to others and their environment. The environment prompts a certain behaviour, but humans seek mastery over the environment (perhaps by building a mound, or flattening a bump); so, we get to field forces and opposing pressures that can either be worked with or released.

Lewin's ideas influenced Bronfenbrenner's ecological model; we can begin to see how the field forces tensions exist not only in the mesosystem (as a range of microsystems jostle for priority, exerting force as they do so) but that there is a 'force field' between all concentric spheres of influence. This opens our thinking to the understanding that not only does the ideology influence the community which influences the family which exerts influence on the child, but the forces operate the other way too. So, the child exerts influence upon the family, friends and ultimately the culture and ideology in which he or she exists. Each exertion of pressure or 'force' instigates a particular process and resultant unique behaviour as a response to these interactions.

Lewin further expands his understanding of 'force' at play through a consideration of physics and rules of 'force'. He highlights how, if 'rules' were applied evenly, and a child was faced with two equal choices, say chocolate and toy, in classic, balanced theory alone, the child would reach neither, but take a trajectory in response to both forces giving a pathway between the two. Usually, however, a child releases one force and follows the other to reach the chocolate or toy. Conception and agency play a part and the forces bend. Where the child wants to get to the piece of chocolate and forces get in the way – an object or perhaps a dog crossing the intended path, then the trajectory is adjusted to enable the child to reach their goal in a roundabout way. Lewin argues that the totality of the forces in the field, the attractive object, others and the physical barriers, will together control the direction of the process. Bronfenbrenner's model, drawing initially on, and then moving beyond, Lewinian field force theory, effectively moved the understanding of 'what is' in human development to 'what could be' according to social context. With all this complexity behind his model, Bronfenbrenner expressed dismay at its simplistic use with an over-emphasis on shaping the contexts for development to the extent that often the child's role in the developmental process was discarded. In part, this focus that he bemoans was generated by his own work in 1988, in which he argued for a strengthening of the family systems:

> children need the consistent and reliable care of their parents ... but to provide that care the parents need the support of employers, schools and society as a whole ... Just as we are becoming more aware that we have the capacity to destroy the natural environment and must take vigorous steps to preserve it, we must use our growing knowledge of the ecology of human development to protect and strengthen it in the face of threats we have unwittingly created.
> (Bronfenbrenner, 1988, p. 260)

Whilst this placed the child at the centre of an ecological consideration, this also placed the adult human in a controlling position, detached from the subject (the child) and able to put in place measures to increase play – a position in which adults 'make the right decisions' for the benefit of children at the centre of the ecosystem. So, whilst child and environment are recognised as interacting for development, the model also acknowledged children as the 'subjects' directed to an adult purpose (successful future adulthood).

Thinking about power and space: Who makes the decisions about the play opportunities in your setting? How far are you able to allow children to develop their own policy solutions in relation to play spaces and places?

Lefebvrian considerations of space as sites of tension and interpretation

If play is about children's freedom to explore, experiment, generate, create (Hughes, 2012), and the UNCRC is calling for more play that is spontaneous, how is this opportunity constrained by the adult concentric environments generated in an adult-centred productive ecological systems model? Might the spaces be generated in line with Bronfenbrenner's concern to protect the ecology of the child, but, perhaps also for the best reasons, by adults with a structured, instrumentalist, systemic approach? Have you ever wondered why playgrounds are where they are? Is it sometimes about keeping children away from certain areas so that there is no disturbance? Is fencing to keep dogs out, or to keep children in?

Bronfenbrenner argued that the developing child also begins to change its environment with the internal becoming external and transformed during the process. Lefebvre (1974/1991) offers us a model by which we may consider how children may understand places and spaces differently from their intended purpose. A departure from Bronfenbrenner's systems theory, critical theory can be used to assist in the initial consideration of powerful constraints and opportunities impacting on children's access to play and playful spaces – a different kind of tension between fields of power. It is the child that lives in a 'milieu of potentiality' (Sturrock, 1997, p. 36) whilst the adult still generates spaces within which the child has opportunity to engage with play. Adults become 'habitual', conforming to norms of societies less and less attuned to the need for play, yet it is these adults who shape the children's spaces and access to play. Sturrock

(1997) asserts that children are spending more and more of their time in institutionalised contexts, play spaces and nursery settings, which he saw as symbols of adult hegemony to children. Yet again this nods to Bronfenbrenner's dual process and potentialities; children can 'kick back' against the design of the spaces, challenging or 'owning and living' in them.

Conceived, perceived and lived space

Lefebvre acknowledged that there is a difference between spaces conceived for a purpose by those in power, spaces perceived through the symbols, and spaces 'lived' and owned by the users of those spaces (1974/1991, pp. 38–39). His model can help us consider the binary tensions between those who conceive of spaces and those who acquisition and appropriate spaces for their play use.

1. Conceived space refers to the design of space for purpose by those with power. These are instrumental spaces designed to shape people's behaviour, and the way they live their lives. Lefebvre refers to the space of planners, urbanists and 'technocratic subdividers' (1974/1991, p. 38). Planners and architects will reflect on need and design play spaces for purposes. So, playgrounds may be designed to direct young people away from residential areas for ball games, or with physical health in mind. A conceived space is led by conceptual understandings of what that space is supposed to do.
2. Perceived space on the other hand is about how space is lived in and understood by those who live in it. So, the designed space can be perceived as controlling, or anarchic if children are alienated by the space they are given. Children may say things like 'Our park is great, it keeps us out of trouble', adopting the conceived purpose; or they may say, 'The playground is not proper play because the adults stop it.' They may then choose to play in alternative spaces.
3. Lived space is a space of representation, creativity, escape from and an alternative to conceived or perceived spaces. Space here becomes interpreted and makes use of symbolic objects and signs to 'inhabit' the space and make it one's own.

How does this translate to children's play spaces? In terms of conceived space, there are the readymade playgrounds, carefully designed within walking distance of a community, with dogs fenced out, and perhaps with parking nearby to ensure easy accessible for families. Signs may warn users to use the equipment appropriately, to keep the gate shut so that dogs cannot enter, and to play no ball games. They may say that some equipment is for younger children and others for older children. They may indicate that there should be no play outside of this area. Fences and barriers ensure that the equipment can only be used in the way intended. Careful thought would have led to climbing, swinging and rotating equipment being in place. The spaces have been conceived and put in place by planners and surveyors according to current guidance and with perhaps some consultation with children. They may equally cut across children's former play spaces, divide up areas or fence across pathways.

Conceived space in a nursery garden may be one laid out to encourage areas of learning, or perhaps physical, social, creative and elemental play. A forest school is conceived in terms of the formula of trees, fire pit, logs around the fire which also act as a barrier to running across the fire, and perhaps a shed to keep the 'forest school' equipment in it.

Why not pause here and reflect on any play space of which you are aware. What is its conceived purpose? Does it have a range of areas designed to shape the way that children behave in them? Have you some conceived 'formulaic' areas to be used only in a certain way?

Perceived spaces may be designed for a purpose or appropriated for a purpose. A flat area of grass in front of houses, even without goals, can be perceived as a football pitch. The bars designed to retain shopping trolleys can – when empty – be perceived as bars for acrobatics and swinging upside down. I have observed children creating 'trails' at the borders of conceived play spaces, perceiving that the liminal areas of bushes, banks and trees offer greater play opportunity than the mown areas, purposeful structures and safety bark.

Lived spaces in terms of free, roaming play are often identifiable by the symbols that inform people that children are playing here. Lived space can be indicated by symbolic placement of things (that old ladder used to get over a park wall to the open space beyond, the bucket or tyre hanging up as a swing, the old blanket and curtains hung over bushes indicating a 'den'). Lived space can also be about chalk marks on the floor, 'This is my home, keep out' or 'No adults here' on the shed.

Children may also generate future culture and conceived spaces through their use of space. Children building and using a skateboard area from rubbish, pipes and planks near to their homes may in time lead to the local authority deciding to construct a skate park within walking distance with a conceived purpose of providing what the children want and have articulated that they need, but of moving it to a more appropriate position. There may be a secondary conceived purpose of keeping children off the roads. Children may not have an official role in relation to designing spaces for 'spontaneous play' (UNCRC, 2013) but can still influence through creative, lived activity. Spaces can therefore be used in a conformist way, or children may 'disrupt' their intended use.

Reflective moment: Do children challenge conceived space in your setting? Where does this occur? How can you support this agentic challenge?

Juxtaposition of two very different conceptual models, Bronfenbrenner's ecological system and Lefebvre's critical conceptualisation of space, allows us to look both at the control of children's space and the challenges to cultural understandings of space purpose, and may go some way to 'regaining' the paradigm of ecological interaction. In both of these models, however, the 'human' adult or child remains at the centre. Let us now try pushing a little further Bronfenbrenner's statement that,

> From its beginnings, development involves interaction between organism and environment. Moreover, interaction implies a two-way activity.
>
> (1993, p. 177)

Postmodernism and posthuman materiality

Imagine now that the power binaries of Lefebvrian post-Marxism and the 'adult: child' or 'family: community' binaries of Bronfenbrenner can give way to 'immanent entanglements' (Deleuze & Guattari, 2005) as the human (child and adult) is 'decentred' and placed alongside material things, creatures and landscapes on an equal footing. It is no longer 'man's role' to shape the future, but rather the present is shaped through the process of play itself, by processes of engagement and intra-action. This shift to a non-anthropocentric position attempts to recognise that humans are only one species amongst many in the world and that life itself is a self-organising system. A shift to a non-anthropocentric way of thinking can decentre the adult perspective on children's play, reducing the potential for adulteration, but also enabling consideration of material influences and elemental persuasions of the potentiality of play. Becoming posthuman involves the shift from a consideration of subjectivity to the production of subjectivity and a capacity to reciprocally change with the environment and to affect and be affected in a relationship of commutation (Athanasiadou, 2018, p. 86, citing Deleuze, 1988b, p. 124).

Commutation can be here referred to as 'exchange'. The 'exchange' may be person to person, or intra-active response to landscapes that slope, rock that warms, elements that intrigue, bushes and seeds to spread. There are some similarities to the two-way interaction between organism and environment that Bronfenbrenner refers to above, but rather than two-way this is many-way, each subjective moment being the result of the potentialities of intra-actions of that moment. Quantum physics has offered an understanding of the world that indicates it is not always predictable, following set rules, but that there are moments of exchange that generate something new. Think of a wave hitting a wave and generating a higher peak and lower trough merely through the moment of intra-action and combined energy. The peak and trough are not there before the intra-active moment of potentiality as the two waves meet. Play itself may be that moment of generation and differentiation.

This may also be an affirmative, equitable approach that helps in the balance of 'adult: child' or 'human: animal' conceived imbalance. In a decentred posthuman approach, all bodies – not just human, adult bodies – count. Taguchi (2010) describes this approach as not being 'in the world' as onlooker and actor looking down and labelling and knowing, nor as an approach that is engaged with social dialogue co-constructing social meaning but as a way of being of-the-world, embedded and engaged with it. In terms of pedagogy, adult and child can engage together as equals, and play is not planned and purposeful but spontaneous and vital as the play moment is not leading anywhere but is spontaneously unpredictable. Related to such a model are conceptualisations of play as not merely activities to be labelled with taxonomies of types, but as a moment of vitality, generating the 'wobble' to the striated existence in conceived spaces (Lester, 2018).

So, what might this mean for play, play policy and pedagogic practice? Bronfenbrenner's nested system becomes reclaimed interactively anew, but the power relationship is rescinded. It may also require a decentring of the observational perspective of the child to consider the agentic matter around the child or what many call a 'diffractive' analysis (Barad 2007; Murris 2016). A child playing on a log on a day without wind may be very different to a child playing on a log on a windy day when balance is difficult and there is an affective excitement in the strength of the elements. The entanglements and intra-actions stimulating the play moment should be considered. One moment I observed was the chance finding of a chair, the stimulation of the wind on the top of the hill, a dog, tall grass and other children. The intra-action of these led to an armchair placed on top of a knoll facing the wind and shaping the strength of the wind such that the children playing had an affective response of energetic running around, making the dog bark, which generated further giggles and adjustments to the play routes around the running dog.

The importance of such decentred, immanent positionality and new materiality offered by the posthumanist philosophers and authors such as Braidotti (2013), Barad (2007), Taguchi (2010) and Murris (2016) offer a new way not of 'development' but of 'becoming' together as we are all becomings, one that is equalising and generative. This latter positionality moves the adult human to side-frame, enabling the spontaneous generation of play moments.

References

Athanasiadou, L. (2018). Commutation ontology. In Braidotti, R., & Hlavajova, M. (Eds.), *Posthuman Glossary*. London: Bloomsbury, pp. 86–88.

Barad, K. (2007). *Meeting the Universe Halfway: Quantum Physics and the Entanglement of Matter and Meaning*. Durham, NC: Duke University Press.

Braidotti, R. (2013). *The Posthuman*. Cambridge: Polity Press.

Bronfenbrenner, U. (1977). Lewinian space and ecological substance. In Bronfenbrenner, U. (Ed., 2005). *Making Human Beings Human: Bioecological Perspectives on Human Development*. London: SAGE, pp. 41–49.

Bronfenbrenner, U. (1979). A future perspective. In Bronfenbrenner, U. (Ed., 2005). *Making Human Beings Human: Bioecological Perspectives on Human Development*. London: SAGE, pp. 50–59.

Bronfenbrenner, U. (1988). Strengthening family systems. In Bronfenbrenner, U. (Ed., 2005). *Making Human Beings Human: Bioecological Perspectives on Human Development*. London: SAGE, pp. 260–273. Paper presented at the Biennial Meeting of the Society for Research in Child Development, Kansas City, Missouri, April 27–30, 1989.

Bronfenbrenner, U. (Ed.) (1989). The developing ecology of human development: Paradigm lost or paradigm regained. In Bronfenbrenner, U. (Ed., 2005). *Making Human Beings Human: Bioecological Perspectives on Human Development*. London: SAGE, pp. 94–105.

Bronfenbrenner, U. (1993). Heredity, environment and the question 'How': A first approximation. In Bronfenbrenner, U. (Ed., 2005). *Making Human Beings Human: Bioecological Perspectives on Human Development*. London: SAGE, pp. 174–184.

Bronfenbrenner, U. (Ed.) (2005). *Making Human Beings Human: Bioecological Perspectives on Human Development*. London: SAGE.

Deleuze, G., & Guattari, F. (2005). *A Thousand Plateaus: Capitalism and Schizophrenia*. Translated by Brian Massumi. London and Minneapolis, MN: University of Minnesota Press.

Hughes, B. (2012). *Evolutionary Playwork: Reflective Analytic Practice* (2nd Ed.). London: Routledge.

Lefebvre, H. (1974/1991). *The Production of Space*. Translated by D. Nicholson-Smith. Oxford: Blackwell.

Lester, S. (2018). Bringing play to life and life to play: A vitalist line of enquiry. In Russell, W., Ryall, E., & MacLean, M. (Eds). *The Philosophy of Play as Life*. London: Routledge, pp. 13–26.

Lewin, K. (1931). Environmental forces in child behaviour and development. In Murchison, C. (Ed.). *A Handbook of Child Psychology*. Oxford: Clark University Press, pp. 94–127.

Lewin, K. (1935). *A Dynamic Theory of Personality*. New York, NY: McGraw-Hill.

Lewin, K. (2013). *A Dynamic Theory of Personality: Selected Papers*. Redditch: Read Books.

Murris, K. (2016). *The Posthuman Child: Educational Transformation Through Philosophy with Picturebooks*. London and New York, NY: Routledge.

Sturrock, G. (1997). Play is peace. In Sturrock, G., & Else, P. (Eds, 2001). *Therapeutic Playwork Reader One*. Eastleigh: Common Threads, pp. 29–39.

Sturrock, G., & Else, P. (2001) The Colorado paper: The playground as therapeutic space – playwork as healing. In Sturrock, G., & Else, P. (Eds). *Therapeutic Playwork Reader One*. Eastleigh: Common Threads, pp. 73–104.

Taguchi, H. L. (2010). *Beyond the Theory Practice Divide*. London: Routledge.

United Nations Committee on the Rights of the Child. (2013). *General Comment No. 17 (2013) on the Right of the Child to Rest, Leisure, Play, Recreational Activities, Cultural Life and the Arts (Art. 31)*. Geneva: Committee on the Rights of the Child.

Woolley, H.E., & Griffin, E. (2015). Decreasing experiences of home range, outdoor spaces, activities and companions: changes across three generations in Sheffield in north England. *Children's Geographies*, 13 (6), pp. 677–691.

12
MICRO-POLICIES OF ADULT–CHILD JOINT PLAY IN THE CONTEXT OF THE FINNISH ECEC SYSTEM

Maiju Paananen and Anna Pauliina Rainio

Research supports the role of reciprocal imaginative play in developing a sense of 'togetherness' and empathy (i.e., Hännikäinen, 2007) and promoting social justice in preschool classrooms (Ferholt & Lecusay, 2010). In the Finnish National Curriculum guidelines on early childhood education and care (ECEC) 2016, adult participation in children's play is recognized as valuable from the perspective of equity and in its own right. Teachers are encouraged to create joint playworlds together with children. Simultaneously, in line with a worldwide trend, preschools in Finland have met rising expectations of efficiency, leading to pressures to demonstrate performance. Under such conditions, it is more difficult to ensure that play activities in preschools occur with adult involvement in children's play. National policies provide a context for making decisions concerning ECEC arrangements. These policy spaces have not been widely examined from the perspective of the daily life of people influenced by them. In this chapter, we highlight how possibilities for play are formed in complex interactions between national and local policies. Through two case studies, we explore the potential and challenges of different kinds of play-based pedagogical activities to persist under pressures from intensification measures and scarcening resources.

In the newest Core Curriculum (2016) that regulates Finnish ECEC, adult–child joint play and adult participation in children's play is recognized as valuable from both a developmental and an equity perspective. The significance of play for children also lies in the play itself: children 'structure and explore the surrounding world, create social relations and form meanings based on their experiences ... construct ideas of themselves and others through play and experiment with different roles and ideas which they could otherwise not carry out' (ECEC Core Curriculum, 2016, p. 63). The curriculum suggests that pedagogical activities (drama, storytelling) can be combined in developing play and constructing imaginary worlds. Play is constructed as neither only instrumental nor only important in its own right, but as a combination of both. Thus, the curriculum illuminates how Finnish ECEC, in addition to being built on Pestalozzi's and Froebel's tradition (see Onnismaa & Kalliala, 2010), reflects the influence of Vygotsky's (1978, 1987) theories of play.

The Core Curriculum also gives guidelines for adults' role in play. It is stated that 'the personnel must acknowledge the significance of concentrated exploration, spontaneous creative expression as well as boisterous play and physical games on children's well-being and learning'. The personnel must ensure that each child gets an opportunity to participate in playing with others according to their skills and capabilities and support the development of children's play by either guiding it from the outside or participating in it (2016, p. 64). Teachers construct play opportunities ensuring equity, in particular the societal function of ensuring social justice: that every child feels included in the group, is being heard, and gains experiences of belonging and joy (Paananen, 2017a).

In line with global trends, however, preschools have to respond to increased pressures to demonstrate performance (Paananen, 2017a). Research indicates that under such conditions, it is more difficult to ensure long-term play activities in preschools with adults in children's play (Paananen, 2017a). These national policies provide a context – a policy terrain – for making decisions concerning ECEC arrangements. Previous literature has explored how policies become translated and adapted when they are moved from one context to another (McCann & Ward, 2011, 2012), sometimes in surprising forms at the national level (Hay, 2004).

As we will demonstrate, national policies that strongly support and emphasize play do not necessarily lead to practices where play has an important role. Rather, they become entangled with local policies and lead to varying practices. We examine how play is simultaneously constrained and made possible by micro-policies. By micro-policies, we mean how decisions concerning the daily practices of preschools are made: how different policy aims become mediated into actual practices; how national and local policies are interpreted; what is considered important when making daily decisions; whose perspective counts, and why?

We use evidence from two ethnographic case studies of Finnish public preschools to establish our argument. We will show – drawing on the first author, Maiju's, study (Paananen, 2017a, 2017b) – how competing aims in national- and municipal-level policies may overrule aims related to play. Then, using the second author, Anna's, data (Rainio, 2010), we will examine the potential conditions in which play remains strong in the daily life of these settings. Contrasting these two examples allows us to ponder what can be done to support adult–child joint play in early childhood settings.

- What does your national curriculum state regarding children's play in early learning and adults' role in children's play?

Example 1: Micro-policies that make play yield to other aims in the daily practices of preschools

In the first study, Maiju used multiple data-generation methods to examine micro-policies in the site: the role of different kinds of governing tools, such as curriculum documents, calendar markings, and schedules – as well as interpretations related to them – to make decisions concerning daily life and practices of the early childhood settings. She asked 13 teachers to keep a diary for one work day and to allow the researchers access to their planning for individual children. Maiju used document-aided interviews of participant teachers to obtain more information concerning the situations they described in their diaries. Interviews were recorded and transcribed verbatim.

Observation data were generated over a four-month period at a small public preschool. Maiju observed daily life in a group of 26 three- to five-year-old children and four adults. Two of the group's staff members worked as preschool teachers. The other two were nursery nurses. Three of the children needed special support. Consent to conduct the study was gained from the children's parents, staff members, and the municipality. Maiju also attended weekly meetings of the group when possible, collecting the meeting minutes, plans created, and staff instructions.

All the situations related to play were selected for analysis. While examining this dataset, it became evident that play and aims that tied closely with children's play seemed to be in turmoil (see also Paananen, 2017a).

Participant teachers described play situations in their diaries. Based on this data, one can definitely say that play has a central role in the daily life of preschools in Finland; but strikingly, the observed situations consisted, almost solely, of situations in which children engaged in role play, or played with toys or other construction sets in groups of two to five children with no adult participation. If adults participated, they were mainly visiting the play situations briefly to solve a problem or suggest a new element in the play, or as temporary participants, such as customers in a shop.

In interviews, the importance of play was emphasized, especially when speaking about children with special needs and children whose social skills did not meet preschool expectations. Teachers felt that some children needed adult help joining and engaging in joint play to develop a sense of belonging and agency; thus teachers viewed play as essential to ensuring equity.

When examining the situation from the perspective of individual children, however, the situation seems a bit different. In Maiju's field notes, some children almost never engaged in play activities with other children. One of these children was a four-year-old child we will call Oliver. He had difficulties communicating with others. It was also agreed in his individual ECEC plan[1] that adults help him in transition situations and engaging in play with other children.

The following is based on Maiju's ethnographic field notes and describes one morning with Oliver:

> Oliver is eating breakfast with a teacher and 12 other children. He is trying to start a conversation with the teacher: "Listen, do you know *Pippi Longstocking*?" The teacher does not answer. She gives advice to other children. Oliver tries again, but the teacher does not respond. Oliver makes eye contact with another boy, and they begin making faces. They giggle and start to waggle more and more wildly. A breakfast roll Oliver is eating falls from the table.
>
> Now the teacher notices Oliver and reacts: "Your breakfast is finished. It is time to go to the toilet, and then get dressed for the outdoor play." However, while some other children follow the instruction, the teacher directs Oliver to a reading corner instead as it is agreed in Oliver's individual

early childhood education plan that Oliver needs adult help in transitions. Oliver can go to dress-up when a nurse from another group, Hanna, comes to help him. Oliver is reading when Hanna comes. He does not want to leave just yet; he has not finished reading the book he has selected. Hanna does not have much time since she needs to go back to her own group. Oliver can't finish his reading.

Later, outdoors, another boy, Simo, is pushing a wheelbarrow. Oliver tries to sit on the wheelbarrow. "Simo can't give you a ride with a wheelbarrow. You are too heavy," says a nurse. Oliver leaves the situation.

Oliver wanders around the yard alone and follows others' play. He starts to collect stones and sand with his bare hands. Suddenly, he overbalances and, as a result, turns around and accidentally makes a pirouette. At first, he seems confused, but then he starts to spin with an expression of joy on his face. He stretches his arms wide as he spins around and extends the stretch to his fingers and opens his hands. The sand and stones from his hands shoot quite far. "Oliver, you cannot throw sand!" yells the nurse. Oliver seems frightened and bends over. "Shhh ..." he whispers.

During this morning, Oliver's play initiations and clues that would have allowed adults to develop joint play with Oliver went unnoticed. The teacher ignored Oliver's conversation initiative about the fictional character Pippi Longstocking, who is very well known in Finland. The second play initiative, giggling and waggling with the other boy, which was likely interpreted as misbehavior that needed to be interrupted rather than encouraged, was interrupted by the teacher. Hanna, a nurse from the other child group, did not seize the opportunity to ask what Oliver was reading to engage in an imaginary world with him. When Oliver arrived at the playground, other children were already engaged in different kinds of activities. No one helped Oliver join in play activities. He tried to play with Simo but was interrupted by the nurse. Finally, when Oliver found his own spontaneous 'dizzy play'[2] (Kalliala, 2005), the nurse noticed the danger related to throwing sand and stopped Oliver rather than encouraging him to continue without sand and stones in his hands.

When examining Oliver's morning, it seems heartbreaking. We cannot help thinking that the staff could have better supported

Oliver's play initiatives and joining in play with his peers. When we examine the situation from the micro-policy viewpoint, however, the situation is more complex.

Based on field notes, diaries, and teacher interviews, we see that staff members tried to create structures that would best serve the needs of the children. Their interactions were typically very sensitive. On the morning described above, they seemed to have their hands full. One staff member was on sick leave, and others arranged to cover the absence; Oliver's first initiative went unnoticed because teachers were discussing these re-arrangements. The municipality's policy was that when a sudden absence of a staff member occurs, they will take care of the situation with internal arrangements instead of calling in a substitute, meaning staff members of the other groups offer help when needed, and they reorganize their work shifts accordingly. This is why Hanna, instead of an adult from Oliver's own group, came to help Oliver. Thus, helping Oliver was a disruption to Hanna's day: she probably had other duties waiting to be addressed in her own group and wanted to help Oliver go outdoors as quickly as possible. The policy of individual ECEC plans, which in Oliver's case involved an agreement to support Oliver individually during transitions, became entangled with the policy related to staff sick leave. Together, they formed a micro-policy that inhibited Oliver from entering outdoor play at the same time as his peers.

Outdoors, when Oliver arrived, a nursery nurse supervised the yard alone. She engaged in conversations with other children, ensured safety, and provided materials and equipment needed by the children. It is possible that she was distracted by another responsibility when Oliver arrived and, therefore, could not immediately help Oliver join in a play activity. The nurse was in the yard alone since the teacher of the group had consultative meetings with a special education teacher and one child's parents. There is a policy that teachers develop and annually update an individual ECEC plan in cooperation with the child's parents. If needed, other professionals, such as a special education teacher, physiotherapist, or psychologist, take part in crafting the individual plan. Usually, in this preschool, meetings related to individual plans were held during the afternoons when children had their nap and quiet time, but were sometimes held at other times if that suited the other professionals or the parents better.

The personnel expressed feelings of exhaustion and were unhappy with the quality of ECEC they were able to provide. In the interviews, they reported that engaging in play activities with the children was something they felt was lacking. In situations involving competing aims, aims related to play seemed to yield to other conflicting priorities (Paananen, 2017a). Activities that were more directly organized by teachers (e.g., planting a vegetable garden) were usually selected when the teacher needed to decide between engaging in different activities. The teachers stated that play still 'happens' even if it receives minimum input from the adults. These findings are in clear conflict with the curriculum's strong emphasis on adult–child joint play.

Furthermore, in this municipality there was a new policy related to the number of children allowed per square meter. The policy had increased the number of both children and adults in child groups. This policy has led to the requirement to stagger the use of spaces. When there are too many children and adults to share the same premises at the same time, such as the dining area, they take turns. Hence, the adults need to have an agreement on the responsibilities of each adult at any given time to ensure smooth transitions. If a teacher is having lunch with one group of children and ensuring they will finish before another group's scheduled lunch time, another staff member needs to ensure the other children are engaged in meaningful activities while waiting. This means, however, that there is little leeway for making decisions based on a teacher's contextual evaluation. For example, it is not always possible to continue fruitful play, even if it would support meeting the aims set for the ECEC, without interfering in the smooth operation of daily activities; the pre-fixed schedule needs to be followed (Paananen, 2017a), as in this example:

> There is this tension that we have to … We have 1 to 1.5 hours to be indoors [for play and other activities in the mornings]. Even though they have wonderful and fruitful play going on, we can't stay inside and continue it because the next group is coming in, and we need to go out. Although we stagger [the use of different spaces], have a very good learning environment, and are a child-paced kindergarten, there are preconditions that cannot be ignored. Sometimes, it feels that it is kind of covered or hidden by saying that in our preschool, you don't have to do this and that, but when we really look closely, we can see that for sure you have to.
>
> (Teacher K)

These findings lead us to ask: under what conditions would adult–child joint play sustain its prominent role in preschools' daily activities, and under what conditions would it be able to resist pressures from recent demands on preschools?

Example 2: Micro-policies that help sustain play in the daily activities of a preschool

In this section, we examine micro-policies in a preschool class that actively used adult–child joint play in its daily activities. The examples are drawn from an ethnographic study by Rainio (2010) that was conducted in a multi-age preschool class in a Finnish elementary school in a small town in 2003–2004. Consent to conduct the ethnographic study was gained from the children's parents, staff members, and the municipality. All names used are pseudonyms.

The group was a result of a longitudinal pilot study (1996–2003) that aimed to study, develop, and promote children's transition from preschool to school through a model of narrative learning and play pedagogy (see Hakkarainen, 2004). The class in which the study was conducted combined the normally distinct educational levels of Finnish ECEC (children aged four to five, the pre-primary education class for six-year-olds, and the first two grades of elementary school), thus including children from the ages of four to eight years and a multi-professional teacher team. The class that the second author of this chapter, Anna, studied was established in 1999.

In the fall of 2003, when Anna encountered the site, there were 30 children, of which 15 were five- to six-year-old preschoolers, and the remaining 15 were first and second graders (seven- to eight-year-old children). An elementary school teacher worked with the first and second grades, and a kindergarten teacher and a nursery nurse worked with the preschoolers. There was also a part-time nursery nurse who helped with children's afternoon activities and mealtimes. Teachers had participated in a three-year in-service education, and the pedagogical activities and daily curriculum of the classroom had thus been developed in collaboration with the researchers.

The preschool class followed its own local curriculum based on the national ECEC curriculum but was also influenced by theoretical underpinnings of the playworld pedagogy (see Hakkarainen, 2004). The week was organized around different activities that had their own place in the weekly order. The seven- to eight-year-olds spent one to two hours per day in regular classroom activities (e.g., reading and maths); the remainder of the time was spent in common narrative- and play-based activities for the whole group (e.g., playworlds[3]).

In her ethnographic study, Anna paid attention to the particularly persistent nature of play-based activities in the group despite the challenges they constantly faced (see Rainio, 2008a, 2008b; Rainio & Hilppö, 2017). Adult–child joint play generally had a central role in the class. The playworld activity took place every week at the same time, and it rarely, if ever, had to be cancelled or changed. In socially-demanding situations, such as quarrelling between children, or chaotic situations, the playworld activity was generally sustained (for examples of such situations, see Hakkarainen, 2009; Paananen & Rainio, 2018; Rainio, 2008a, 2008b). These ethnographic findings created an interesting contrast with Maiju's study, in which play yielded to other conflicting aims in the group. This led us to ask what kinds of micro-policies were in action that helped to support the execution of the play-based curriculum at Anna's site, and what can we learn from them?

We explore this issue by using data from Anna's site. Our data are from an Annual Report (2002–2003) that teachers wrote based on the experiences from the final year of their pilot project. We have conducted a thematic analysis of the annual report to shed light on the micro-policies of play in this setting. We first made note of all instances where the teachers described children's play, adult–child joint play, or activities that contain elements or relate to play activities in the group. Then, we separated instances where teachers mentioned a challenge or a difficulty in their preschool's activities and setting that could influence play activities in the group. Finally, we marked all instances in which the teachers described how the difficulties encountered were examined further. Particular attention was paid to any kind of *governance tool* (see Paananen, 2017b) that played a role in executing the planned play activities. Additional ethnographic field notes from Anna's study during the 2003–2004 school year were used as complementary data to contextualize the findings.

Most play-based activities in the group had a stable place in the weekly schedule, which teachers were committed to following. The children also knew the schedule (see Rainio, 2010). In contrast, in Maiju's study, although there was a weekly schedule, plans were often cancelled; for example, when a staff member was absent. At Anna's site, the playworld activity took place every Wednesday and

Thursday morning after breakfast (approximately 9.30–11 am). Similarly, city play, another central play activity in the class, had a permanent place on the weekly calendar, although it was also a flexible form of play that they often initiated if there was extra time available during the day. Adults had an active role in both of these play activities, although it was different in each of them. The teachers describe city play in their 2002–2003 Annual Report as follows:

> City Play turned into a shared activity for us when the adults started to take an active role in developing it. Children got very intrigued by this turn, and then the play started to develop fast. On the other hand, one strength of this form of play is that there is no ready-made model for it, and the adults don't really participate in developing the plot. Everyone can "live" this play in their own way, like families live their lives ... City Play is a secure choice if we have "free" days between our projects. City Play does not even suffer if it has been forgotten for some time; the children are always equally pleased to construct the town ... City Play in this class is children's own form of play that we hope will have its place here in the future too.
> (From the Annual Report, 2002–2003)

In this excerpt, one can detect the established place of city play within the group's daily activities. The construct was established in such a way that it has become a governing tool; the children know how to engage in city play even if adults do not participate as much as they did previously. The children have an adequate understanding of what city play entails, although there is room to develop it further.

In Maiju's study, one finding was that when the children's individual ECEC plans became entangled with other kinds of local policies, they formed micro-policies that inhibited the children's participation in shared play activities (e.g., in Oliver's case described above, it had been agreed that Oliver would not exit the building to go outdoors at the same time as his peers). In the class that Anna studied, special supports for individual children were typically built into developmental tasks for the teachers to work on within the play activity. The teachers describe such a situation in relation to playworld planning:

Parallel to the objectives (for playworld) we set for the whole group, we used children's individual plans. We chose two child groups that were different from the other kids and needed adult guidance and support. We decided to follow the first group more carefully; it included four children who were reserved and needed encouragement. The other group consisted of four children who experienced significant challenges in collaboration and social interaction. Two of them were hyperactive with a tendency to act impulsively ... These follow-up groups were very different, and we deliberated on how we could create a play activity that supports the developmental plans of all these children. We ended up creating characters (played by adults) within the play, who would act in very similar ways as these children. Simultaneously, we followed the children's actions and reactions in different situations. Originally, we developed three adult characters: one shy; one inconsiderate type who is hyperactive; and a "Who cares, I want it all" type. These plans went awry because of the sick leave (of the personnel), so we combined two of these roles into one. The result was a character called *Ines*, who was shy and reserved, and *Mirkku*, who was hyperactive, impulsive, and curious.

(From the Annual Report, 2002–2003)

In contrast to Oliver's case, at Anna's site national policies of play and national policies related to the individual support of children were intentionally combined in the local playworld activity. The needs of children requiring special support were considered when planning the play and supported during the play. Yet, the playworld remained open in such a way that it was not only the teachers who could decide what happened there. More specifically, these two national policies materialized in the daily life of the class as a governing tool of playworld – a certain shared understanding of organizing daily life. The governing tool aspect of playworld seemed to lead to a micro-policy of resilient play where surprising interferences, such as absent staff members, did not prevent playing it, and the children's varying abilities did not prevent anyone from being part of the play.

When challenges were encountered in Maiju's example, the play activities remained on the schedule; however, they often had to modify them. In Anna's example, teachers had to change their original plan for the characters because several personnel were absent. This required improvisation *in situ* to collectively re-plan the activity at short notice. To do so, there needed to be a place for continual planning in the teachers' schedule and a chance to re-negotiate situations. In such situations, the teachers actively chose to retain the playworld. The playworld activity was adequately flexible in its combination of improvisation and careful preplanning (see Lindqvist, 1995). The teachers conducted a weekly planning session where they reflected on the week's play activities and loosely prepared the next week. During these meetings, teachers followed up the motivation of each group and individual children (Rainio, 2010). We claim that teachers need established long-term structures and other continual supportive elements that enable the sustainability of play in situations involving conflict and overlapping aims. In-service education and regular consulting support for the teacher team, for example, provided by the city in collaboration with the university, helped develop these practices as a regular part of the class.

Indeed, the local city administration and leaders of the school were very supportive of this group's play-based pedagogies. It thus received clear external support. In their annual report, teachers described how they felt that the support from both the school's principal (Maria) and the head of the municipality's ECEC services (Leila) were central to developing their work:

> The most tranquil phase in our team counseling started at the end of the second year when Leila returned to work. For the first time, we had a situation in which both our advisors, Leila and our school principal Maria, full-heartedly supported our team. The next one and half years we were very productive, not even the replacements in our personnel slowed down the progression in the contents of the pilot study.
> (From the Annual Report, 2002–2003)

Today, 15 years after the study and with about two-thirds of the personnel replaced, the class still follows the play-based curriculum in the school and develops city play and playworlds in the class. We suggest that the supportive structures created on the local political level in collaboration with research- and theory-based in-service education have created a preschool culture in the class that sustains itself year after year despite challenges currently facing the sector.

The crucial question now is: what can be learned from this case? How can such sustained and persistent play-based practices be embedded in ECEC classrooms more widely?

- What kinds of practices and arrangements would help you to participate in or follow children's play?

Conclusion

We have examined how different levels of policy aims become mediated and turned into micro-policies shaping pedagogical choices made by teachers in the daily activities of preschools. We have shown how possibilities for adults to participate and support children's play are entangled with other policy aims, leading to either inhibiting or enabling this participation. As we noted in the first case study, although the national policy highlights play, and the personnel consider play an important part of daily activities of the ECEC, it does not necessarily lead to practices in which play is actively supported. The second case illustrated that for play to have a more secure placement in daily activities, it needs to be intentionally and carefully combined with other local policies and aims posed. This is not an easy task if we want to avoid play having only an instrumental value.

Although there were other elements in Anna's study that possibly contributed to making play such a sustained activity in the classroom (see Ferholt et al. in Chapter 2 of this volume; Lindqvist, 1995; Rainio, 2008b) we have focused on the *micro-policies* that helped make play sustainable. We conclude that at least four policy-level factors seemed crucial for play to receive such persistent recognition:

- Play activities turned into governing tools with an established place in the routines of the class. There were named, recognized, and shared play activities with their own rules and ways of acting that were actively chosen by the children and adults each week: city play and playworld.
- These play activities were based on explicit and supported long-term development work by practitioners, the city municipality, and the researchers.
- Teachers received external support and had a dedicated space and time for team counseling during the pilot study.

- There was a secured place and time for teacher planning, reflection, and documentation weekly and long term. In these sessions, many other ECEC policy aims and tasks could be integrated into the schedule and to these play activities. The challenges faced by the teachers in their work could also be dealt with in ways that did not easily destroy or cancel shared play.

Making meaningful pedagogical choices in preschools is not just a matter of goodwill or the preschool teachers' pedagogical competence. It is also not solely a matter of support from the national ECEC policy. Instead, there is a need for explicit, supportive local policies helping teachers create governing tools that help achieve desired pedagogical aims (e.g., adult participation in play) while meeting other competing ECEC aims (such as efficiency) that often contradict pedagogical goals. In this chapter, we have given some perspectives on such micro-policies in relation to play. There remains a need to systematically study different play-based curricula in various settings, both in Finland and internationally, to learn from the persistency of these cases and develop appropriate teaching practices to support play.

Notes

1 Every child ought to have an individual ECEC plan that aims to consider the child's individual needs and opinions and the parents' views in arranging the child's education and care. The plan includes an agreement on important aims for the child, and how the individual's needs are taken into account in the preschool's activities.
2 'Dizzy play' describes the creation of disorder and reorder within playful experiences. Elements of dizzy play are full body exploration and humour. It can involve tussling, spinning, or rolling over each other on the grass (Kalliala, 2005).
3 Playworlds is an educational practice based on a creative pedagogy of play developed by the Swedish scholar Gunilla Lindqvist (1995). Playworlds can be described as a form of adult–child joint play in which adults and children enter into a common fantasy that is designed to support the development of both adults and children (i.e. Ferholt et al., Chapter 2 of this volume). Adult–child joint play is typically structured around a piece of literature or a work of art.

References

Annual Report. (2002–2003). Unpublished annual report written by the preschool personnel for the city administration.

Ferholt, B., & Lecusay, R. (2010). Adult and child development in the zone of proximal development: Socratic dialogue in a playworld. *Mind Culture and Activity*, 17(1), 59–83.

Hakkarainen, P. (2004). Narrative learning in the fifth dimension. *Critical Social Studies – Outlines*, 2004(1), 1–20.

Hakkarainen, P. (2009). Development of motivation in play and narratives. In Blenkinsop, S. (Ed), *The imagination of education: Extending the boundaries of theory and practice* (pp. 64–78). Newcastle-upon-Tyne: Cambridge Scholars Publishing.

Hännikäinen, M. (2007). Creating togetherness and building a preschool community of learners: The role of play and games. In T. Jambor & J. Van Gils (Eds), *Several perspectives in children's play: Scientific reflections for practitioners* (pp. 147–160). Antwerpen and Apeldoorn: Garant.

Hay, C. (2004). Common trajectories, variable paces, divergent outcomes? Models of European capitalism under conditions of complex economic interdependence. *Review of International Political Economy*, 11(2), 231–262.

Kalliala, M. (2005). *Play culture in a changing world*. Berkshire: McGraw-Hill Education.

Lindqvist, G. (1995). The aesthetics of play: A didactic study of play and culture in preschools. *Acta Universitatis Upsaliensis*, Uppsala Studies in Education 62. Stockholm: Almqvist & Wiksell International.

McCann, E., & Ward, K. (Eds) (2011). *Mobile urbanism: Cities and policymaking in the global age*. Minneapolis, MN: University of Minnesota Press.

McCann, E., & Ward, K. (2012) Assembling urbanism: Following policies and 'studying through' the sites and situations of policy making. *Environment and Planning A: Economy and Space*, 44(1),42–51.

National Core Curriculum for Early Childhood Education and Care 2016. Helsinki: Finnish National Board of Education.

Onnismaa, E.-L., & Kalliala, M. (2010). Finnish ECEC policy: Interpretations, implementations and implications. *Early Years*, 30(3), 267–277. DOI: 10.1080/09575146.2010.511604.

Paananen, M. (2017a). The imaginaries that survived: Societal roles of early childhood education in an era of intensification. *Global Studies of Childhood*. Online first. DOI: 10.1177/2043610617704934.

Paananen, M. (2017b). Imaginaries of early childhood education: Societal roles of early childhood education in an era of accountability. *Helsinki Studies in Education* 3. Helsinki: Faculty of Education.

Paananen, M., & Rainio, A. P. (2018). Adult–child joint play in turmoil: Can play overcome the challenges of performativity in Finnish ECEC? A paper presented at the American Educational Research Association (AERA) Conference, 16 April, New York, USA.

Rainio, A. P. (2008a). From resistance to involvement: Examining agency and control in a playworld activity. *Mind, Culture, and Activity*, 15(2), 115–140.

Rainio, A. P. (2008b). Developing the classroom as a figured world. *Journal of Educational Change*, 9(4), 357–364.

Rainio, A. P. (2010). Lionhearts of the playworld: An ethnographic case study of the development of agency in play pedagogy. *Studies in Educational Sciences* 233. Helsinki: Institute of Behavioural Sciences, University of Helsinki.

Rainio, A. P., & Hilppö, J. (2017). The dialectics of agency in educational ethnography. *Ethnography & Education*, 12(1), 78–94.

Vygotsky, L. S. (1978). *Mind in society: The development of higher psychological processes*. Cambridge, MA: Harvard University Press.

Vygotsky, L. S. (1987). Imagination and its development in childhood. In R. W. Rieber & A. S. Carton (Eds), *The collected works of L. S. Vygotsky, Vol. 1* (pp. 339–350). New York, NY: Plenum Press.

EDITORIAL PROVOCATIONS
Engaging readers and extending thinking

Nicola Stobbs

The three chapters in this section focus on the way children, educators and communities respond to systems and policy initiatives. Play, playfulness and the pedagogy of play are brought into sharp relief, and the chapters raise questions, which can be quite unsettling at times, as they challenge how and for whom systems and policies are designed. They help us to critically examine what goes on and to sharpen the focus on the interplay between play and learning. In Chapter 10, for example, Fleet and Reed raise the issue of tensions between systems and practice. They identify how systems really do influence practice and the role of the educator, suggesting that there is:

- a pressure on educators to prove they recognise valuable learning when observing children at play;
- a tension between policy context and educator values; and
- a need to consider carefully the role of the educator when working within systems.

A theme taken up by Mandy Andrews in Chapter 11 is, how do systems attempt to influence children's play through the implicit ideological underpinnings of play space design? These are interesting and unsettling concepts for the educator, but again provoke questions about the way this influences their role. The reflective educator may ponder the nature of play spaces and the way children claim them for their own, impacting on the spaces as much as the spaces impact upon them. A key starting point for an educator considering the impact of what they do in relation to children's learning might be to ask: to what extent does playing help children to forge their own ideology and community of practice?

The educator again appears as central to systems and policy in Chapter 12 by Maiju Paananen and Anna Pauliina Rainio. They take the issue of play and pedagogy further and ask: does successful play-based pedagogy necessitate strong communities of practice and supportive micro-policies? Their views are based upon two research studies undertaken in Finland, often regarded as a nation that has 'got it right' in terms of the balance between pedagogy as social justice and accountability and performativity, due to its high ranking in international educational evaluations. Revisit the case study where adults were unable to enact their values and commitment to play due to logistical demands and the need to work within diminishing resources; a huge issue that will no doubt resonate with educators worldwide. This case study can be compared with the second one in the chapter and provide insight and optimism for educators. In this context, staff were under the same national demands and logistical pressures but managed to maintain their commitment to play-based pedagogies. Consider how the commitment of those closely involved in the setting, combined with a collaborative community, practical in-service education from local government agencies and academic consultative support, resulted in a positive outcome. This process enabled the pedagogy of play to become established beyond the drive of an individual; in fact, I go as far as to say this: it took on a life of its own, not dependent on daily decisions but truly established. I therefore end my review by proposing that systems influence educators, but educators also can, and should, influence systems.

CODA
Thinking forward

Michael Reed and Alma Fleet

Prior to reading this volume – or at least having dabbled in some sections of it – you may have wondered: in what sense is 'Play' a pedagogical issue? With an age-old adage about 'play being children's work' (generally attributed to Maria Montessori) and research establishing that, certainly by the first years of school, children have been shown to be very clear about the difference between work and play (Wing, 1995), the scene had been set for this exploration.

Twenty-three authors and a four-person editorial team from nine different countries have offered provocations from their research and experience related to rethinking play as pedagogy. Perhaps you noticed that the core term – 'play' – is contested; i.e. it is defined differently in varying contexts, with strong contextual influences on the conceptualisation of this apparently straightforward concept. Language use is slippery, with authors sliding across 'play', 'playing', 'playful pedagogies' and 'playfulness'. Subtleties of interpretation become apparent as authors unpack the layers from their provocations. 'Common sense' notions of play, 'romanticised' notions of carefree play, demeaning notions of play as a frivolous use of time, and contextualised versions of play as exploratory, creative, intellectual and socially satisfying, all vie for attention.

Looking at the content from this vantage point, we – the series editors – invite you to re-look at how play as pedagogy has been offered to you: from the perspectives of being alongside children, thinking with those who educate, embedding families and communities, and considering the relationship between institutional systems and children's 'rights' to play. These diverse perspectives invite us to foreground a consideration of children's rights as offered in this volume, noting, for example, the provocations in the 2016 publication exploring the relationship between children's rights and educational research (Gillett-Swan & Coppock, 2016). We wonder where you might see the intersections between pedagogy and research in this context.

This brings us to the jumping-off point for future thinking. Where might these considerations take you? Might you wish to look for other work written by these authors to learn more about their geographical locatedness and areas of specialisation? Might you look across chapters and sections for points of connection/comparison, or contrast? Which ideas have jumped out at you as needing further consideration/clarification? Which projects or points of view excite you and/or offer opportunities for impact on your studies and your professional practice?

A comment has been made that this Coda has a kinetic feel (slipping, sliding and jumping off!); perhaps that's not unreasonable for a volume-ending commentary on play as pedagogy. It also positions us all in the space opened by Peter Moss in his 2015 article exploring 'contestation and hope in early childhood education'. Following a critique of 'the growing influence of neoliberalism on politics and economics', he moves to 'the disruptive potential of a discourse of hope' (p. 226). This volume may be viewed through that lens: acknowledging the complexities in which children, their families and educators find themselves, while also offering snippets of richly realised experiences of play as purposeful/meaningful pedagogy and multi-layered narratives of possibility. Perhaps seeing yourself in this terrain has offered potential for not only joining the debates as an advocate for young children's ways of being, but also positioning yourself on the hopeful field of playful pedagogy.

References

Gillett-Swan, J., & Coppock, V. (Eds). (2016). *Children's Rights, Educational Research and the UNHCR: Past, Present and Future*. Oxford: Symposium Books.

Moss, P. (2015). There are alternatives! Contestation and hope in early childhood education. *Global Studies of Childhood*, 5 (3), pp. 226–238. Doi: 10.1177/2043610615597130.

Wing, L. A. (1995). Play is not the work of the child: Young children's perceptions of work and play. *Early Childhood Research Quarterly*, 10 (2), pp. 223–247. Doi: 10.1016/0885-2006(95)90005-5.

INDEX

Aboriginal Australians 160–161
accountability 70, 77, 79, 80, 167, 206
action research 122
adult-child joint play 17–18, 19, 21, 23–29, 47–48, 189–202; *see also* playworlds
adult intervention 127–128, 129
adulteration of children's lives 177
Africa 48
agency 60, 62, 64, 165, 173; children's perspectives on play 85; digital drawing 4, 7, 12; force field analysis 181; 'interactive' 3, 15; joint play 192; mythical play 57; playful thinking 15; relational 147–148; socio-cultural pedagogy 92
'agora' 139, 150, 154
Aistear 86–89, 91–92, 93, 95–96, 102–103
Alcock, Sophie 47–49, 53–68, 101–103, 153–154, 164, 168
Allen, Pamela 167
Andrews, Mandy 173–188, 205
anthropology 143
apps 4, 5–6, 7
Aram, D. 94
Armour-Thomas, E. 92
art: digital drawing 3–16; playworlds 23
Artzt, A. 92
Arya, R. 34
Aspelin, J. 18, 19
assessment 80, 81, 83, 167, 168
attunement 48, 64–65
Australia: Aboriginal voices on play 160–161; digital drawing 3; Early Years Learning Framework 70, 76–77, 80, 82, 85, 163–164; music 33, 36; professional development 69–70, 94, 102
autonomy 74, 81, 126

Ball, S. 94–95
Barad, K. 187
Barrett, Margaret S. 33–46, 48
Bateson, Gregory 143
beliefs 92–93, 94, 96, 179
belonging 57, 64, 90, 190, 192
Beunderman, J. 123
Biffi, Elisabetta 139–152, 154
Bjørkvold, Jon 42
Blank, M. 123
Bowman, B. T. 92
Bradwell, P. 123
Braga, Piera 141
Braidotti, R. 187
Braun, A. 94–95
Bronfenbrenner, U. 173, 175–183, 185, 186
Bruner, J. 14
Burgess, J. 88–89, 90
Burns, M. S. 92

Canada 161–162
Canning, N. 103
Cardiff School of Education 121
Cardiff University 121
Carr, Margaret 147–148
chasing 59–61, 64, 65
CHAT *see* Cultural-Historical Activity Theory
Chesworth, L. 159
child-centred approach 92, 93, 95–96
child development 178–179
child-initiated play 43, 79, 128, 129
Child Study movement 143

209

INDEX

childhood 140–141, 142, 143–145, 174
choice 74, 83, 109, 136; Aistear 92; children's perspectives 85; playful pedagogies 81; Playwork Principles 128, 129
citizenship 57
City Play 198, 201
Clarkin-Philips, Jeanette 147–148
co-existence 19–20, 22, 28, 29
co-operation 19–20
Cohen, J. 93
Cohen, L. 61
Colliver, Y. J. 162
Colmer, K. 94
colour 4, 5, 9
communication: with families 113, 119; infants 35; relational competence 29; vitality affects 55
community engagement 69, 134–135, 149–150
commutation 186
conceived space 183–185
confidence 11
Connolly, Mark 121–138
'constants' 28, 29
Cooper, Maria 107–120, 153
Corsaro, W. A. 57
creativity 47, 92, 131
critical theory 182–183
Cullen, J. 93
cultural capital 92–93
Cultural-Historical Activity Theory (CHAT) 40
cultural norms 177, 179
culture 95, 109; co-construction of 88; force field analysis 181; funds of knowledge 109–110; music 39, 40
curiosity 87
curriculum: ACARA 77, 79; Aistear 86–89, 91–92, 93, 95–96, 102–103; didactic approach 91; Finland 189–190; guidelines 165–166; Israel 94; linked with assessment 167; local community needs 150; play-based 91, 165, 202; playful pedagogies 80, 81, 82; primary 87, 88, 90, 93; reform 93, 95; Te Whāriki 108, 110

Dahlberg, Gunilla 144
data projectors 10–12
De Gioia, K. 90
Deleuze, G. 177, 185

Developmentally Appropriate Practice 89
dialogue 112, 147, 154
didactic approach 88, 90–91
digital drawing 3–16, 47
digital footprints 7
digital music technology 36
Dissanayake, Ellen 35
'dizzy play' 193, 202n2
Dockett, S. 94
documentality 144
documentation 83, 139–150, 154, 168, 202
Donovan, M. S. 92
dramatic play 56, 57, 61, 62, 65
drawing 3–16, 47
dreaming 56
Dumitrescu, Sandra 121–138
Dunphy, E. 90

early childhood education (ECE): documentation 140, 142, 145–146, 148–150; ECEC plans 192–193, 194–195, 198, 202n1; Finland 189–190; funds of knowledge 110, 119; Ireland 86–96; micro-policies 191–202; New Zealand 107, 109, 111, 153
Early Years Learning Framework (EYLF) 70, 76–77, 80, 82, 85, 163–164
ecological model 175–177, 178–182, 185
educational change 70, 91, 166
Edwards, S. 91
Einarsdottir, J. 94
Eisner, E. 8
Ellis, Cheryl 121–138
emotions 53–54, 55, 56, 64, 127
empowerment 108
energy 53, 54–55
Engeström, Y. 23
England 162–163, 165, 174
ethnographic research methods 58
experiential learning 102
Explain Everything 5, 7
exploratory learning 22, 90–91

family: ecological model 175–177, 179, 181; engagement with 135; force field analysis 180–181; funds of knowledge 107, 108, 109–119, 153;

INDEX

music 35–36; play as cultural practice 37; *see also* parents
fantasy play 17–18
Fasoli, Lyn 160
Fenwick, T. 92–93
Ferholt, Beth 17–32, 47–48, 101
Ferraris, Maurizio 144
Finland 20, 21, 189–190, 191–202, 206
First Nations 161
Fleer, M. 43
Fleet, Alma 69–85, 88–89, 90, 102, 142, 157–172, 205, 207–208
flexibility 65, 125, 126, 131
force field analysis 177–178, 179, 180–181
forest school 184
formative interventions 23
Foucault, Michel 144
freedom 40–41, 54, 124
Froebel, Friedrich 190
funding 174
funds of knowledge 107, 108, 109–119, 153

Gallant, P. A. 90
games 5–6, 10, 12–14, 71
gender 62
González, N. 110
'good enough' caregiving 57, 62, 64
Goodall, D. 165
governing tools 197, 198, 199, 201, 202
Gray, C. 88
Griffiths, C. 165
group emotions 64
Growing Up Children in Two Worlds project 160
Guattari, F. 177, 185

Hannon, C. 123
Harrison, Linda 163
Hart, R. A. 160
Haughton, Chantelle 121–138
Hayward, L. 167
hazards 128
Hedges, Helen 93, 107–120, 153
Hockney, David 3, 4, 15
holding 53–57, 61, 65, 66–67, 101
holistic development 108
home visits 110–119
Hughes, B. 124
Huizinga, Johan 141

Hunter, T. 88, 93
Hurst, V. 89

Iceland 94
identity 88, 109, 110
ideology 173, 175, 176–177, 180–181, 205
images 7–8, 10–12, 143–144; *see also* photographs
imagination 125, 131
inclusion 72
Indigenous peoples 160–161
infants 33–35, 37
'interactive agency' 3, 15
interpersonal fields 53–56, 58–59, 63, 65, 66–67, 101
invented song-making 41–43, 44
involvement 40
iPads 7, 8–9, 10–12, 14
Ireland 86–96, 102–103
Israel 94
Italy 148–149, 154

Joseph, J. 89

Kemenyvary, Mel 69–85, 102, 158
Kinderling Radio 36
knowledge: co-construction of 88, 90; funds of knowledge 107, 108, 109–119, 153
Kolbe, Ursula 5
Kress, G. 4, 15

language 35, 109, 114
Lansdown, G. 92
Law, J. 95
leadership 76, 77, 80, 84, 95
learning: children's perspectives 72; digital drawing 14–15, 47; dispositions 78, 80, 81–82, 163; early childhood education 88, 89–90; experiential 102; exploratory 22, 90–91; 'learning spaces' 158–159; musical play 37–41; play-based 4, 75–76, 109, 119, 163; socio-cultural view 87–88, 90, 91–92; strengths-based practices 80; teachers' perspectives 74, 75–77, 78; *see also* pedagogy
Lecusay, Robert 17–32, 47–48
Lefebvre, H. 178, 182, 183, 185
Lenz Taguchi, H. 3, 15

INDEX

Lester, S. 122
Levin, I. 94
Lewin, Kurt 122, 173, 177–178, 180–181
Lewis, C. S. 26
Lindqvist, Gunilla 20–22, 23, 30n2, 202n3
The Lion, the Witch and the Wardrobe (Lewis) 26–28
listening 56, 158; pedagogy of 22
Little, H. 168
lived space 183, 184
Loizou, E. 92
loose parts 127, 130, 131–132, 165
'loved companions' 9–10

Maguire, M. 94–95
making things 71–72
Mandela, Nelson 18
Mannello, Marianne 121–138, 154
mark-making 4, 8–9, 47
'material semiotics' 94–95
maternal singing 34, 37–41
Mead, Margaret 143
meaning: digital drawing 15; funds of knowledge 153; hidden 54; meaning-making processes 55–56, 67; singing 41
Meire, J. 124
Melaville, A. 123
mentorship 84
micro-policies 206
Millar, Susanna 141
Mining Minds project 69, 74, 77, 81
Montessori, Maria 207
Moss, Peter 208
motherese 35, 41
movement 6–7, 56, 60–61, 65, 127
movies 5–6, 9
Mozart Effect 36
Mukela, Reuben 48
Murphy, B. 91
Murris, K. 187
music 33–44, 48; invented song-making 41–43, 44; maternal singing 34, 37–41; musical parenting 33, 36
mythical play 57, 62, 63, 65

nature play 82, 127
negative capability 61, 66
New Zealand: early childhood education 107, 109, 111, 153; Te Whāriki 108, 110; teacher participation in play 58, 59, 101
Nicholson, Simon 130
Nilsson, Monica 17–32, 47–48
Nixon, Mark 9
Nuttall, J. 91

O'Donoghue, Margaret 86–100, 102–103
Office for Standards in Education, Children's Services and Skills 162–163
Open All Hours project 121, 123, 126–136, 154
Organisation for Economic Co-operation and Development (OECD) 90–91
outdoor play: adulteration of children's lives 177; barriers to 124–125, 130; decline in 175; school grounds 121–123, 126, 130–136, 154; spaces 183–185
overhead projectors 10

Paanen, Maiju 189–204, 206
Paley, Vivian 30n1
parentese 35, 41
parents: cultural norms 177; ecological model 179; maternal singing 34, 37–41; Open All Hours project 123, 130, 132, 134; pedagogical documentation 145, 147–148, 150; *see also* family
participant observation 56
participation 92–93, 148, 150, 153, 189
partnerships 108–109
Pascal, C. 165
Patterson, C. 90
pedagogical documentation 139–150, 154, 168; *see also* documentation
pedagogy: creative pedagogy of play 20, 21; early childhood education 89–90, 119; Finland 206; linked with assessment 167; of listening 22; play as 207–208; playful pedagogies 69, 79, 80–83, 84–85, 207; posthuman perspective 186; relationship-based approaches 119; socio-cultural 91–92; systems 169; utilitarian concepts of 180; *see also* learning
peer groups 57
perceived space 183, 184

INDEX

performance 40, 41
Perry, B. 94
Persson, S. 19
Pestalozzi, Johann 190
photographs 7–8, 9, 143–144, 146, 148, 161
Piaget, Jean 141
planning 199–200, 202
play: adult-child joint play 17–18, 19, 21, 23–29, 47–48, 189–202; adult intervention 127–128, 129; barriers to 124–125, 130; CHAT perspective 40; children's perspectives 71–73, 85, 102, 158; creative pedagogy of 20, 21; culture of 141–142; definition of 126; digital drawing 11, 12–14, 15; early childhood education 88–89, 92, 108; ecological model 178; grounded in real-life experiences 112–113, 115, 117–119; importance of 123–124, 192; micro-policies 189–202, 206; musical 35–44; observing and interpreting 53–67; pedagogical documentation 139, 140, 142, 145–152; as pedagogy 207–208; Playwork Principles 128–129; policy 159–164; posthuman perspective 186–187; postmodern perspective 177; professional development 70; rich play environment 109, 127; right to 121, 122–123, 125, 136, 154, 157, 163, 174, 207; scholarship 159; school grounds 121–123, 126, 130–136, 154; as a social construct 174; spaces 183–185, 205; spontaneous 167–168, 175, 182, 185, 186; systems 165, 169, 205; teacher participation 54, 56–67, 101; teachers' perspectives 73–80, 85, 102; understandings of 101
play-based learning 4, 75–76, 109, 119, 163
Play England 174
Play Wales 121, 123, 136
playfulness 59, 64; Aistear 87; language use 207; playful pedagogies 69, 79, 80–83, 84–85, 207
playgrounds 183–184; *see also* school grounds
playtime 89
Playwork Principles 128–129

playworlds 17–18, 20–22, 23–29, 47–48, 196–200, 201, 202n3
policy 159–164, 165, 205; ecological model 176–177; enactment 94–95, 102–103; England 162–163, 174; interactive/intra-active perspective 173, 174; Ireland 91, 93; micro-policies 189–202, 206; statements and strategies 93; Wales 154
Pond, Donald 42
posthumanism 173, 176, 178, 185–187
postmodernism 173, 176, 177, 178, 185–186
power 162, 165, 168, 182; Lefebvre 178, 183; mythical play 57, 65; reversal of power relationships 65; shared group emotions 64; vitality affects 60
prenatal music exposure 34
pretend play 53, 54, 57
problem solving 131, 168
professional cultures 92
professional development 69–70, 82, 94, 102; curriculum reform 95; family and community engagement 135; policy enactment 102–103; policy strategies and funding 93
professionalism 18, 109, 166
projection 10–12
provocations 82, 85, 168
psychosocial wellbeing 92
'pure play' 164

quantum physics 178, 180, 186

Rainio, Anna Pauliina 189–204, 206
reading 20
Reed, Michael 103, 157–172, 205, 207–208
reflection 103
reflective practice 82, 83
Reggio Emilia 20, 22, 76, 77, 144
regulation 166
relational agency 147–148
relational competence 17, 18–20, 21–22, 23–30, 48, 101
relationships 108, 119, 165
resilience 87
resistance 57, 60, 61, 178
resourcefulness 131
responsibility 64

INDEX

rights-based approach 92, 93, 95–96, 122–123, 125–126, 136, 207–208
risk 125, 129, 130, 134–135, 154, 168
rituals 36
Robertson, Janet 3–16, 47
Robson, S. 87, 91
Rogoff, Barbara 142
role-play 21, 22, 24, 27, 192
rough-and-tumble play 60–61, 65–66, 67, 101, 127, 168
rules 40–41, 57, 64
Russell, W. 122
Ryan, A. 88

safety 124, 128, 168, 175
Sandseter, E. B. H. 65–66
Santer, J. 165
Sarwar, Sian 121–138
Scacchi, V. 87, 91
scaffolding 74, 75
scheduling 195, 197–198
school grounds 121–123, 126, 130–136, 154
screen time 3
Seesaw 7
self-esteem 92, 131
self-regulation 66
senses 33–34, 127
Shah, B. 123
shared memory 146
Singer, E. 165
singing: children's memories 71; invented song-making 41–43, 44; maternal 34, 37–41; role of 34
site culture 77–78
social capital 92–93
social change 122
social justice 189, 190, 206
socio-cultural view 87–88, 90, 91–92
socio-dramatic play 56
Sole, M. 41
spaces 158–159, 182, 183–185, 205
spatial awareness 131
staff ratios 79
stereotypes 144–145, 150
Stern, Daniel 55
Stobbs, Nicola 205–206
stories 6, 47, 57
Storli, R. 65–66
strengths-based practices 80
Sturrock, G. 182–183
Sumsion, Jennifer 163

Sverdlov, A. 94
Sweden 20, 21, 22–26
symbolic play 141
systems 165–169, 173, 205, 206

Taguchi, H. L. 186, 187
Talking Pictures project 160–161
task-scapes 6, 12–14
Te Whāriki 108, 110
'teachable moments' 74
teachers: digital drawing 12, 47; empowerment of 90; funds of knowledge 108, 110, 111–119; Ireland 88; micro-policies 191–202, 206; observing and interpreting play 53–67; parent engagement 147–148; pedagogical documentation 148–149, 150; perspectives on play 73–80, 85, 102; playful pedagogies 80–83, 84–85; playworlds 22, 23–29, 47–48; preschool to school transition 70, 83–84, 196; pressures on 159; relational competence 17, 18–20, 21–22, 23–30, 48; staff ratios 79; values and beliefs 91–94, 96
technology: digital drawing 15, 47; music 36
time 66, 125, 132, 136, 168
Tobin, Joseph 142
toys 145, 192
transitions 61, 195
Trevarthen, C. 35
trust 29, 53, 65, 118, 158
Tyrie, Jacky 121–138

United Nations Convention on the Rights of the Child (1989) 92, 125–126, 140–141, 154, 160, 163, 174–175, 182
United States 20, 21, 23, 26–29
Unwin, L. 93
Urban, M. 87, 91

values 91–94, 96, 205
Van Oers, B. 40
visible thinking 13
vitality affects 53–56, 59, 60–61, 62–66, 101
vocalisation 35, 38, 40, 41
voice 146, 150, 158
Vygotsky, L. S. 20, 40, 190

INDEX

Wales 121–136, 154
Walker, R. 166
Walsh, G. 88, 93
Weisz-Koves, Tamar 107–120, 153
Wenger-Trayer, E. 166
Where the Wild Things Are (Sendak) 64, 66
The Wiggles 36

Winnicott, Donald 55, 141
wonder 87, 126
Wood, E. 43, 159, 165
Wunungmurra, Alison 160
Wyver, S. 168

Zuccoli, Franca 146

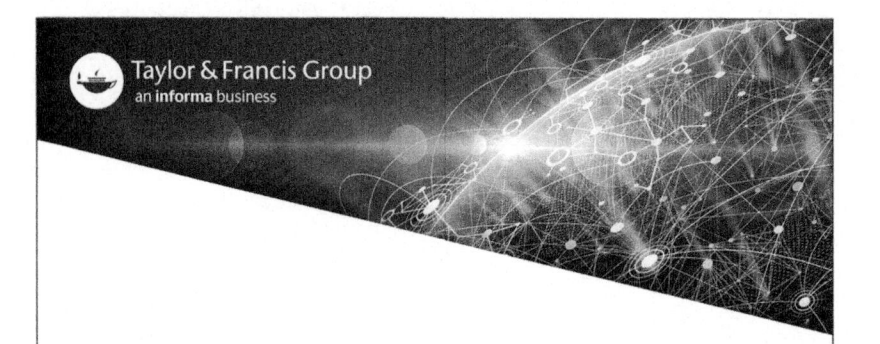

Printed in Great Britain
by Amazon